PENCIL DRAWING
PORTRAITS

Learn to draw faces, features, and more with
step-by-step pencil projects perfect for beginners

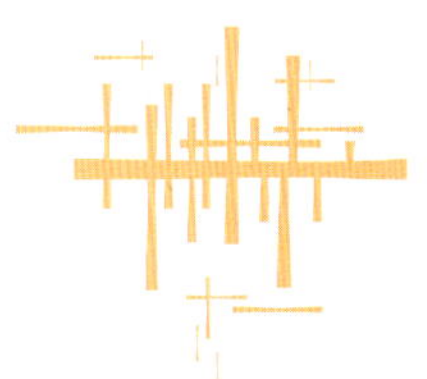

SAMET TÜRKAN

Walter Foster

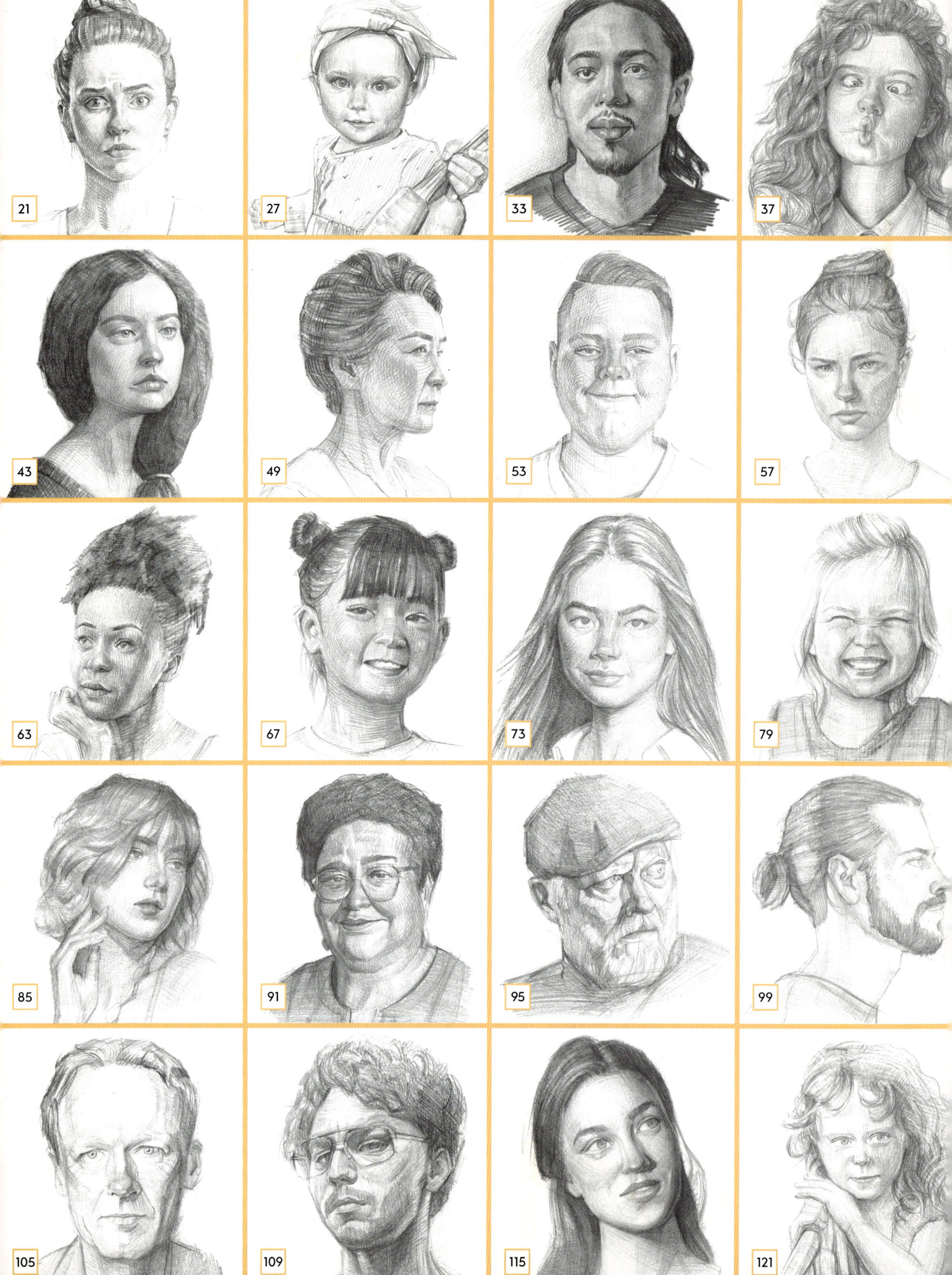

21
27
33
37
43
49
53
57
63
67
73
79
85
91
95
99
105
109
115
121

CONTENTS

PORTRAITS

INTRODUCTION

Portraiture, a prominent branch of figurative art, entails creating a detailed drawing of the human face. Initially, it is important to understand the basic anatomical features of the face when drawing a portrait. Drawing the eyes, nose, mouth, and other details in the correct proportions and placement is the key to a successful portrait.

In portrait drawing, the artist must work in detail to reflect the subject's disposition and emotions. The management of light, the use of shadows, and the details of expression greatly affect the feeling of the portrait. The artist must skillfully use visual expression to emphasize the subtle nuances of facial features to reflect the mood and personality of the sitter.

Portrait drawing requires not only technical skills, but also keen observation skills and the artist's unique creativity. When drawing a portrait, the artist's goal is to go beyond the physical characteristics of the person to reveal their emotions and uniqueness.

Portrait drawing is a process of expressing the power of art through human expression and establishing a connection with the viewers, offering a unique opportunity to understand and share the human experience. The artist must constantly practice and pay attention to their observations in order to develop their own style and add emotion, depth, and realism to their portraits.

PORTRAIT DRAWING IS A PROCESS OF EXPRESSING THE POWER OF ART THROUGH HUMAN EXPRESSION AND ESTABLISHING A CONNECTION WITH THE VIEWERS.

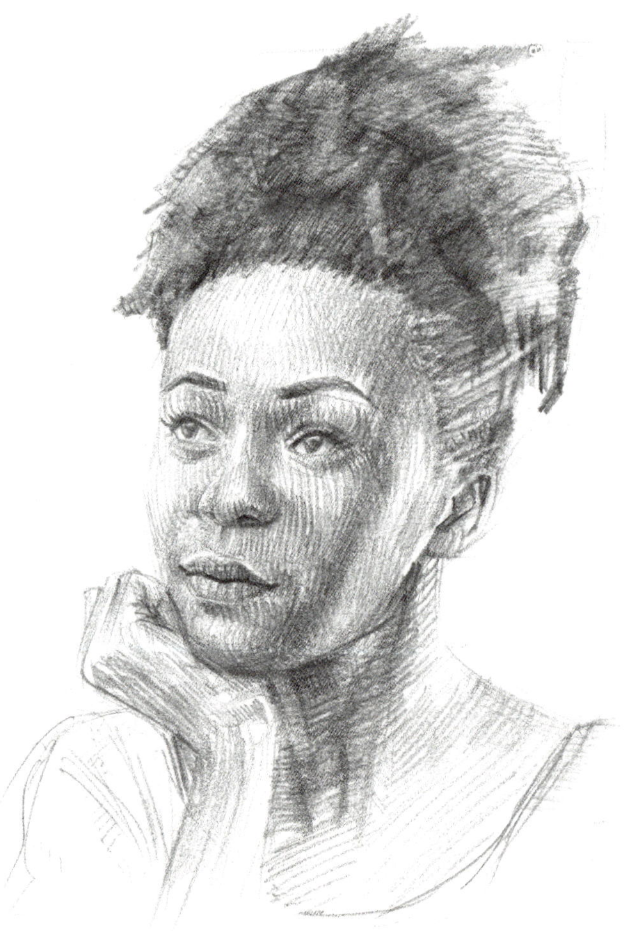

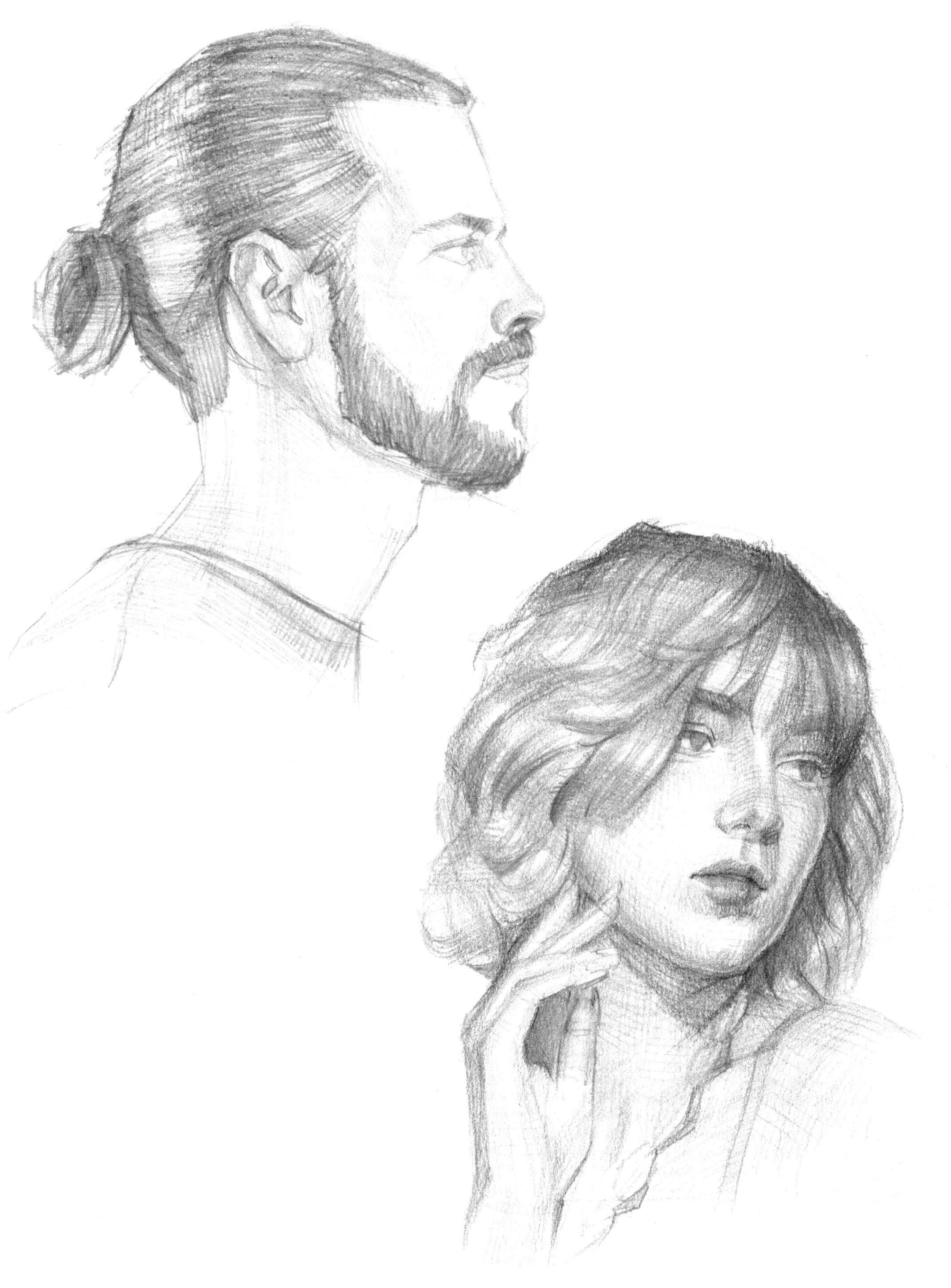

TOOLS AND MATERIALS

Portraiture is an expressive art form that requires the ability to express character through subtle shading and detail. Choosing the right materials is essential for successfully executing this style of drawing.

PENCILS

A high-quality pencil drawing set is a basic requirement. This set should include pencils of different hardness that give the artist the flexibility to add various gradations and details. Pencil hardness varies from very soft (9B) to very hard (9H). A good starter set includes a 6B, 4B, 2B, HB, B, 2H, 4H, and 6H.

Charcoal pencils for shading and toning are also important for creating depth and volume in a drawing. Like graphite pencils, you can use soft, medium-hard, and hard charcoal pencils to achieve different tones and add realism to the portrait.

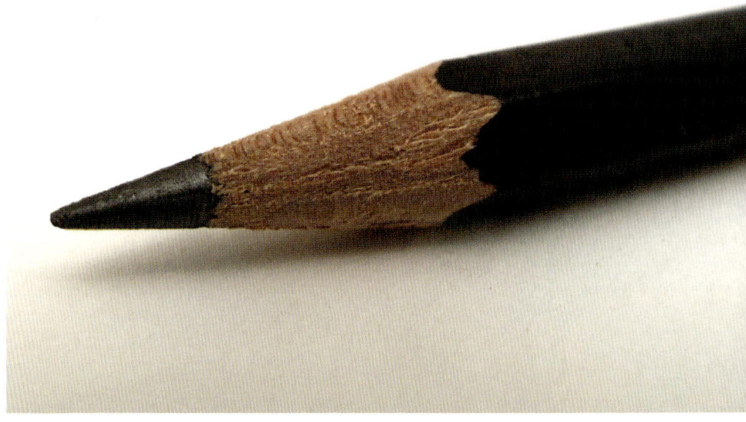

Here's the order of pencils I usually use when I draw a portrait: H–HB–B–2B–3B. I find don't need softer pencils to achieve darker tones, as I usually get the darkest tones by applying pressure; however, you can also use 4B, 5B, and 6B pencils if you desire.

Pictured here are gradations of 8B, 4B, HB, and 4H leads over medium drawing paper, allowing you to see the differences in stroke quality and darkness.

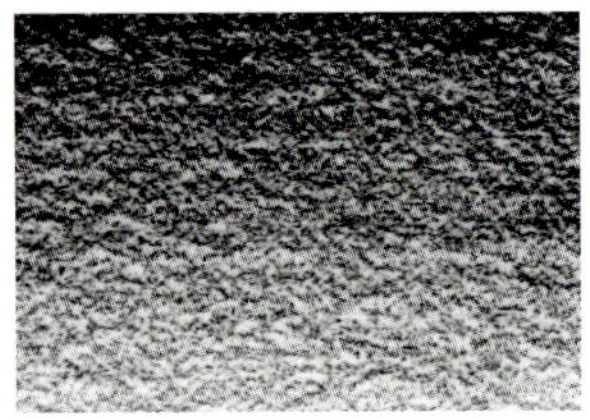

8B

4B

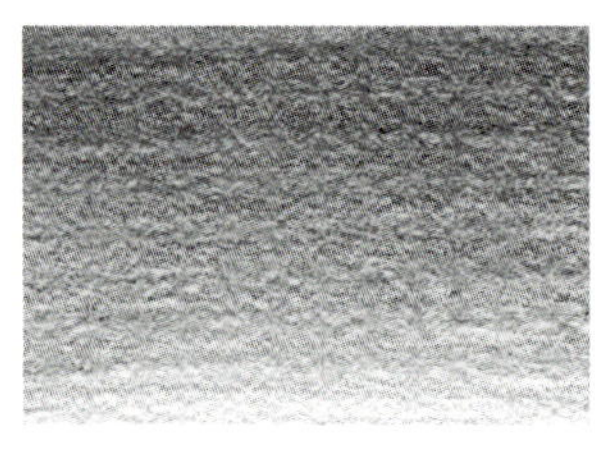

HB

4H

PAPER

The paper for pencil drawings should also be carefully selected. Drawing paper is available in a range of surface textures, including smooth grain (hot pressed), medium grain (cold pressed), and rough. A thick art paper with a dense and smooth surface is preferable for portraiture. This type of paper responds better to pencil shading and allows the fine details in the drawing to be better defined.

ERASERS & BLURRING TOOLS

Your choice of eraser is also important. Using a fine-tipped eraser to correct delicate details or emphasize light and shadow effects can improve the quality of the drawing. Erasers are available in a variety of materials. Plastic erasers are useful for removing hard pencil marks and large areas. Kneaded erasers can be molded into different shapes and used to dab at an area, gently lifting tone from the paper.

Some artists may also prefer blurring tools, such as paper napkins or blending stumps to make gradations softer and more natural.

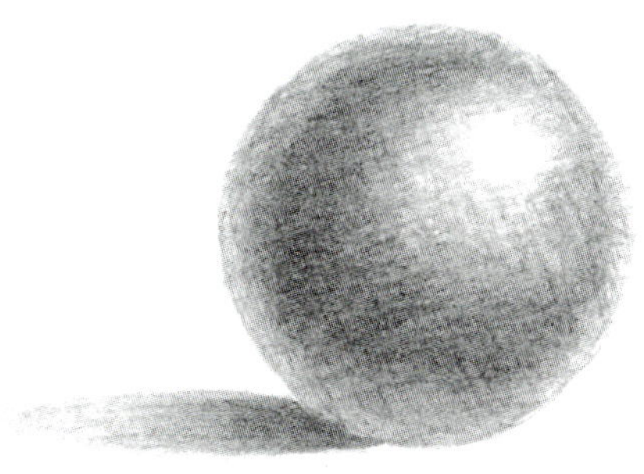

SMOOTH

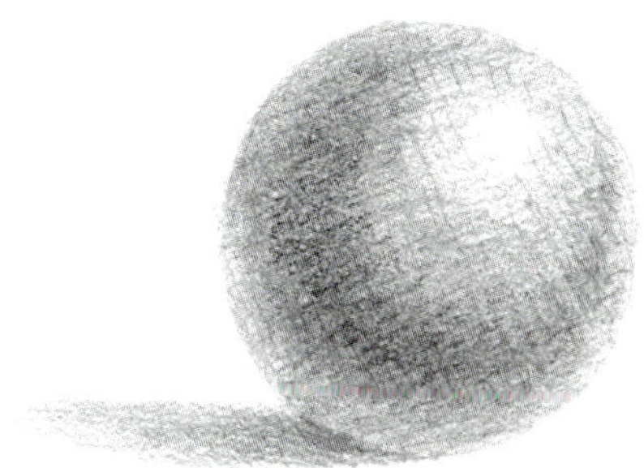

MEDIUM

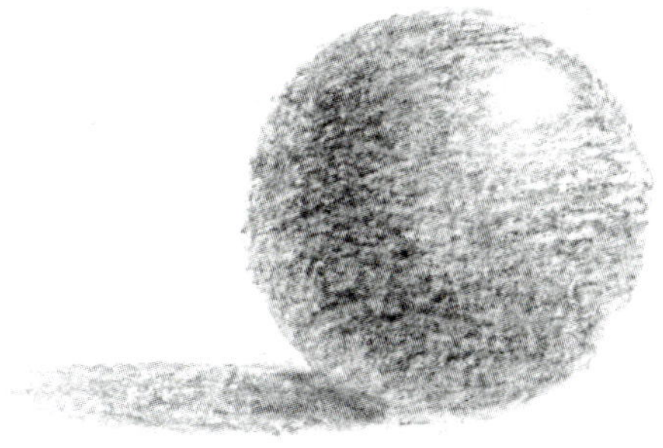

ROUGH

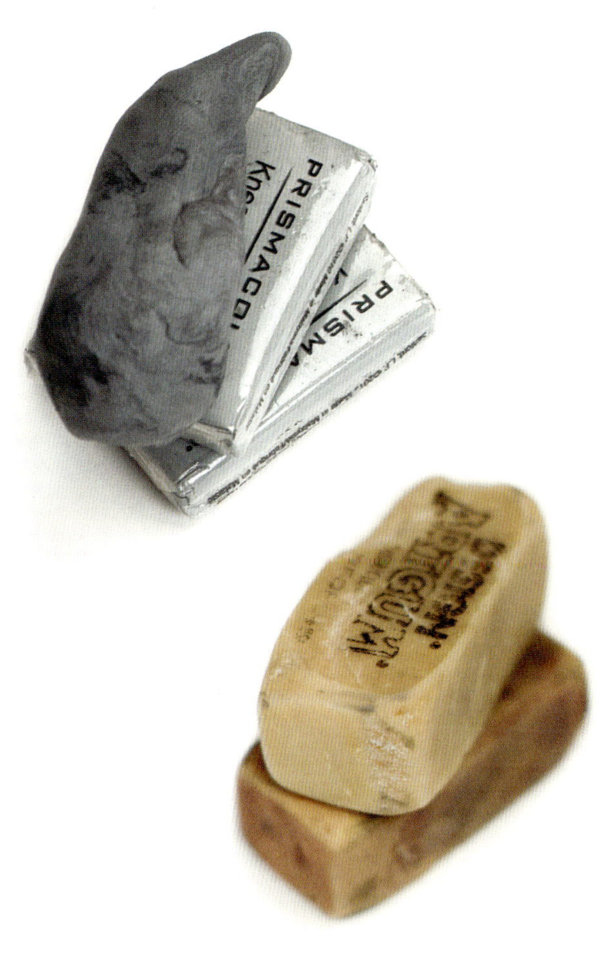

BASIC PENCIL TECHNIQUES

Basic pencil drawing techniques give the artist a strong foundation in toning, detailing, and shading. You should always start with thin lines made with light strokes to help you identify the basic lines. These lines are guidelines, which can later be erased, and determine the overall composition of the drawing.

REFLECTING LIGHT AND SHADOW

Toning in charcoal involves varying the pencil pressure to reflect light and shadow in the drawing. Lighter tones are used in areas where the light falls, while darker tones are preferred in areas of shadow. This gradation is important in creating a sense of volume and depth in the drawing.

USING LINE TO CREATE TEXTURE AND DETAIL

Using diagonal lines, or hatching, is effective in balancing the overall tone of the drawing and creating texture and shading. Quick, freehand diagonal lines make the drawing look more dynamic and energetic.

In addition to using thin lines to add detail, it's also important to use contour lines to indicate shaded areas. Contour lines focus on specific areas of the drawing, directing the eye to the main focal point.

ERASER TECHNIQUES

Use of an eraser is also an important technique in pencil drawings. Artists can use an eraser to emphasize white areas and better control light. The different surfaces and tips of various erasers can help make precise corrections to different parts of the drawing.

STICK ERASERS are ideal for erasing small areas and "drawing" with the eraser to create light details.

KNEADED ERASERS can be molded into a fine point, an edge, or a larger flat or rounded surface. They are useful for pulling graphite off the paper in a dabbing motion.

PLASTIC ERASERS remove graphite well and are gentle on your paper. This type of eraser works well for erasing large areas or doing a final cleanup of your finished drawing.

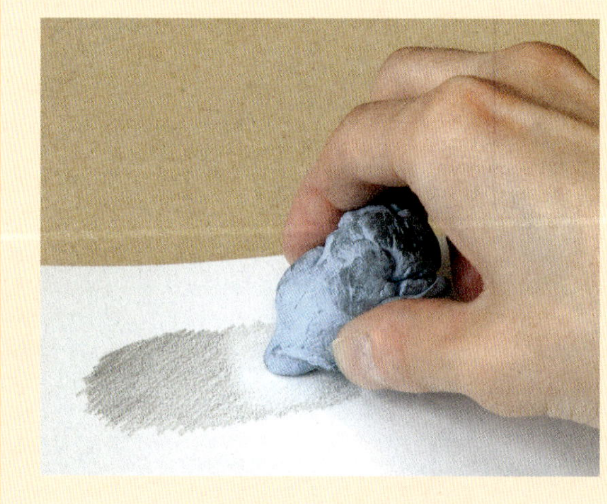

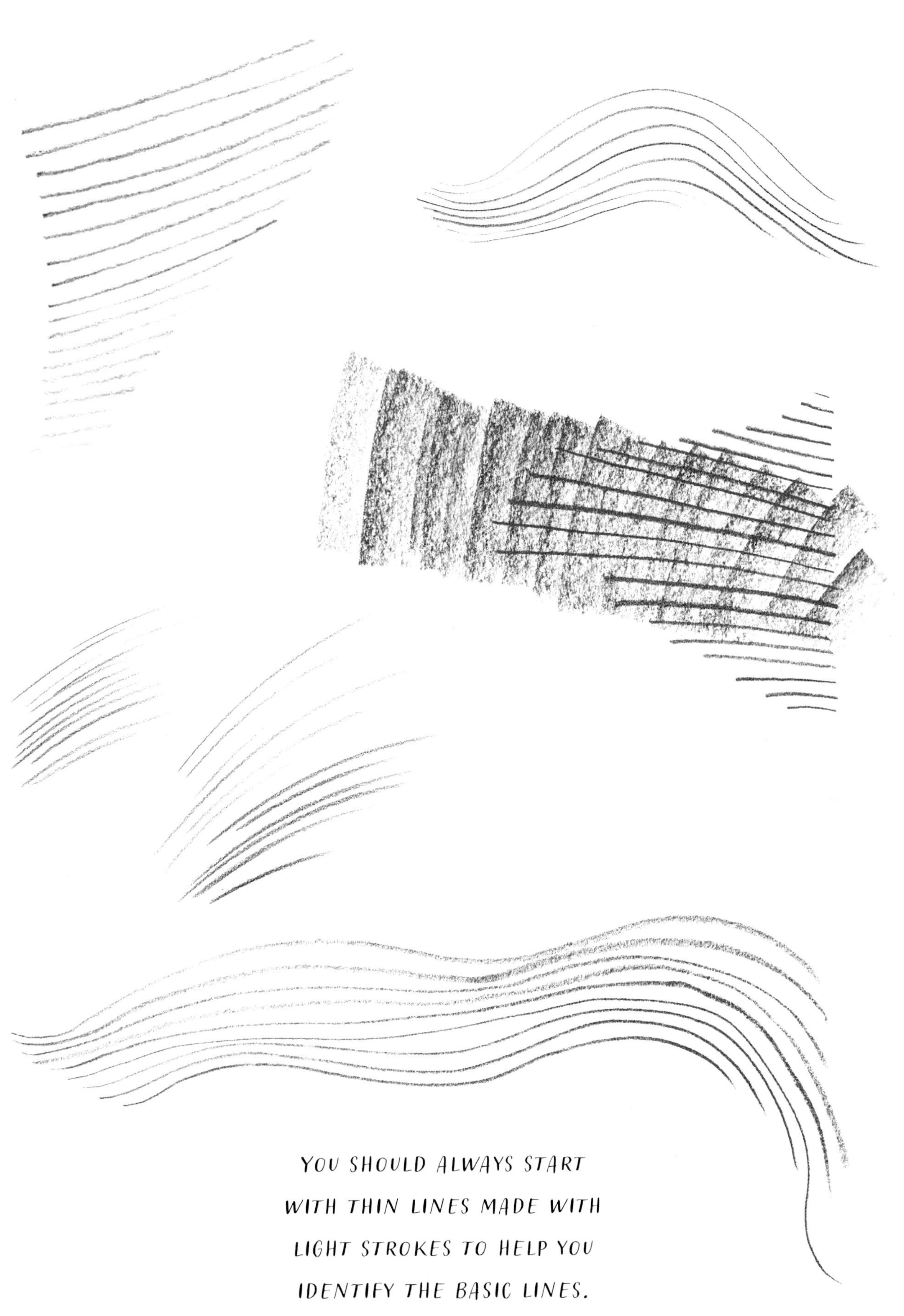

YOU SHOULD ALWAYS START
WITH THIN LINES MADE WITH
LIGHT STROKES TO HELP YOU
IDENTIFY THE BASIC LINES.

PROPORTIONS

Basic portrait drawing rules of proportions and facial features are important in helping artists express the human face accurately and expressively. A good portrait requires accurate drawing of the eyes, mouth, and other details to capture facial expression and character.

The direction of light and shading techniques are also important in portraiture, as these elements play a critical role in adding volume and depth to the face. Understanding the basic rules of portraiture gives artists a strong foundation for creating realistic and expressive portraits.

ANATOMY OF THE HUMAN FACE

A key component of portrait drawing is understanding the makeup of the human face. It's important to draw the face, eyes, nose, mouth, ears, and other features in the correct proportions and placement to create an accurate and lifelike rendering.

Here is a breakdown of the general proportions of the human face:

- The length from the forehead to under the chin is proportional to the width of the chin.
- The eyes are located in the center of the face, and the distance from each other is the width of one eye.
- The nose starts below the eyes, and its relationship with the mouth is also important.

PROPORTIONS AND MEASUREMENTS OF THE HUMAN HEAD

The proportions and measurements of the human head are important for realism and harmony in portraiture. The anatomical measurements of the head guide artists in correctly placing the different features of the face.

Here is a guide to general head proportions and facial feature placement:

A. The width of a head is usually equal to the length from the forehead to the cheeks, two-thirds its height (excluding the height of the hair). Picture the head contained in a rectangle with a width of 2½ units, and a height of 3½ units.

B. If you divide the human head into 3½ parts with horizontal axis lines starting at the top of the skull, the section from the beginning of the hair to the bottom of the chin consists of three mostly equal parts: (1) between the hairline and the eyebrow line, (2) between the eyebrow line and the line under the nose, and (3) between the line under the nose and the line under the chin.

C. The section between the top of the skull and the hairline is half of the third section.

D. The space between the eyes is the width of one eye. The eyes are in the center of the head.

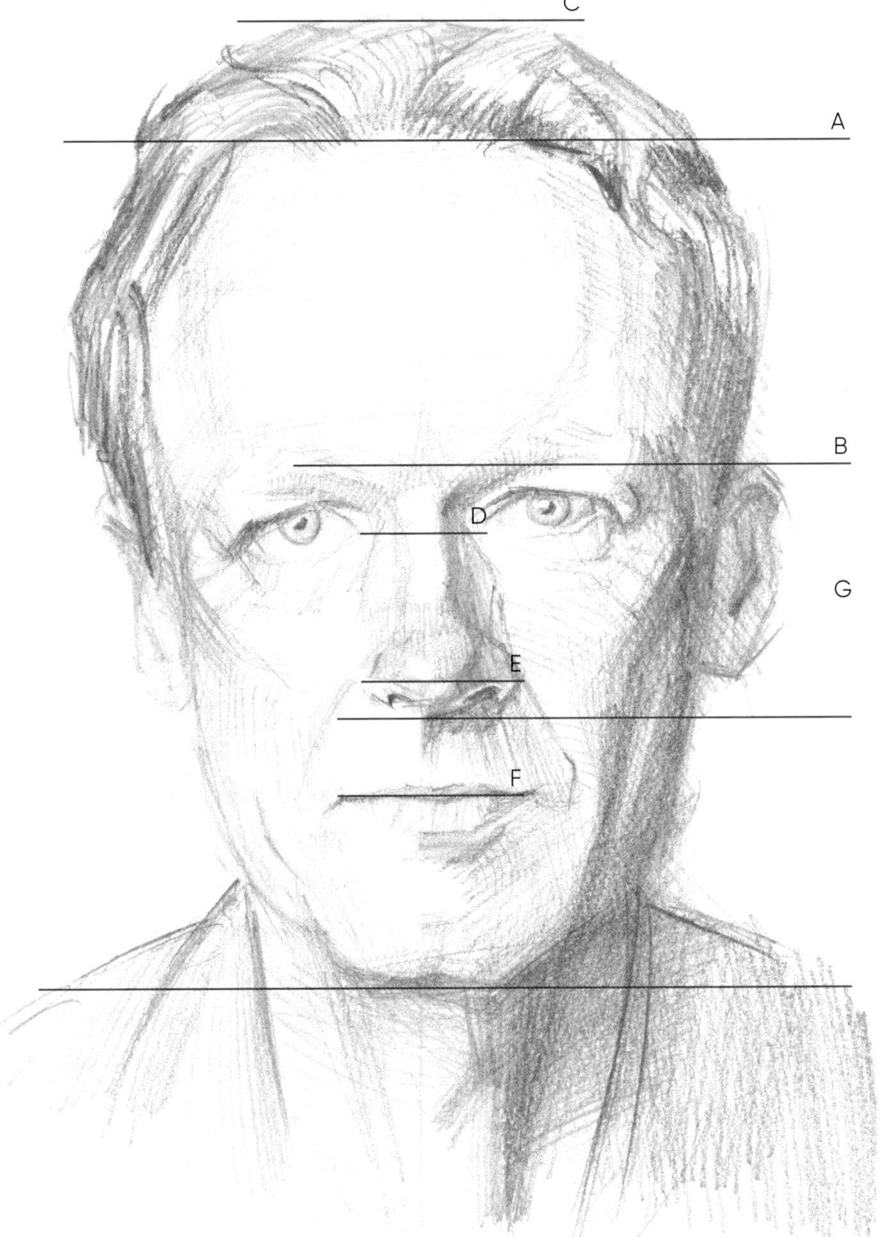

E. The width of the nose is the width of one eye. The nose starts below the eyes and is usually aligned between the inner and outer edges of the eyes.

F. The mouth starts under the nose. The distance between the tip of the chin and the top of the nose usually is close to the width of the mouth.

G. The ears are usually located between the upper edge of the eyes and the lower edge of the nose.

Following these proportions helps ensure the head is drawn in its correct anatomical proportions and that the portrait leaves a true impression on the viewer. The proportions and measurements of the human head provide a basic guideline for artists to achieve successful expression and balance in portraiture.

COMPOSITION AND PERSPECTIVE

COMPOSITION

A successful portrait composition tells a story to the viewer, captures the essence of the subject, and achieves an aesthetic balance. Composition in portrait drawing is a form of expression the artist can use to create an emotional impact. A portrait composition that draws the viewer in, moves them, and makes them think can maximize the power and expressiveness of art. Composition in portraiture plays a critical role in adding meaning and depth to the artwork.

First, the artist should consider the placement of the main elements that will be used in the drawing: the position of the model, the point of view, and any other elements of the drawing. Placing the model at eye level, and the overall composition of the drawing, is very important in order to convey to the viewer the artist's desired emotional effect. The choice of position in the drawing can guide the viewer's interaction with the model.

The background also affects the composition. A simple and plain background can direct the viewer to focus more on the model's facial expressions and details. On the other hand, a more complex background can add depth to the portrait and enrich the overall atmosphere of the drawing.

The balance between the eyes and other elements in the drawing is another important element of composition. The use of light, shadows, and gradations should be carefully arranged to emphasize the model's facial expression and give the drawing a three-dimensional appearance.

PERSPECTIVE

Perspective is a concept that refers to the changing size and shape of an object or scene depending on distance. When drawing a portrait, taking perspective into account will make your drawing look more realistic and accurate.

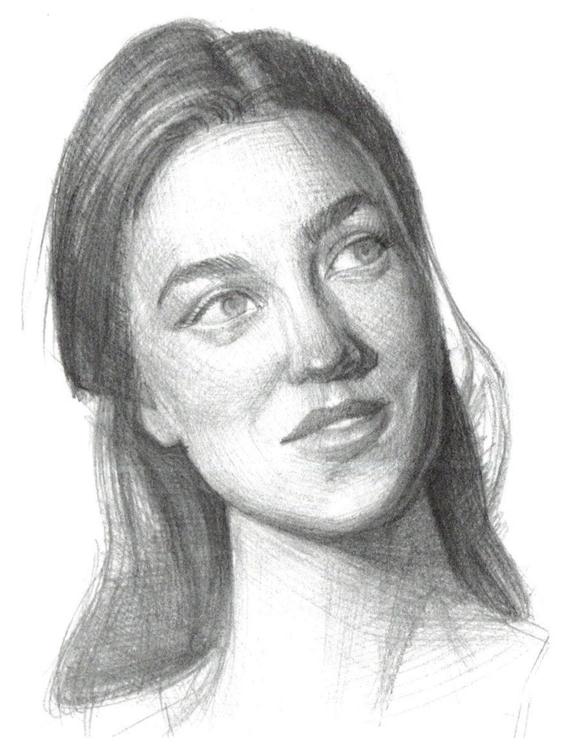

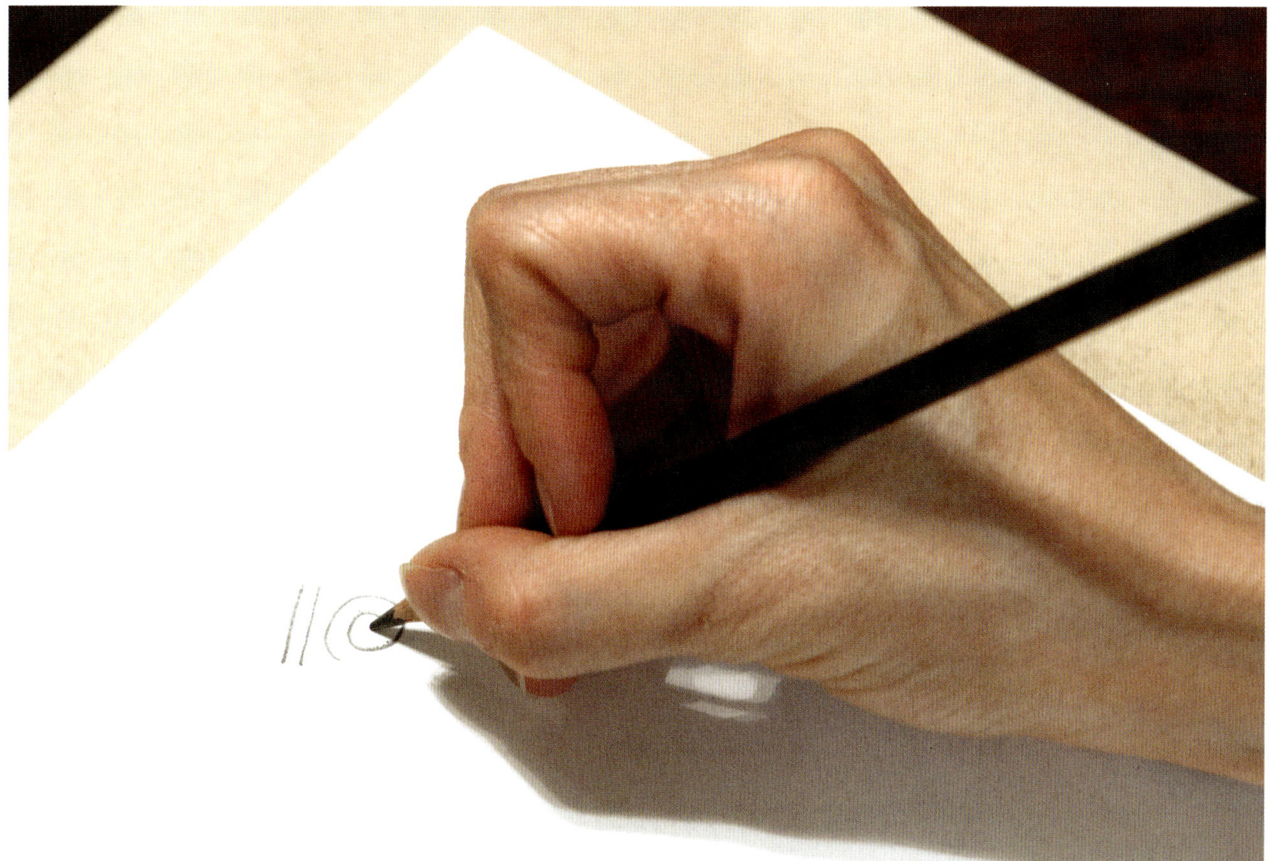

To understand perspective, hold your paper out at eye level and think about where your portrait will go. Based on the eye level, you can understand how objects will appear and how the perspective will change.

It is important to understand how objects shrink in relation to distance and how they fit into perspective. Objects that are farther away appear smaller. Therefore, the details and features in your portrait should decrease in direct proportion to the distance of the objects.

If the objects in your portrait appear upright, it's important to draw the perspective lines correctly. For example, to accurately express the perspective of parallel objects, such as bricks on a wall, you can use accurate perspective lines that show these parallel lines moving closer or farther away from each other in a straight line.

You can emphasize perspective using shadows and depth effects. For example, you can use shadows to show how objects are shaded in relation to distance and how they contain less detail. You can also increase the sense of depth by drawing background objects more faintly or indistinctly to enhance the depth perception of perspective.

> **TIP:** When creating light and shadow, your work will improve if you use fine lines, not broad strokes.

STEP-BY-STEP DRAWING TECHNIQUES

STARTING WITH A LIGHT SKETCH

When starting a portrait drawing, beginning with light sketches is an important step in the process of determining the basic lines. This stage allows the artist to accurately measure facial features and pay attention to proportions. Light sketches make it easier to make corrections and changes in the early stages of drawing.

Start by lightly sketching the general contours of the face. This includes baselines to define the forehead, chin, cheeks, and jawline. Light lines help accurately place the overall proportions of the facial features without initially weighing down the drawing.

Next, add light lines to determine the placement of the eyes. Lightly marking details such as the distance between the eyes, the size, and the shape of the eyes plays a critical role in laying the foundation for the drawing. At this stage, the focus is on features such as eye contours and the position of the eyebrows.

Continuing with light sketches, determine the outlines of the nose and mouth. Draw the nose starting below the eyes, and add the mouth, paying attention to the proportion between the nose and the chin. At this stage, light lines help determine the placement of details.

Finally, add the other features with light lines to complete the facial features and further elaborate the drawing. In particular, it is important at this stage to mark the soft transitions and gradations of the facial features.

Starting with light sketches provides a foundation for adding sharper and more defined lines in the later stages of the drawing process. This gives the artist more flexibility and the opportunity to make corrections as needed to develop the drawing. Light sketches are an effective way to establish a reliable foundation at the beginning, helping to maintain the correct proportions and details in portrait drawing.

UTILIZING BASIC GEOMETRIC SHAPES

Utilizing basic geometric shapes in portraiture is an important strategy in the process of determining the correct proportions, creating the composition, and focusing on details. Basic geometric shapes provide guidance when creating the overall composition of the portrait.

Start with simple geometric forms, such as circles, ovals, and rectangles. A round form represents the head, while an oval shape for the face helps get the proportions right at the beginning. Rectangles and lines can be used to define important features such as facial features and the placement of the eyes.

These simple geometric forms identify focal points for the viewer and balance the portrait. They also help the artist understand perspective and predict how the portrait will look from different angles. Converting details such as a nose or mouth into simple geometric forms allows you to better control proportions and placement.

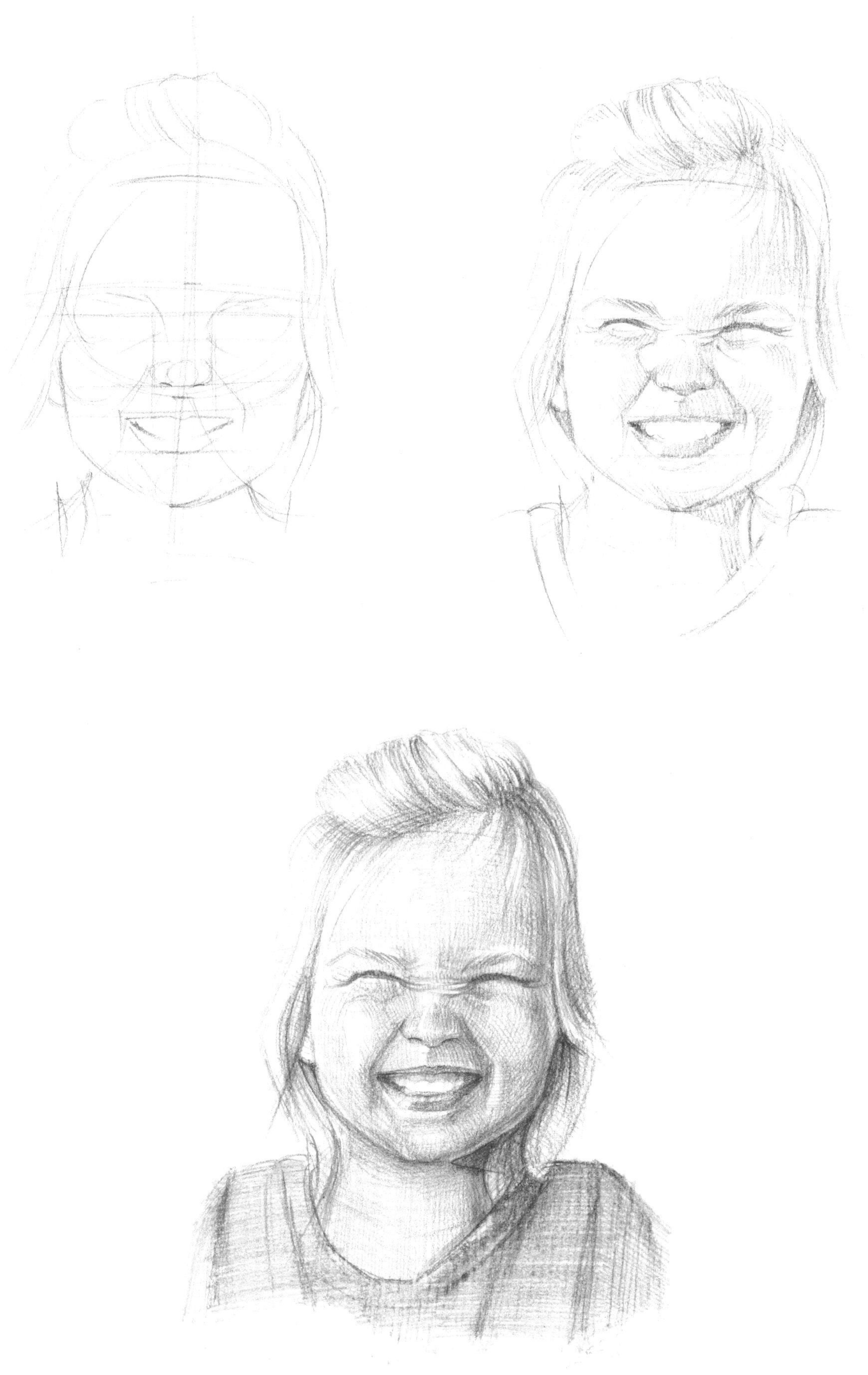

In addition to establishing an accurate frame at the beginning, this strategy also allows you to make corrections during the drawing process and present a more realistic portrait to the viewer.

DETERMINING ACCURATE PROPORTIONS

In order to capture the correct anatomical dimensions of the portrait and express the human figure realistically, it is necessary to draw the proportions correctly. Harmony between each part of the face ensures the overall balance and aesthetic appeal of the portrait, and paying special attention to proportions is the basis for a successful portrait drawing.

The first step is to correctly determine the overall proportions of the face. This includes basic proportions, such as the width of the head, the distance between the eyes, and the placement of the nose and mouth. Initially, you can use basic geometric shapes to determine these proportions, which will help you understand the overall structure and proportions of the head.

The eyes are one of the most important elements in portraiture and must have the correct proportions. The placement of the eyes is usually in the center of the head, and they should be equidistant from each other. The size of the eyes should be proportional to the facial features and the width of the head. These proportions should be fine-tuned to achieve a more realistic and balanced portrait.

The nose and mouth are other important features of the face, and the placement of these details should also be in the correct proportions. The nose usually starts below the eyes, and the distance between the mouth and the chin should also be within a certain proportion. The mouth should be correctly positioned in the lower half of the face, in harmony with the other features.

UNDERSTANDING LIGHT AND SHADOW TO ADD DEPTH AND DIMENSION

Light and shadow is one of the most important elements in portrait drawing. It's crucial to identify the direction the light is coming from and use the tonalities on the surface correctly. The position of the light source, the placement of shadows, and tonal changes are critical in adding depth to the portrait. The right light/shadow effects emphasize the details of the face, making the model's facial expression and features more distinct.

Light Source

Understanding the light source is an important first step. When drawing a portrait, knowing where the light source is coming from helps determine the gradations and shadows on the face. Highlighting emphasizes the model's facial features and contours, while shading emphasizes the depth and form of the surface.

Light and Shadow

The use of light and shadow has a huge impact on adding depth and dimension. The right gradations and shadows create a three-dimensional effect by pushing certain areas of a face into the background while highlighting others. This makes the portrait look more vivid and realistic.

When drawing a portrait, skillful use of light and shadow effects allows you to create a greater sense of depth and dimension. The right gradation and shading enrich the atmosphere of the portrait and more effectively express the various textures on the model's surface. Understanding these concepts and correctly applying light/shadow tonalities is a fundamental skill for professionalism and aesthetic success in portrait drawing.

ADDING DETAILS AND TEXTURES

In portraiture, getting the details right plays a key role in expressing the subject's unique features and emotional depth to the viewer. These details reveal the subject's expression and give you the power to tell a story.

Your observation skills and fine dexterity are of great importance when drawing the details in a portrait. Adding details without exaggeration, in the right proportions and in harmony, preserves the aesthetic integrity of the portrait and allows the viewer to establish a deep connection. These details enrich the impression the portrait leaves on the viewer and emphasize the subject's personality. Drawing these details well demonstrates the artist's talent and skill in revealing the subtleties and beauty of portraiture.

Your first step can be to start with small details in the eyes. Elements such as the fine lines around the eyes, the details of the eyelashes, and the reflections in the pupils affect the subject's expression and mood. Since the eyes are one of the most emphasized points in a portrait, pay special attention to these details.

The details of the mouth also play an important role in portraiture. The curves of the lips, the shadows of the teeth, and the small details that accompany the mouth movements emphasize the subject's expression.

It is also important to focus on details in other parts of the face. The lines of the nose, the subtle curve of the eyebrows, the details of the ears, and the details of the hair strands enhance the realism of the portrait and the authenticity of the subject. Details are especially important in capturing the hair's natural texture and shape.

DRAWING HAIR

Determining the overall volume and style of the hair greatly affects the impression the portrait leaves on the viewer. Wavy, straight, curly, or uneven hairstyles can reflect the personality and story of the subject.

The first step in drawing realistic hair detail is to determine the overall shape of the hair. When starting hair drawing, use broad lines to capture the natural flow and movement of the hair, establishing the overall layout of the hair.

Light and shadow also play an important role in drawing hair. By creating bright areas where light hits the hair, you can emphasize the volume and form of the hair. Adding shadows and tones from the roots to the ends of the hair will make the hair look voluminous and natural.

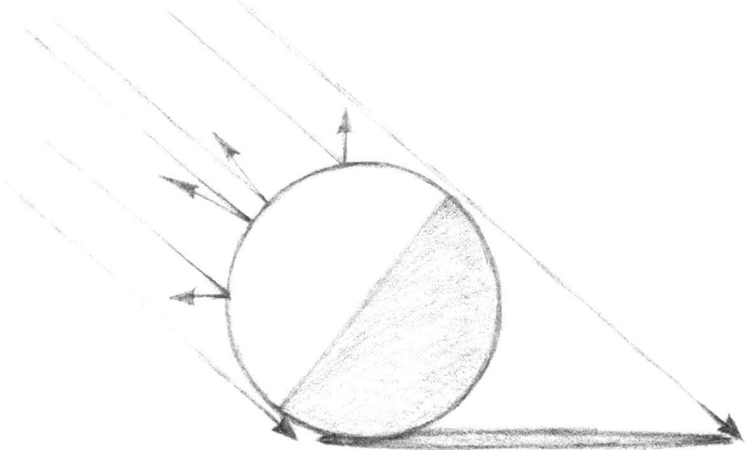

Shading gives dimension to our drawings as we model form with lighter and darker values. A convincing application of these value changes gives the impression of light and shadow. Notice the pattern of light as it bounces off the sphere, revealing cast shadow.

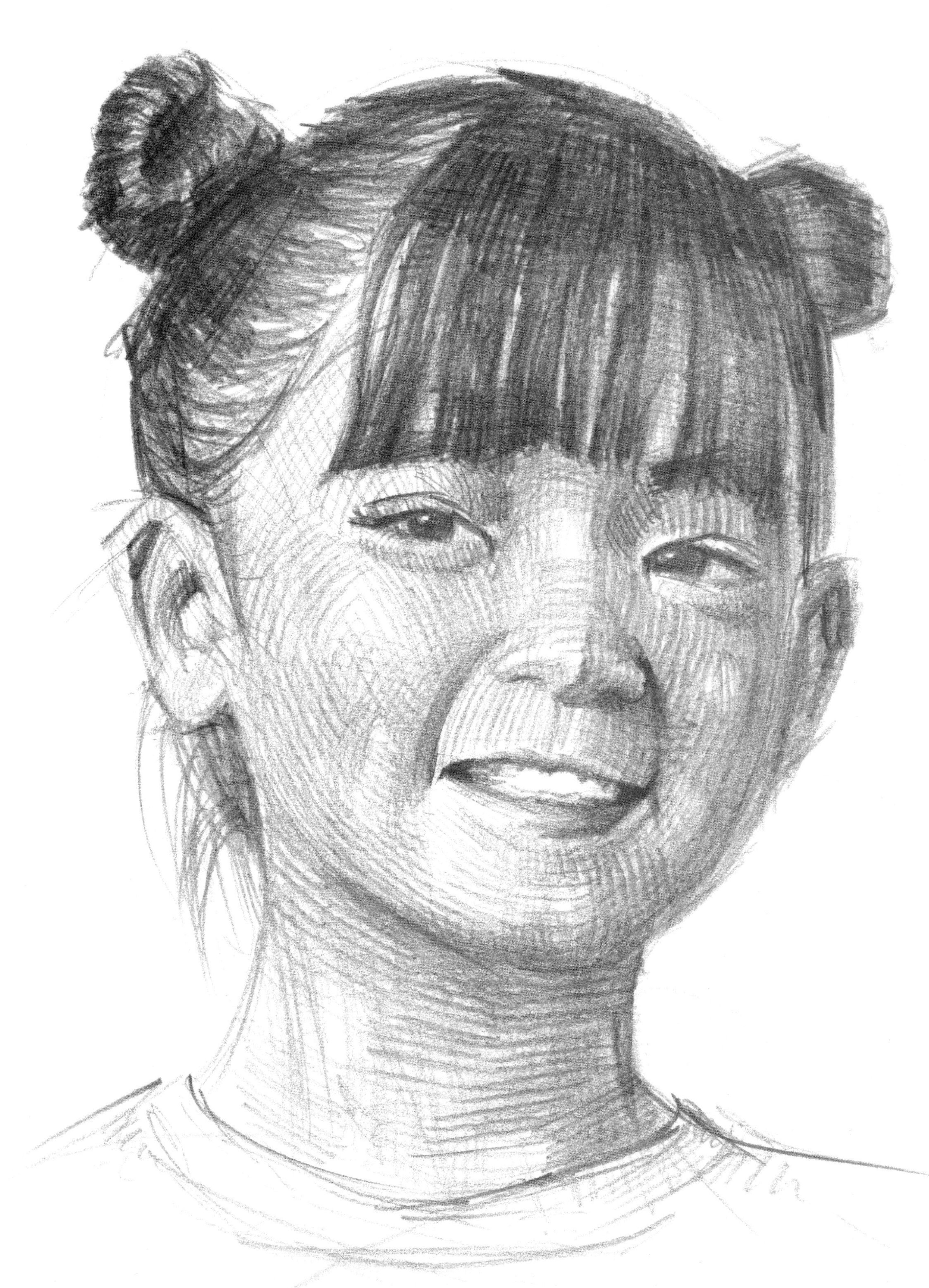

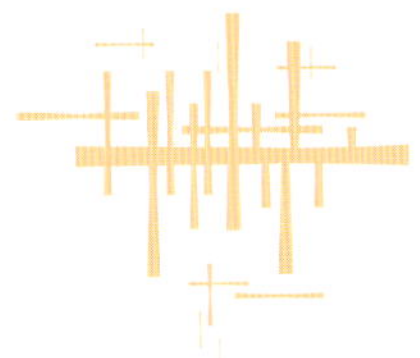

PORTRAITS

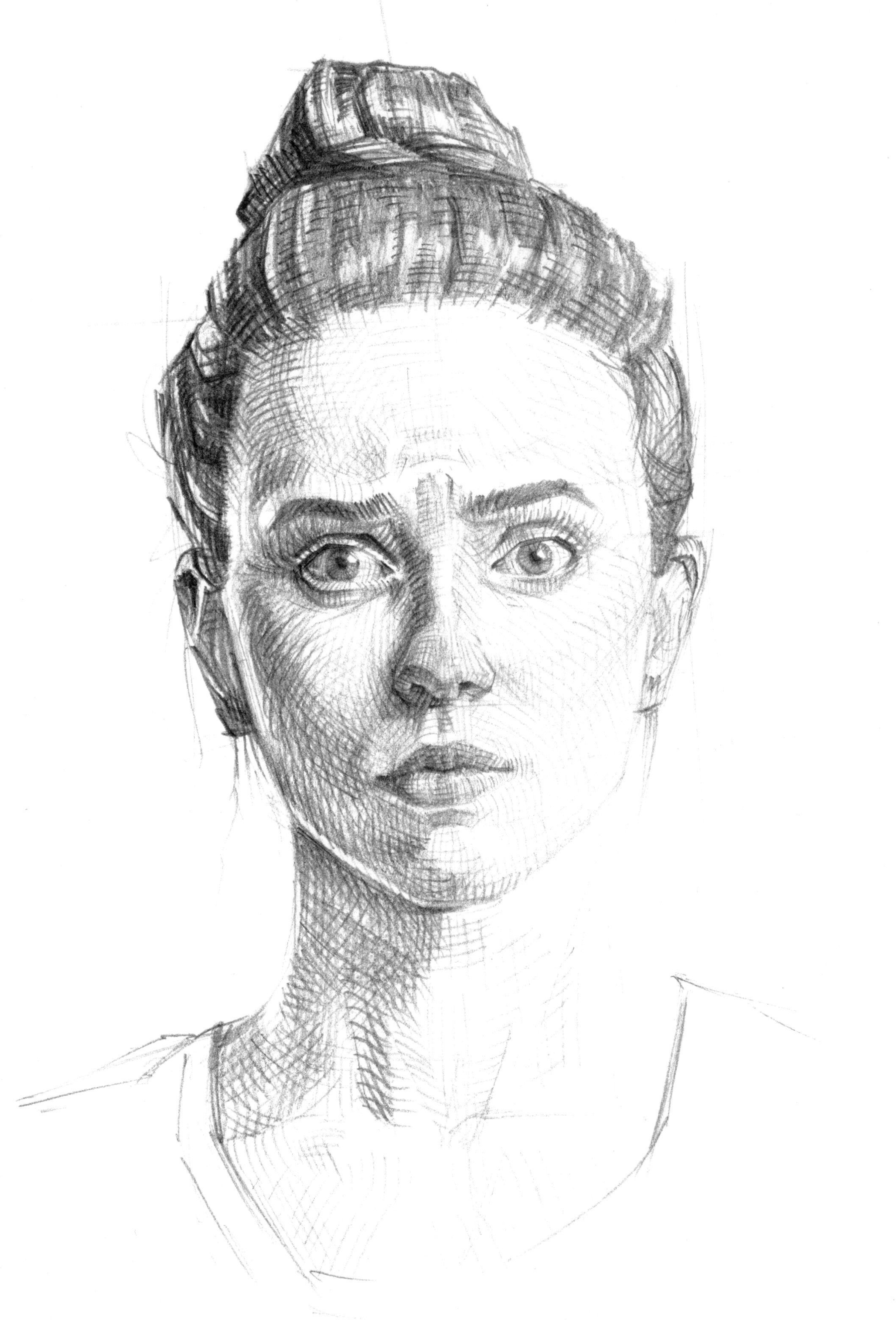

PROJECT 1

SIDE-LIT FRONT VIEW

In this portrait the light is positioned to the subject's side, which creates strong shadows on the face and neck. This type of lighting accentuates the subject's three-dimensional form.

The first step is to decide how the portrait will be placed on the paper and what its dimensions will be. Plan where to place the face and where to draw it on the paper. Next, determine the proportions. Usually, a face is approximately twice as long as its head, in terms of height. So the distance from the eyebrows to the bottom of the chin is twice the distance from the eyebrows to the hair.

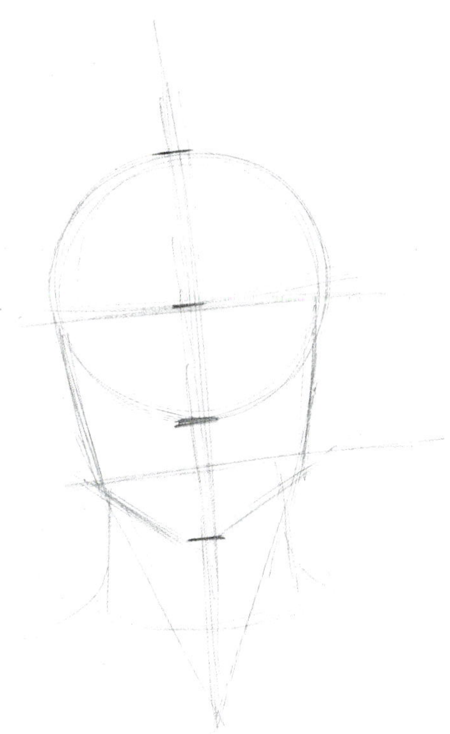

STEP 1

First, draw a circle and divide it with a horizontal line into two equal parts and draw a perpendicular line downward.

This step is preliminary work to determine the basic shape and features of the face. Start by marking the outline of the face and the position of the eyes, nose, and mouth.

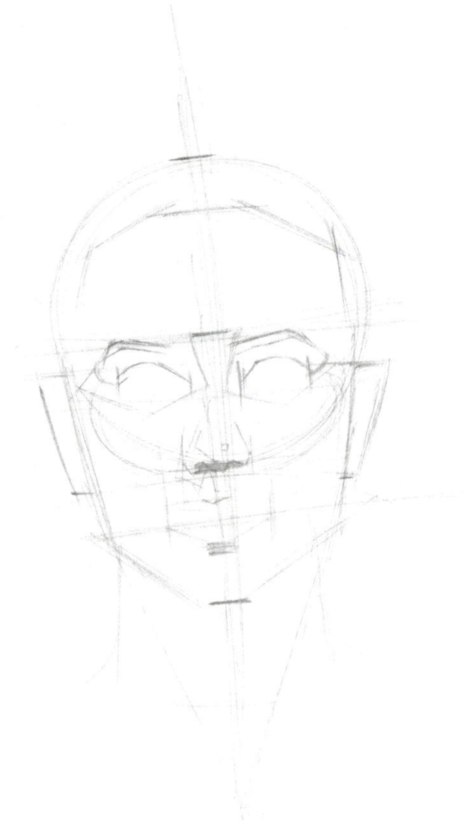

2

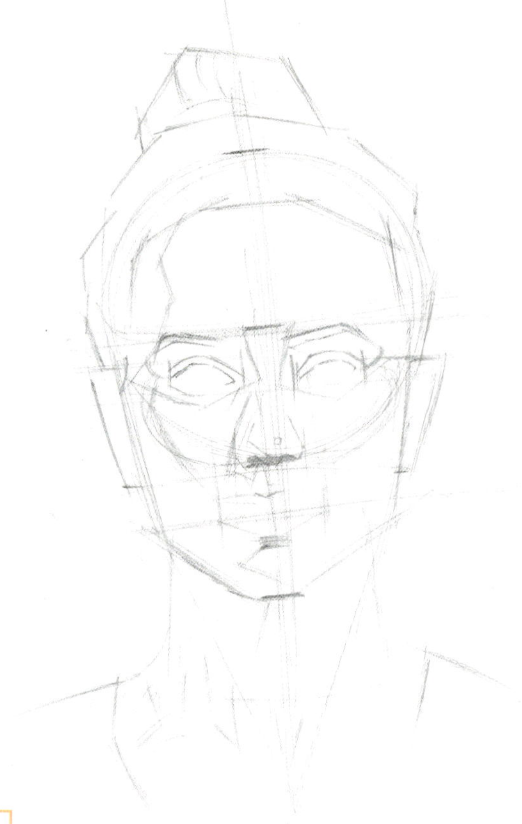

3

STEP 2

Determine the placement of the eyes, nose, mouth, and ears on the face. In this step, place these features, accurately observing proportions and symmetry.

STEP 3

Now that you are sure of the proportions of the facial features, confidently emphasize them over these guidelines. With more precise, more defined lines, shape your portrait. Add the general shape of the hair.

STEP 4

Add the irises, eyelashes, nostrils, lip lines, and other details. In this step, focus on the details that define the expression and character of the face.

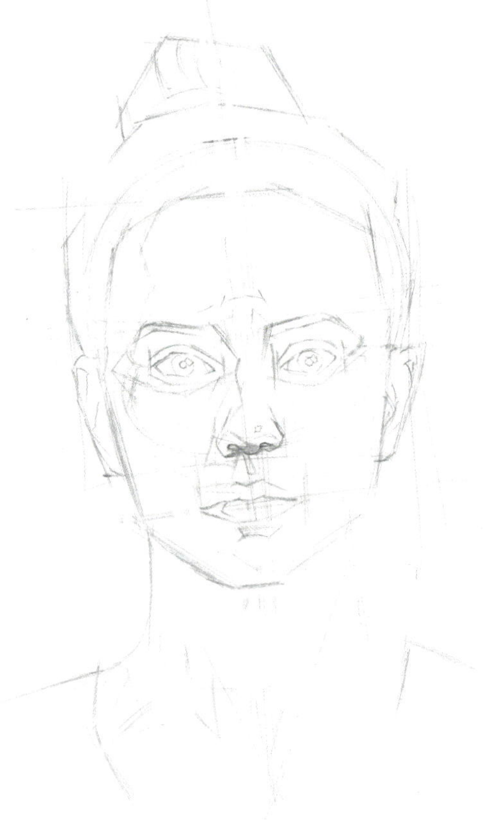

4

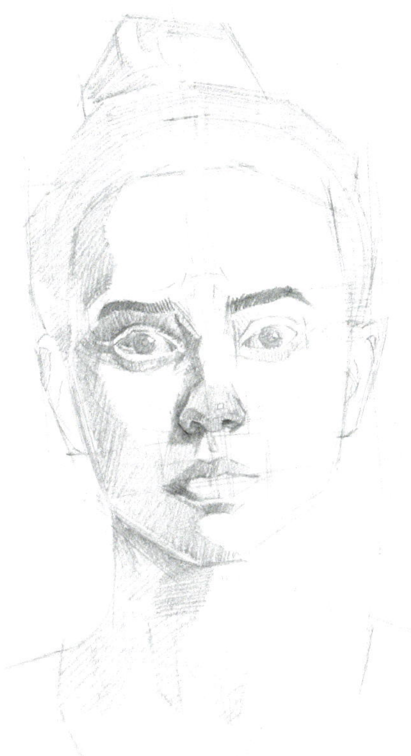

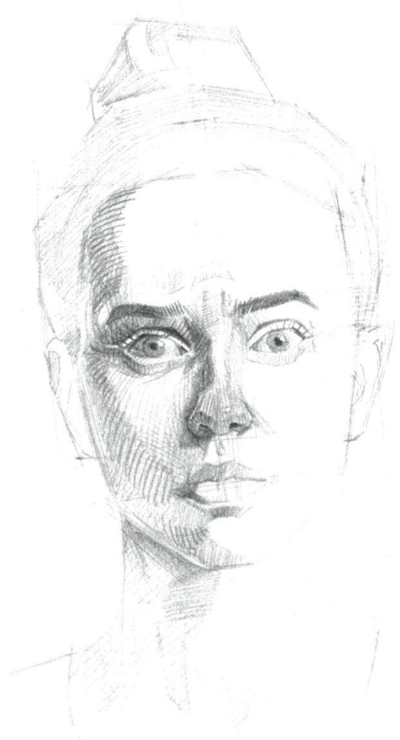

5

STEP 5

Now you have created your portrait with the right proportions and added the characteristic features. Next, identify the shadows and highlights on the face. Thinking about where the light comes from—the right side of the subject—begin to create shadows and light reflections in different areas on the surface.

6

STEP 6

Continue to increase the volume and depth of the portrait by darkening areas of shadow. Create the makeup of the face by emphasizing the protruding features—nose, lips, brow bone. At this stage, shading is very important to show the rotation and volume of the face.

> **TIP:** When creating light and shadow, your work will improve if you use fine lines, not broad strokes, as if you were painting.

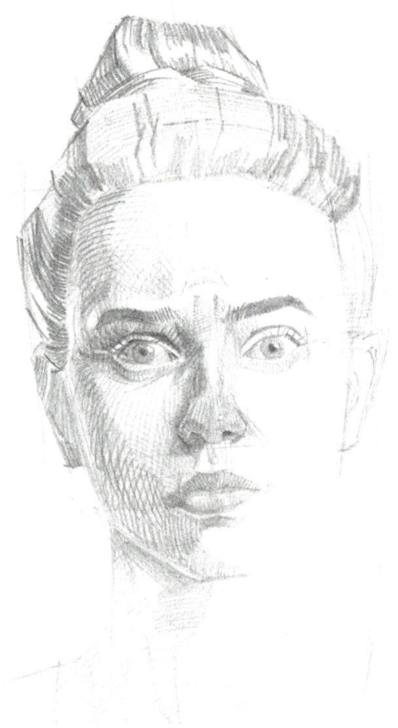

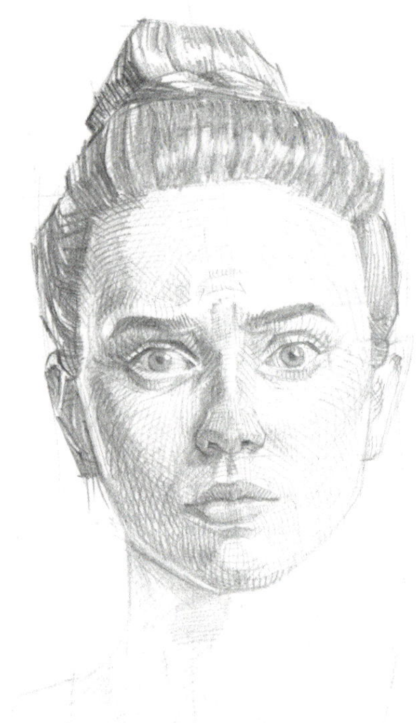

7

8

STEP 7

Review the details of the portrait and make corrections where necessary. Check for symmetry and make the details of the eyes, nose, eyebrows, and lips more prominent.

STEP 8

Next, add even greater detail and shaping to the face, thinking of the portrait in three dimensions. Your drawing marks for the cheekbones, eye sockets, jaw, and nose need to be in the right direction. This is the crosshatching technique. Curve your hatching lines according to the slope, depth, and protrusions on the face. When you curve your lines slightly, you express the makeup of the face much better.

Start drawing the mass and tone of the hair. An easy mistake in portraiture is to create every part of the drawing with the same tones—tone values are very important to avoid a "flat" drawing. In dark tones, the hair should naturally be darker than the tones in the portrait. In this example, the darkest values are in the hair. Since the left side of the hair is in shadow, that area has the darkest values.

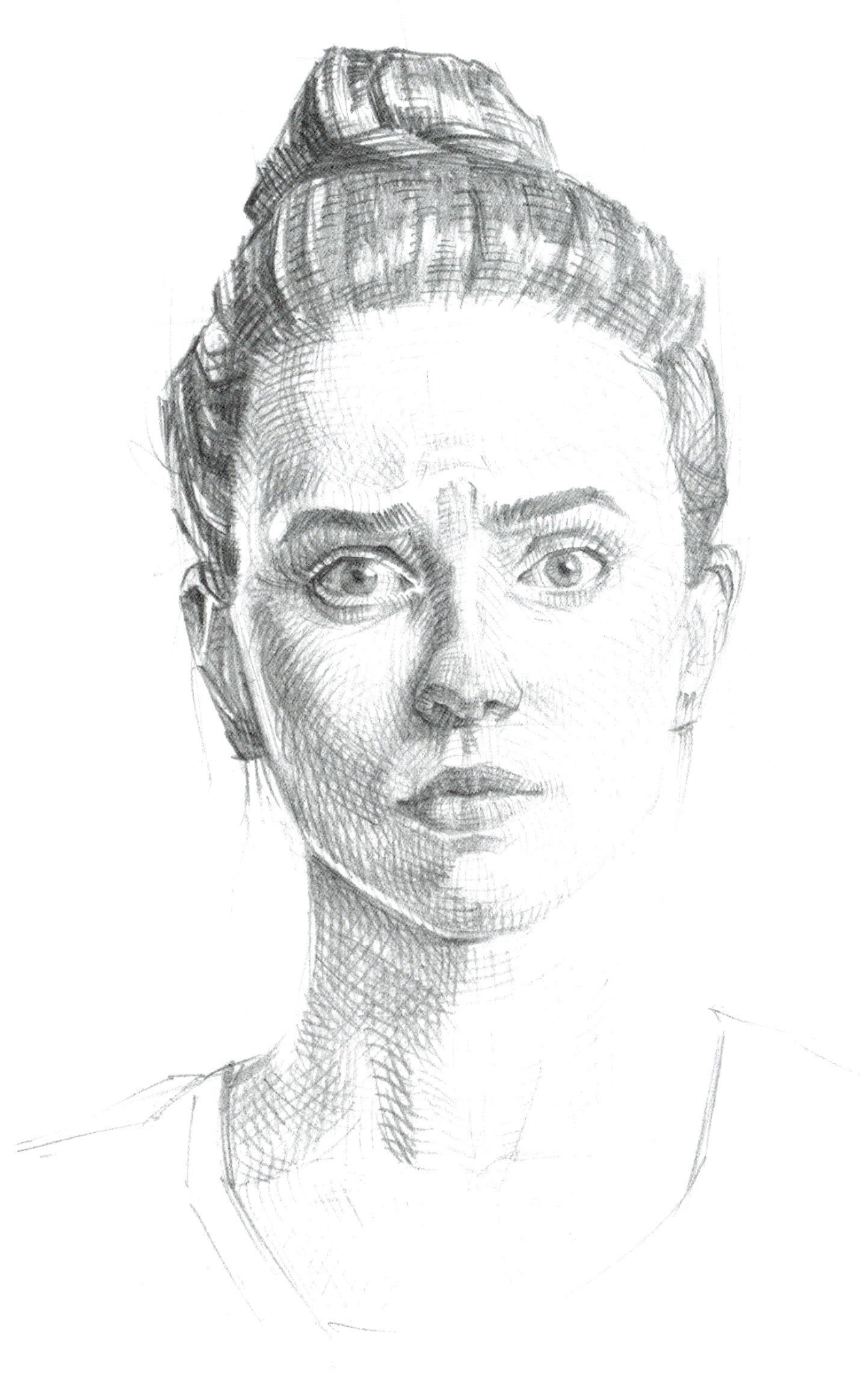

9

STEP 9

Finalize your portrait by creating balance between
soft transitions and clear borders. Check the overall
balance of the portrait and add the finishing touches.
Complete the background or add additional details
to further emphasize the portrait.

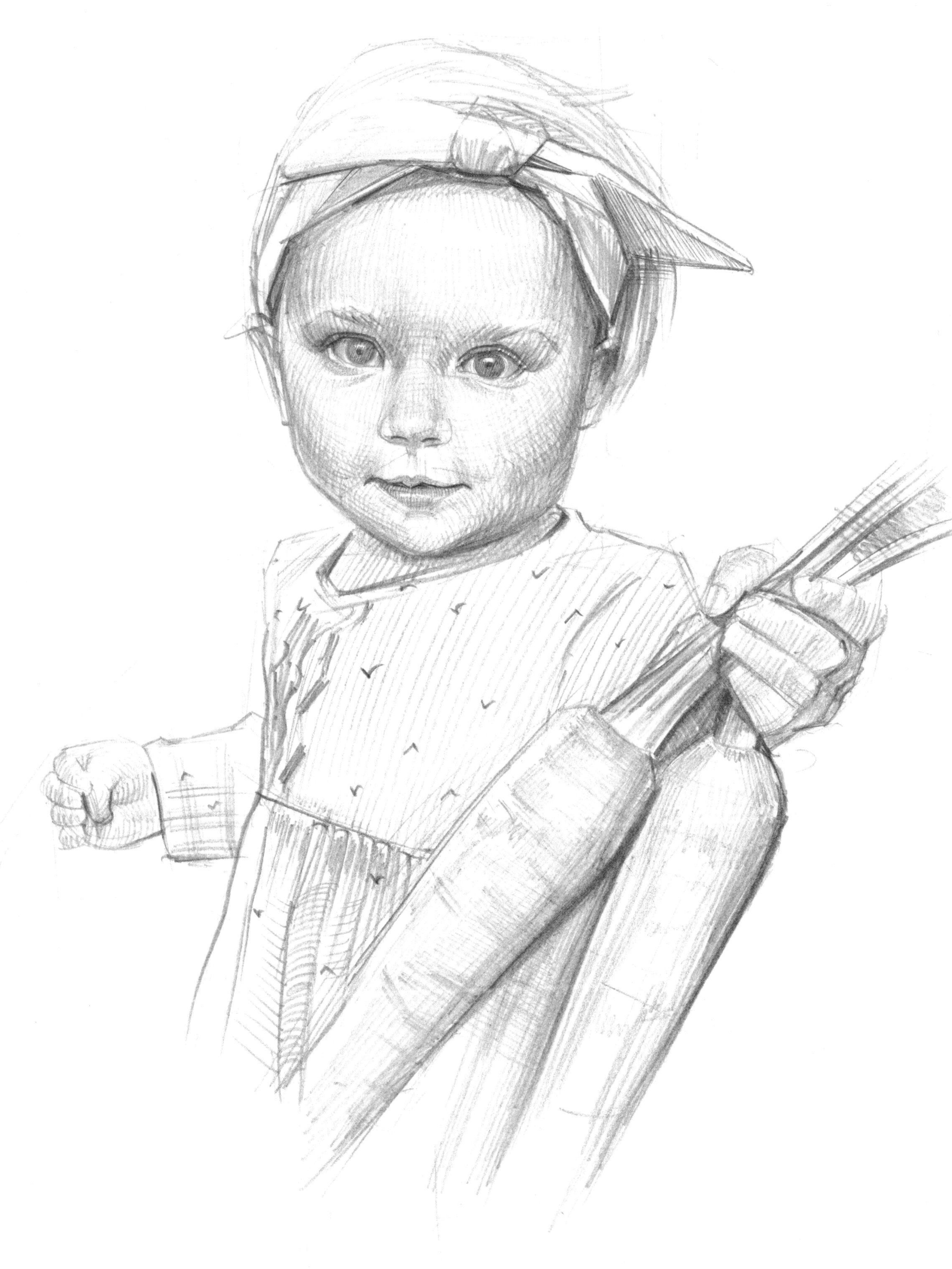

PROJECT 2

TODDLER

Drawing portraits of children requires a different approach than adults because children's facial features and expressions are generally softer and more delicate, so the focus should be on rounded and gentle lines rather than sharp ones. Details that determine expression, such as the eyes, mouth, and eyebrows, should be drawn accurately, as children's expressions can be vivid and emotional. Capturing these expressions increases the realism of the portrait. Also, a child's head is often large in proportion to their body, so pay close attention to get the scale right.

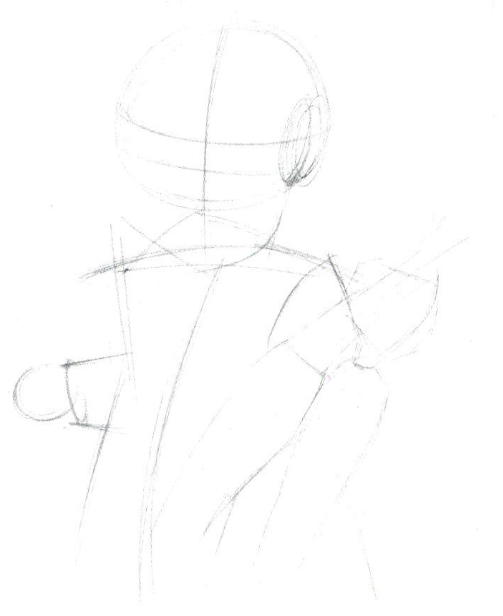

1

TO SUMMARIZE:

- The child has a big head and skull.
- The child has big eyes.
- The nose is small and upturned.
- The jaw bones are underdeveloped.
- The cheeks are full.
- The forehead is high and open.

STEP 1

Draw the horizontal and vertical axis lines and mark the width and height of the head on the axis lines.

Study the head size and neck and shoulder attachments. Don't be afraid to make mistakes—these are simply guidelines that you will go over and correct with darker tones. Use lots of guidelines and try to find the right proportions.

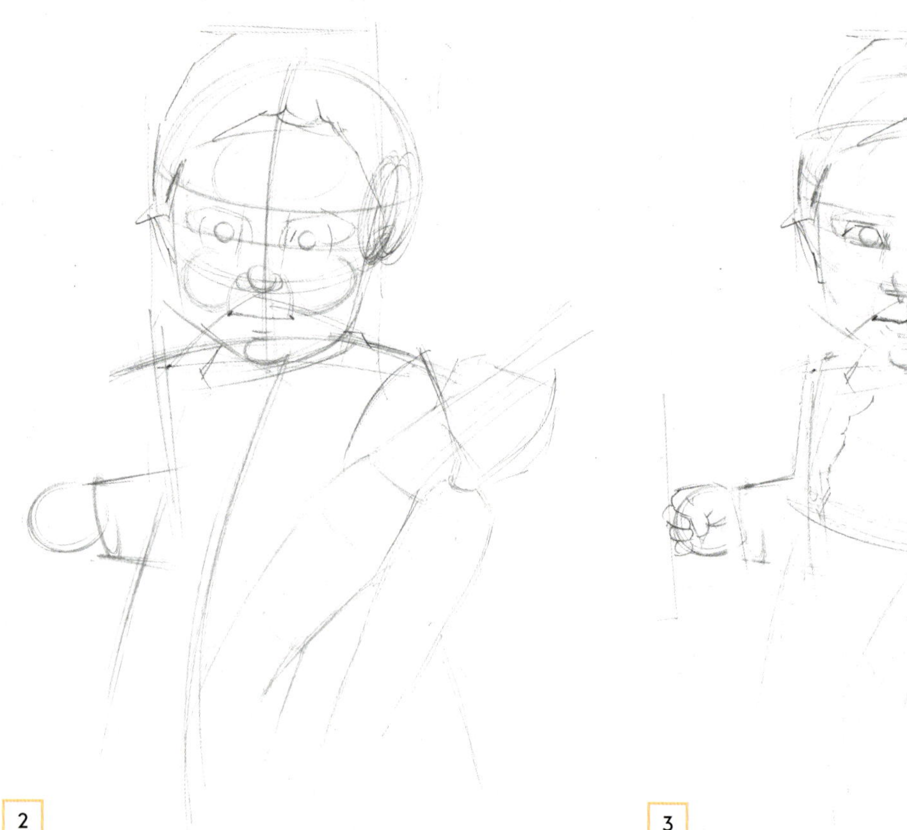

STEP 2

At this stage, determine the location of the eyes, nose, and lips. Make use of geometric shapes. Because children's faces are softer and muscle development is very low, create the outline of your portrait with circles.

STEP 3

Now that you are sure you have drawn the proportions correctly, you can erase the guidelines in the portrait. Add some definition to the hands.

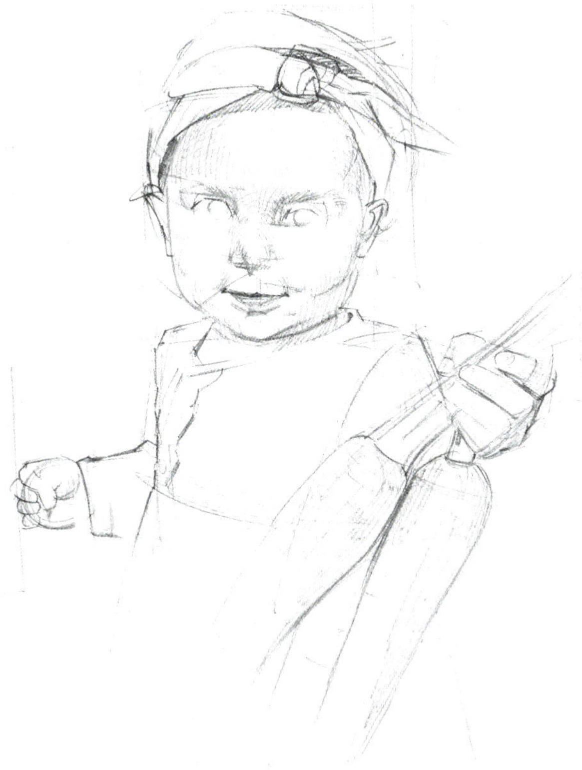

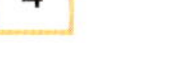
4

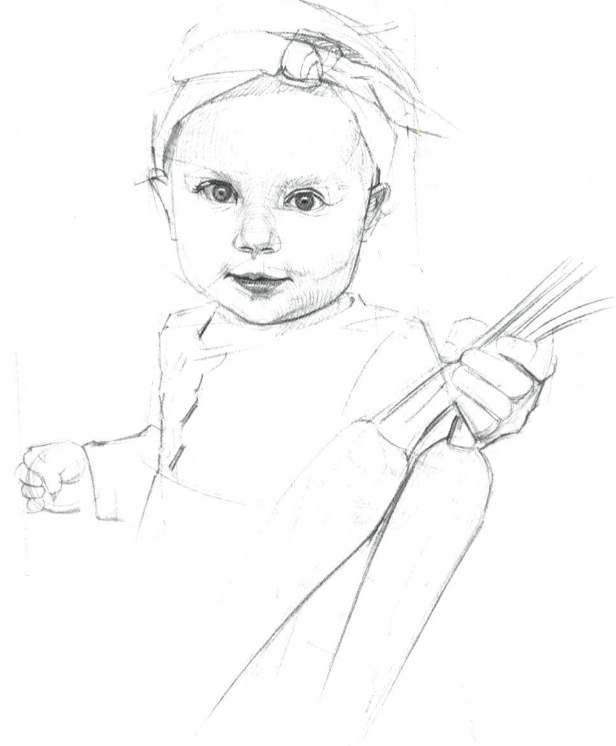

5

STEP 4

Detail the basic facial features. The size, shape, and position of the eyes are important to reflect the child's expression. Then draw the nose and mouth. These details determine the character of the face.

STEP 5

Once you have correctly placed the elements on the face, you can shape your lines according to your reference.

At this stage, begin to comb out the shadowed parts, revealing the eyes and lips. As you work, you gradually size the portrait.

USING CURVED LINES IN SHADING

As you scan the various areas of the portrait to add shading and create volume, imagine a tennis ball. This ball is a circle, and if you want to shade it and draw it in three dimensions, you must use curved lines. Vertical and horizontal lines will not look aesthetically pleasing, and your drawing will be "flat." Always pay attention to the basic shapes you see in your subject, and make your marks accordingly.

STEP 6

Use shading and toning to add depth and dimension to your drawing. Identify your natural light source and determine the shadows and highlights by considering how this light falls on the face. Use curved lines to create the rounded face and features.

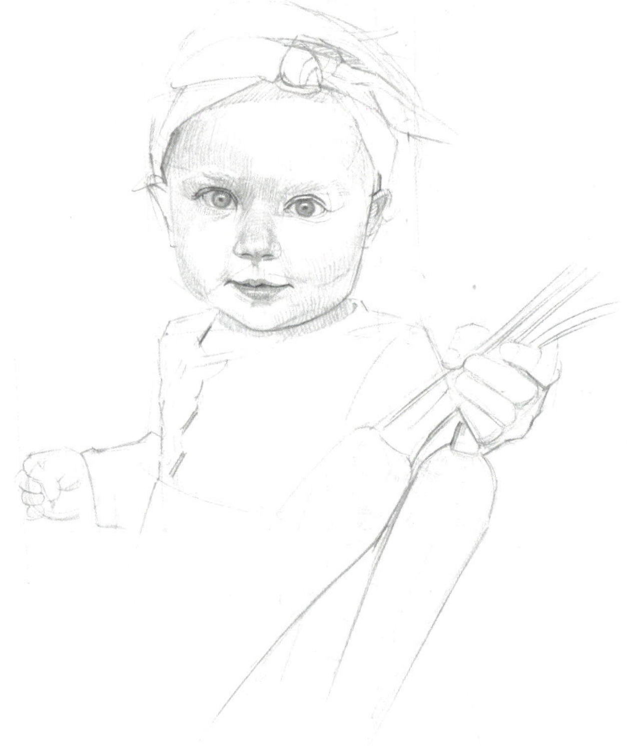

6

STEP 7

As you continue to develop the tones and values in the face, move on to the child's clothes, accessories, and environmental details. These details complete the character and story of the portrait, but don't get too caught up in the minutiae. Keep the focus on the child's face. It is up to the artist to focus the viewer's attention. Often the face is the most detailed part.

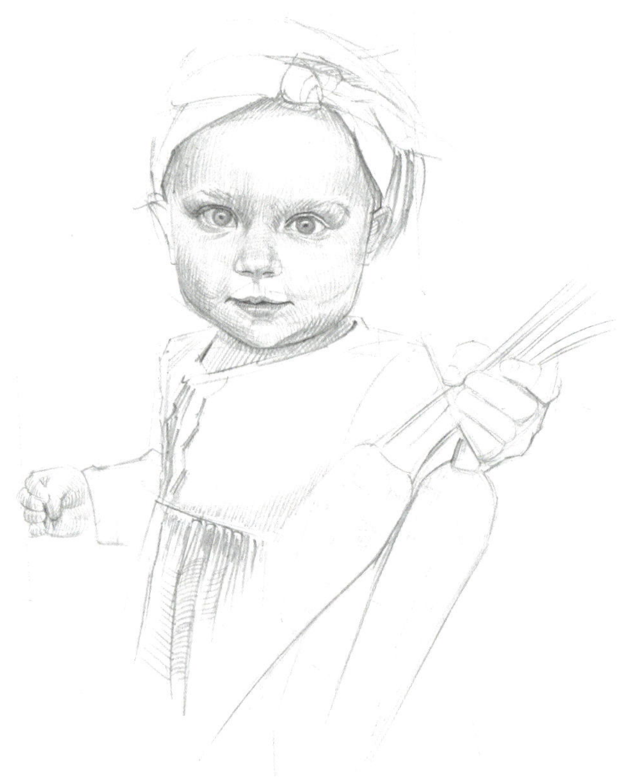

7

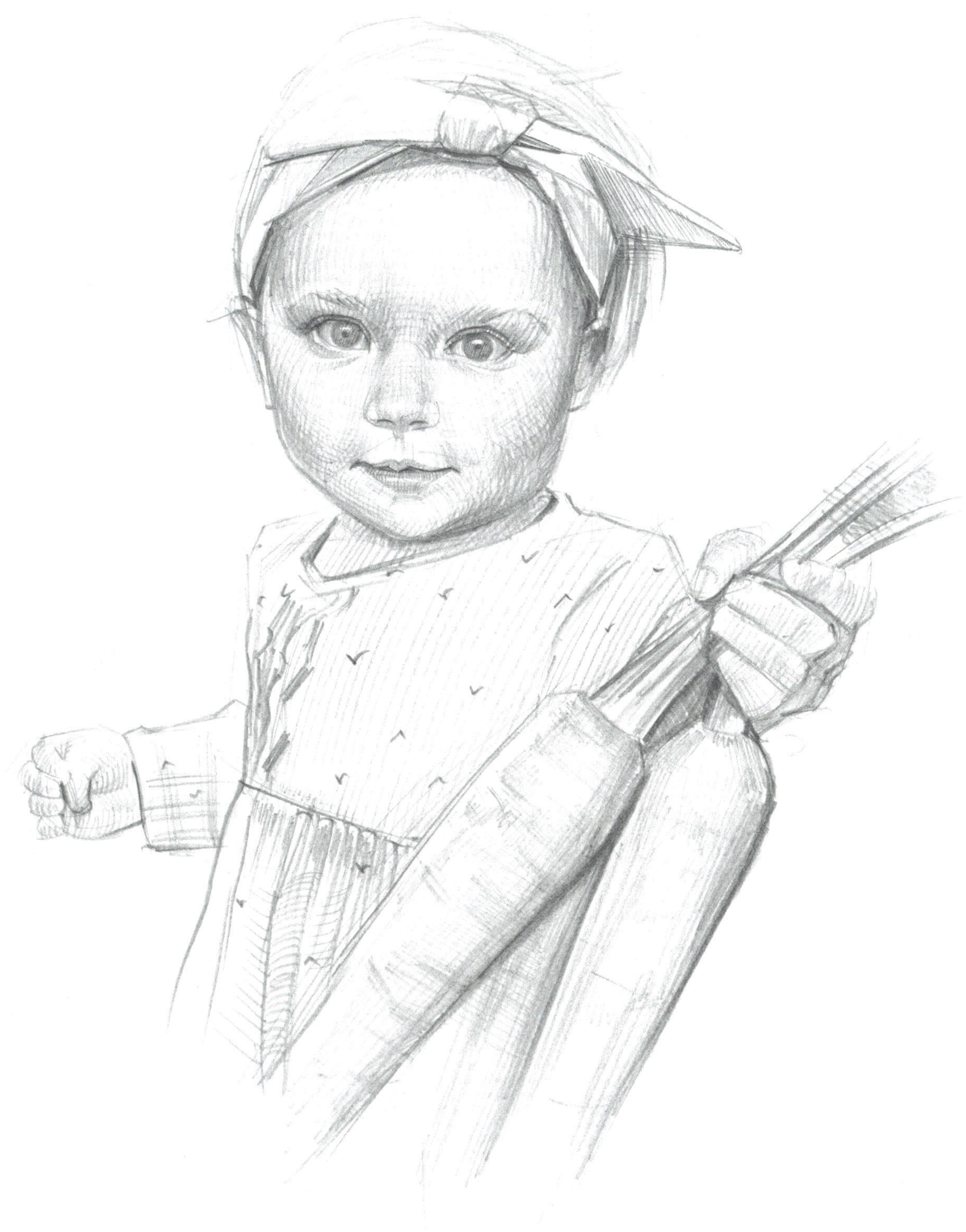

STEP 8

As you finish your portrait, think about perspective. The most detailed part of any drawing is always in the foreground. When adding background details, add as much detail as you do in the child's face. Use lighter lines in the background to keep the portrait in the foreground.

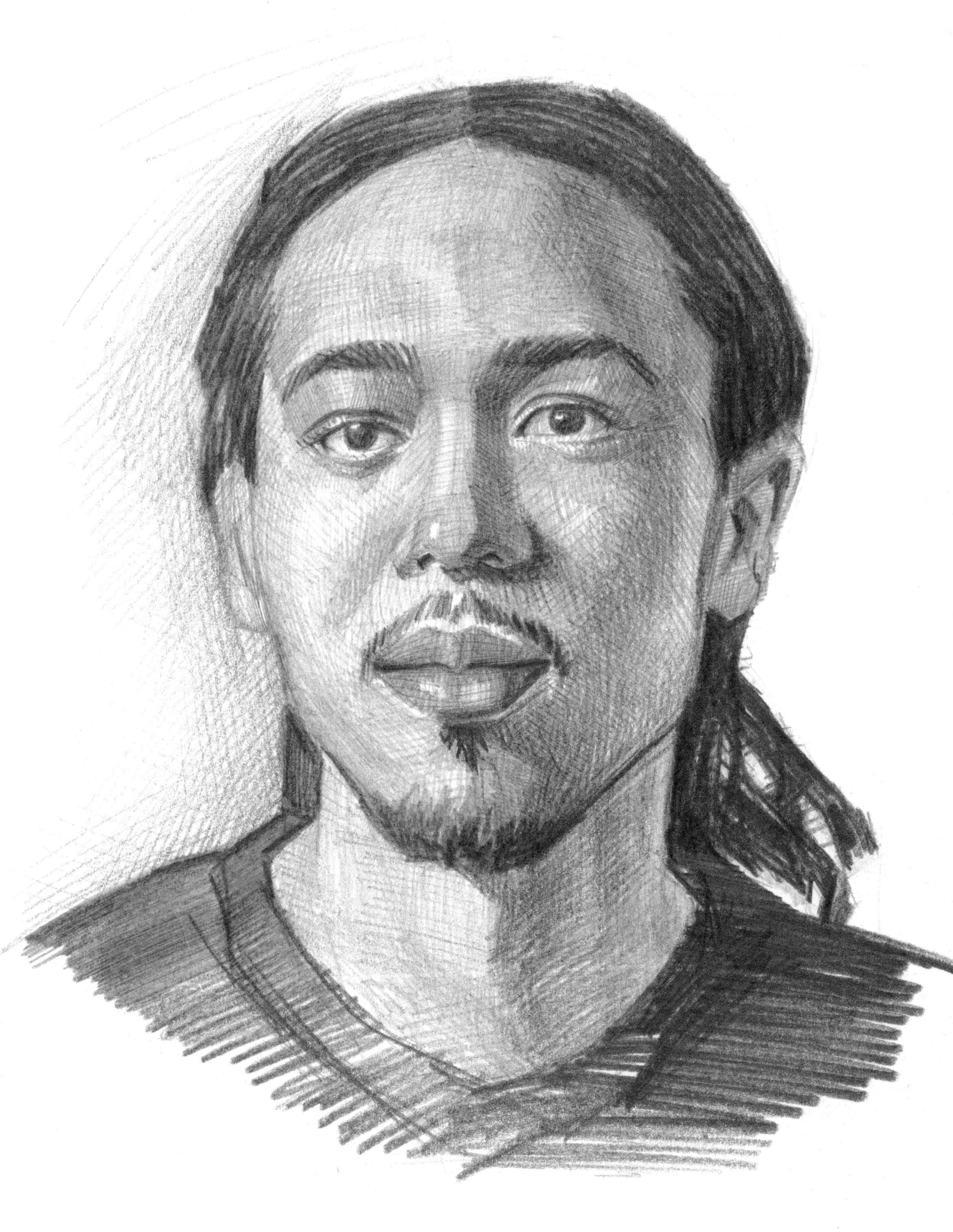

PROMINENT FACIAL FEATURES

While the general rules of proportion and features are helpful guides, these standard measurements won't be accurate for every model. Pay close attention to your reference photo when beginning a new portrait; you may notice different dimensions than those of a "standard" portrait, depending on the shape and size of the person's face and their unique features. In this portrait, for instance, note the bigger nose and lips. These facial features are more prominent in this model.

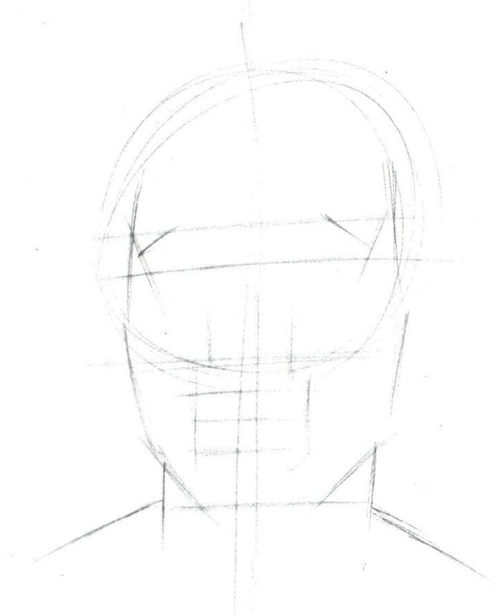

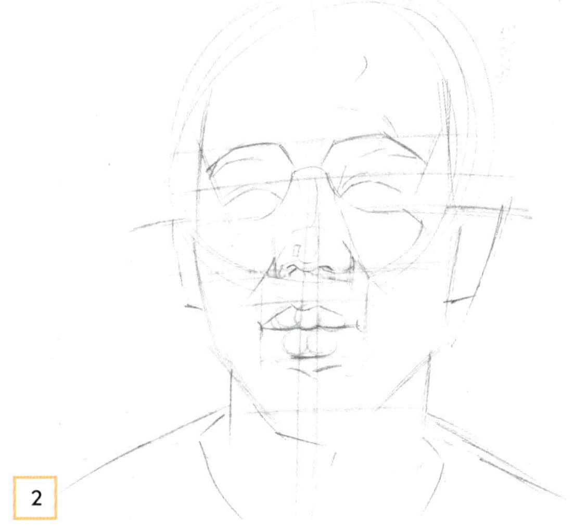

STEP 1

Before starting to draw, observe the direction of the head and express it in simple geometric shapes and lines.

STEP 2

Use your guidelines to locate the eyes, nose, mouth, and other facial features. Since the angle of this portrait is straight on, the face should look symmetrical and balanced.

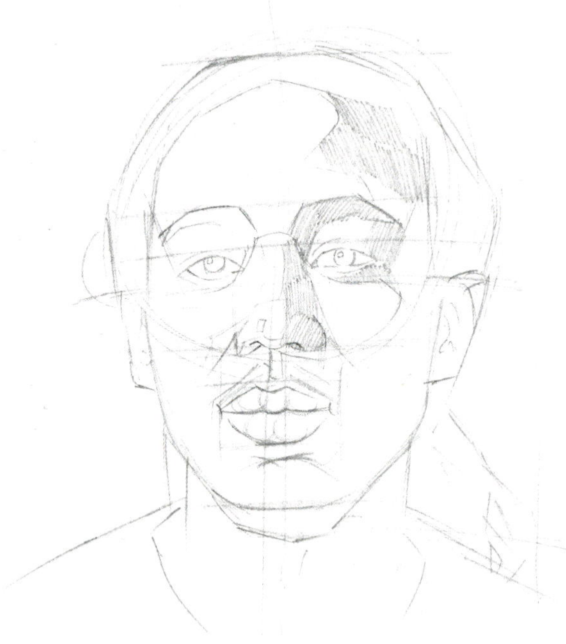

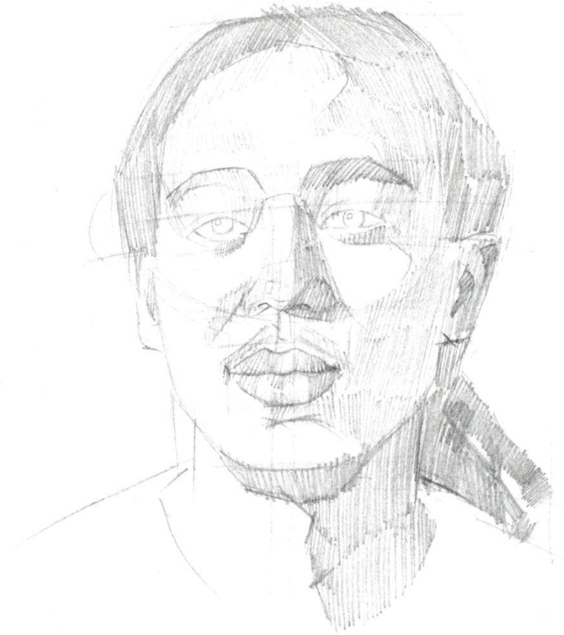

3

4

STEP 3

Add the character's facial and gestural features to the portrait drawing.

STEP 4

Once you have drawn the facial features, look for the areas of light and shadow. In my reference photo, the light shines on the face from the model's left side. At this stage it is not very important which direction you make your marks; you are only detecting light and shadow.

STEP 5

Next, move on to darker tones. Detail the eyes, nose, chin, hair.

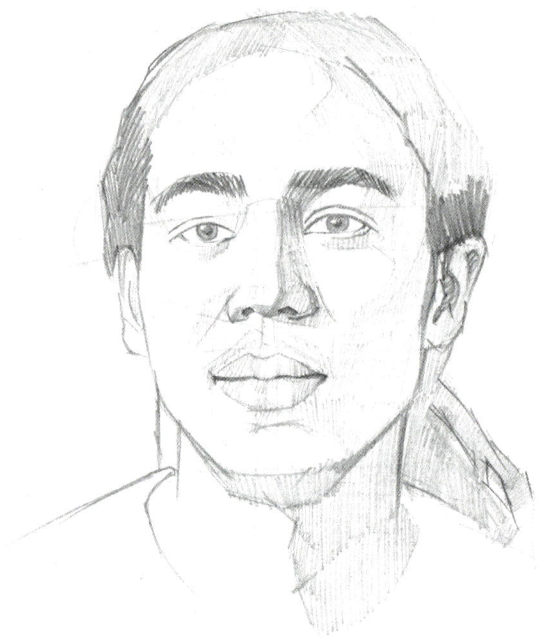

5

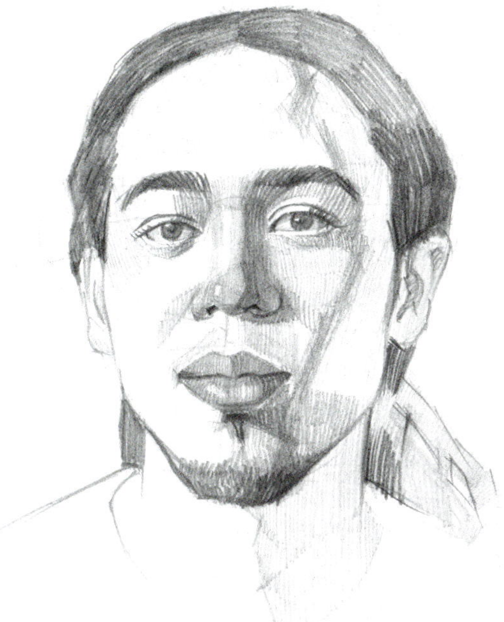

6

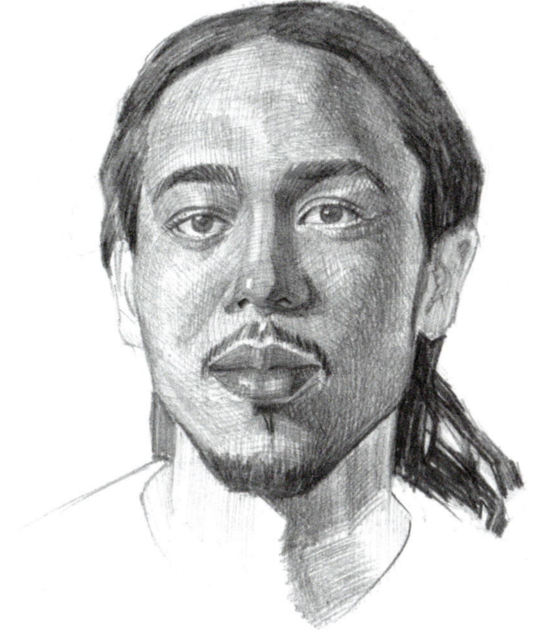

7

STEP 6

Emphasize the volume and depth of the face. With side lighting when you face the model head on, shadows and gradations can be more pronounced; make sure you apply them correctly. Add shadows to areas such as the eye sockets, under the nose, and on the lips.

Determine the overall shape of the hair, and draw the mass of the hair instead of individual strands. Determine the direction of hair growth and work with the natural flow of the hair. Don't forget to add the ears and other details.

STEP 7

Continue toning your portrait, not forgetting the shadowed areas of the face. Pay attention to the beard, hair, mustache, eyebrows, lips, and nose, and note that the shadowed parts are darker.

STEP 8

Finally, identify the darkest areas in the portrait. These areas are usually in the shadows and at the back. Darkening the mass of hair under the ears and behind the shoulders will add depth to your portrait.

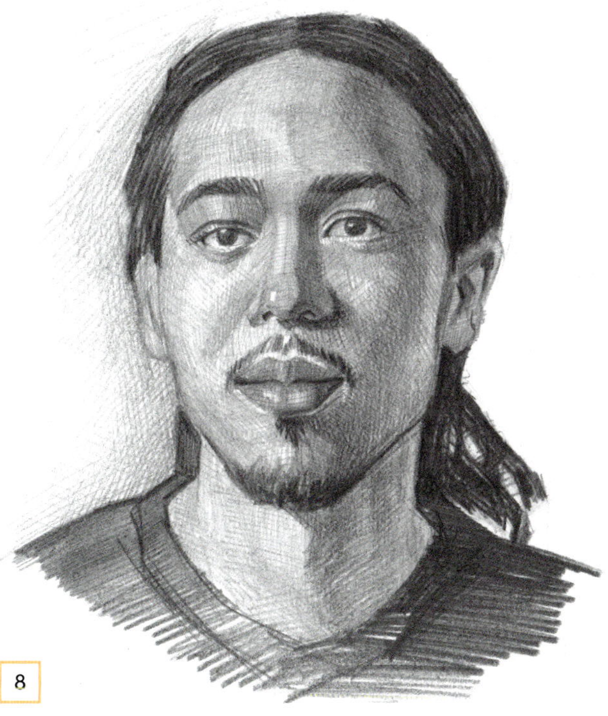

8

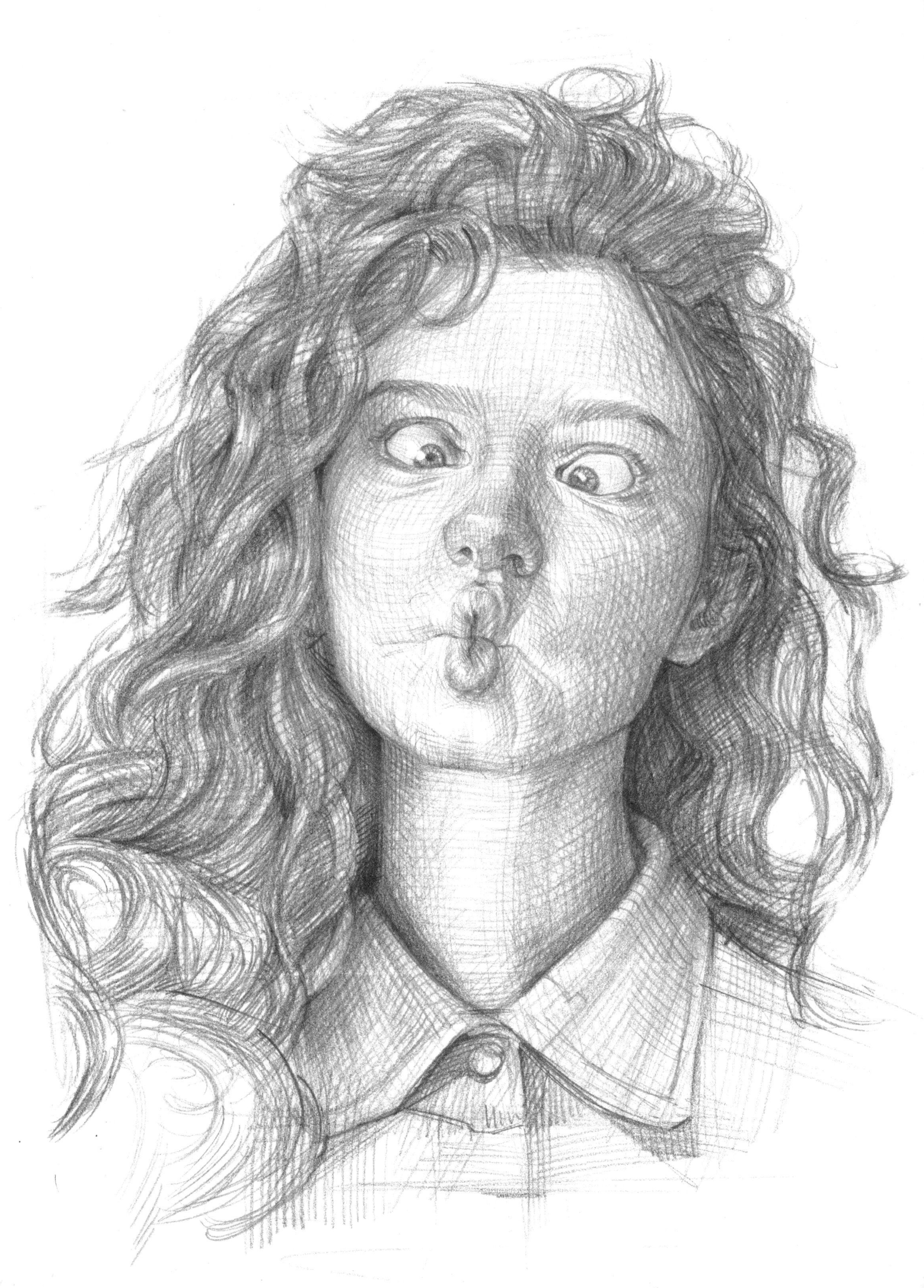

CURLY HAIR

I think the most challenging part of this portrait is the long, curly hair. To create an accurate rendering, first carefully draw the contours and general shape of the hair before creating the darker and lighter tones that create volume and depth.

Toning is an important way to create a sense of depth and volume in pencil drawings. Be patient and improve your skills with practice.

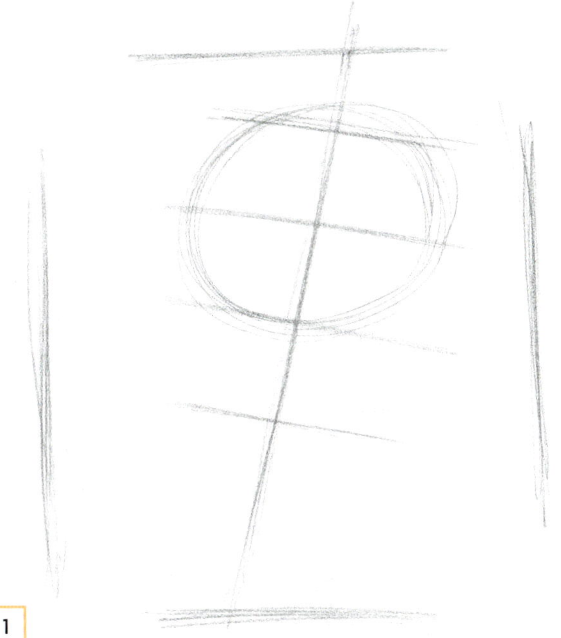

TIP: When beginning a portrait, space the edges evenly to center the drawing with the correct proportions. To do this, draw rough guidelines to create a rectangular working space in the middle of the paper. You will erase these lines when your portrait is finished.

STEP 1

Start by drawing a circle for the head. Look at the inclination of the head and draw an inclined, perpendicular line dividing the circle in this direction.

After dividing the circle into two equal parts, add lines to break up the face into parts, marking the top of the head, under the nose, the chin, and the bottom of the neck.

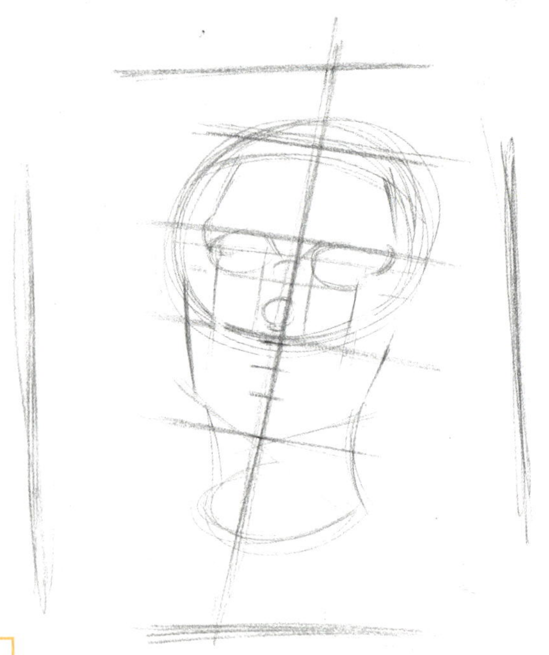

2

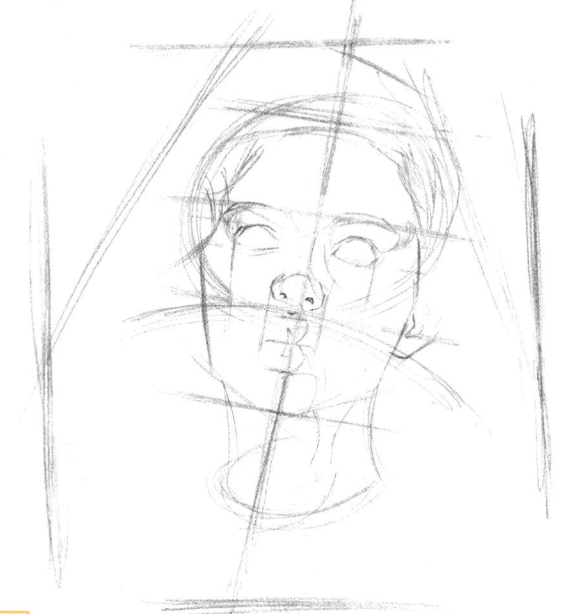

3

STEP 2

Draw the sides of the neck and facial feature contours. Determine the correct position of the eyes, nose, lips, and chin.

STEP 3

Determine the starting and ending points of the eyes, then draw the details of the irises and eyelids.

Draw the basic outline of the lips. Try to accurately reflect the fullness and shape of the lips. Block out the general shape of the hair with straight lines.

STEP 4

Define the shape of the hair without going into too much detail. Roughly show the shirt collar detail.

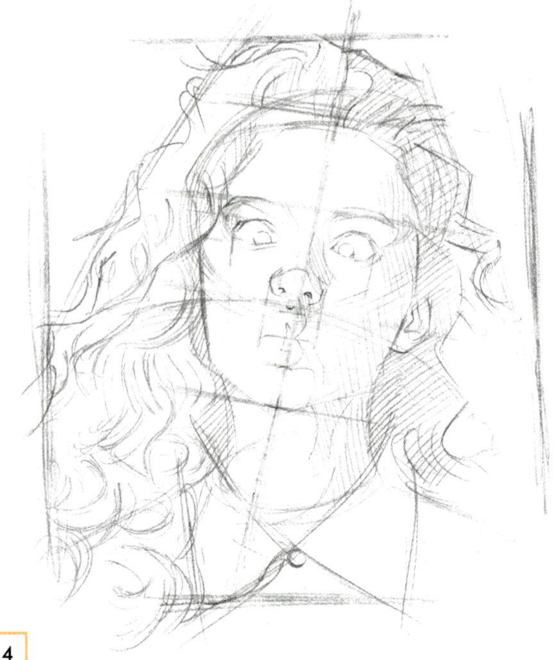

4

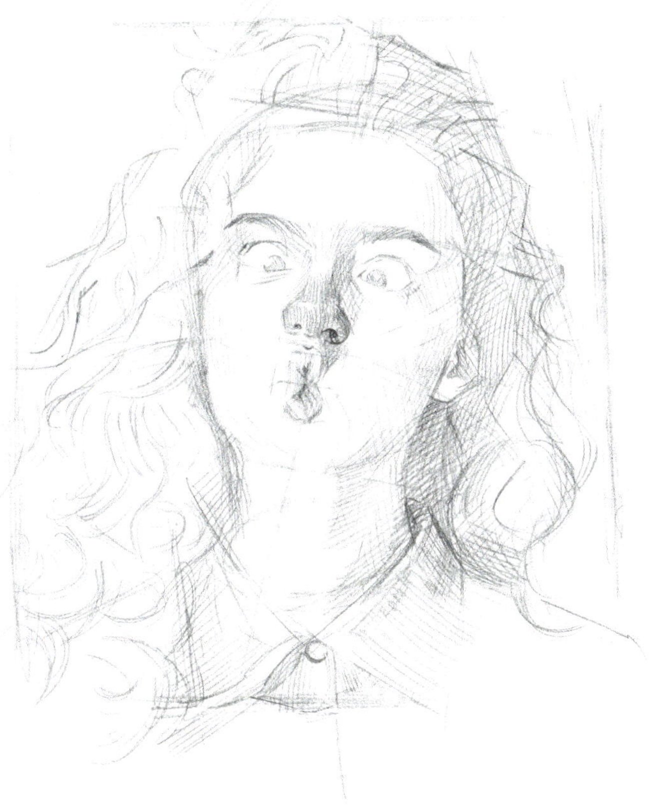

STEP 5

Define the space between the upper lip and lower lip and create the volume of the lips using shadows. Determine the shape of the eyebrows, the contour of the cheeks, and the structure of the chin. These details determine the character of the portrait.

STEP 6

Determine the light source and begin to place the shadows accordingly. Create the volume of the face by applying shadows slowly and in a controlled manner, taking the areas of light and shadow into account.

Shade the pupils, eyebrows, neck, and behind the ears first. Shading these areas will make your drawing "pop" out of the paper, moving from two-dimensional to three-dimensional.

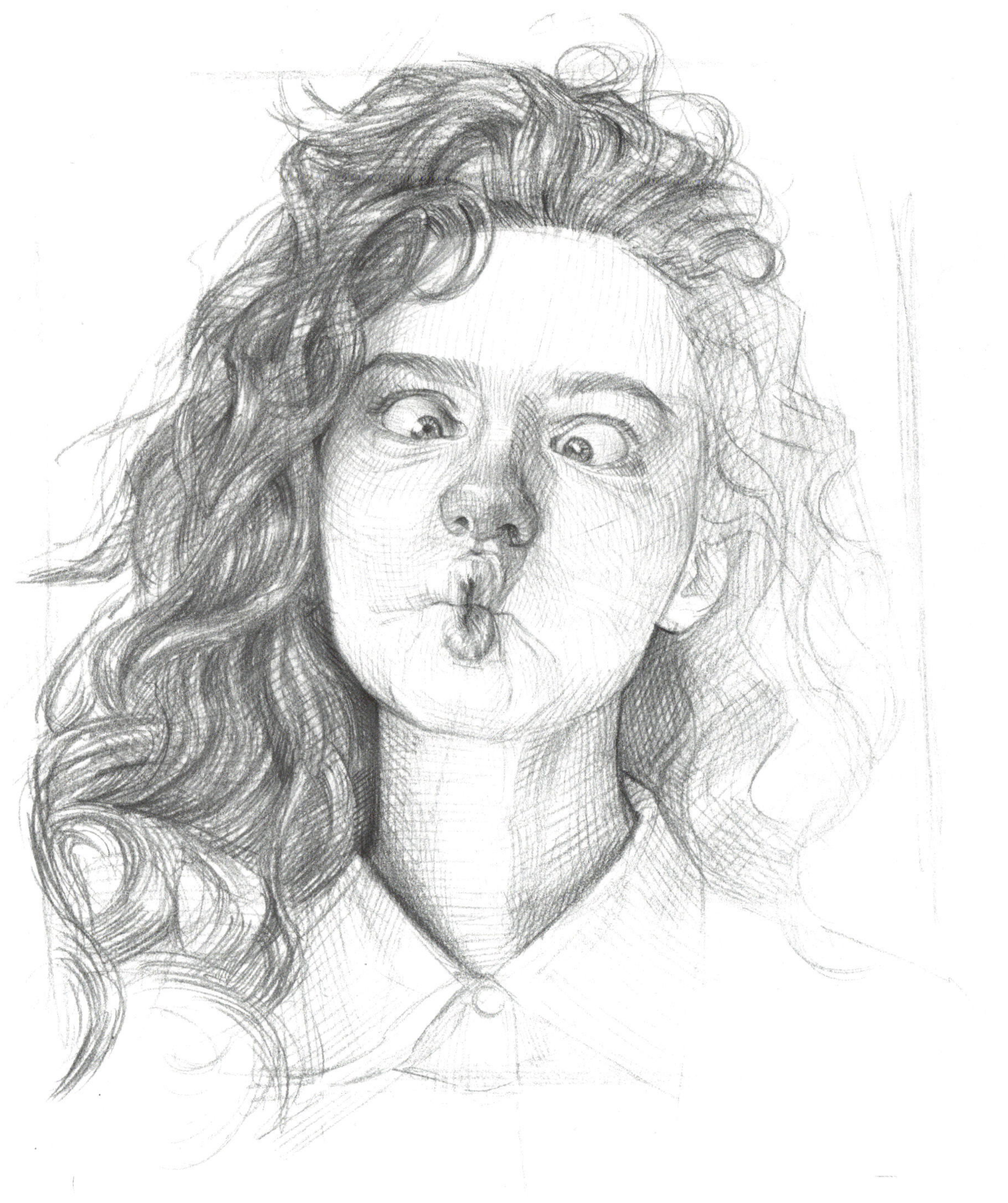

STEP 7

Now you can get into the details. Make the eyes and nose distinct with fine and frequent marks. Observe the lip movement well.

Continue to draw the shape of the wavy hair without going into detail. Pay attention to the direction of the hair growth and mirror it with your marks, leaving the white of the paper in the places that reflect the light. Remember to work in sections of light and shadow, rather than trying to draw individual strands. Create the darker tones by stroking repeatedly in the same direction with your pencil.

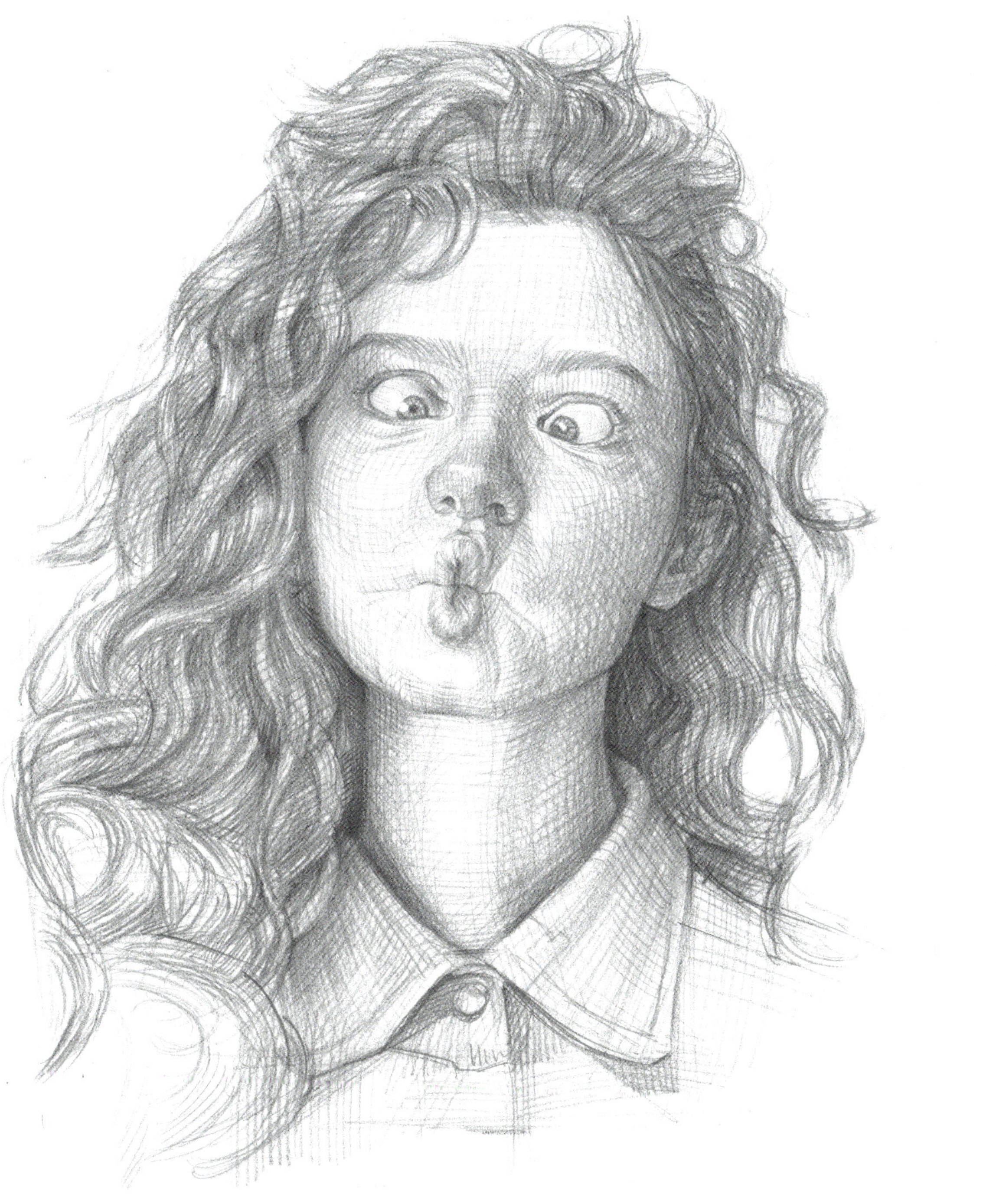

8

STEP 8

Detail the facial features. To add dimension and depth to your portrait, sweep the hair with denser lines. Suggest the shirt detail by paying attention to the areas in shadow, such as the shadows cast by the collar of the shirt. Darken these areas by applying more pencil strokes.

Finally, after the toning process is finished, review your drawing and make corrections, adjust gradations, or enhance details where necessary.

TIP: To create dynamic toning, use charcoal pencils of different hardness. Use harder pencils for lighter tones and softer pencils for darker tones.

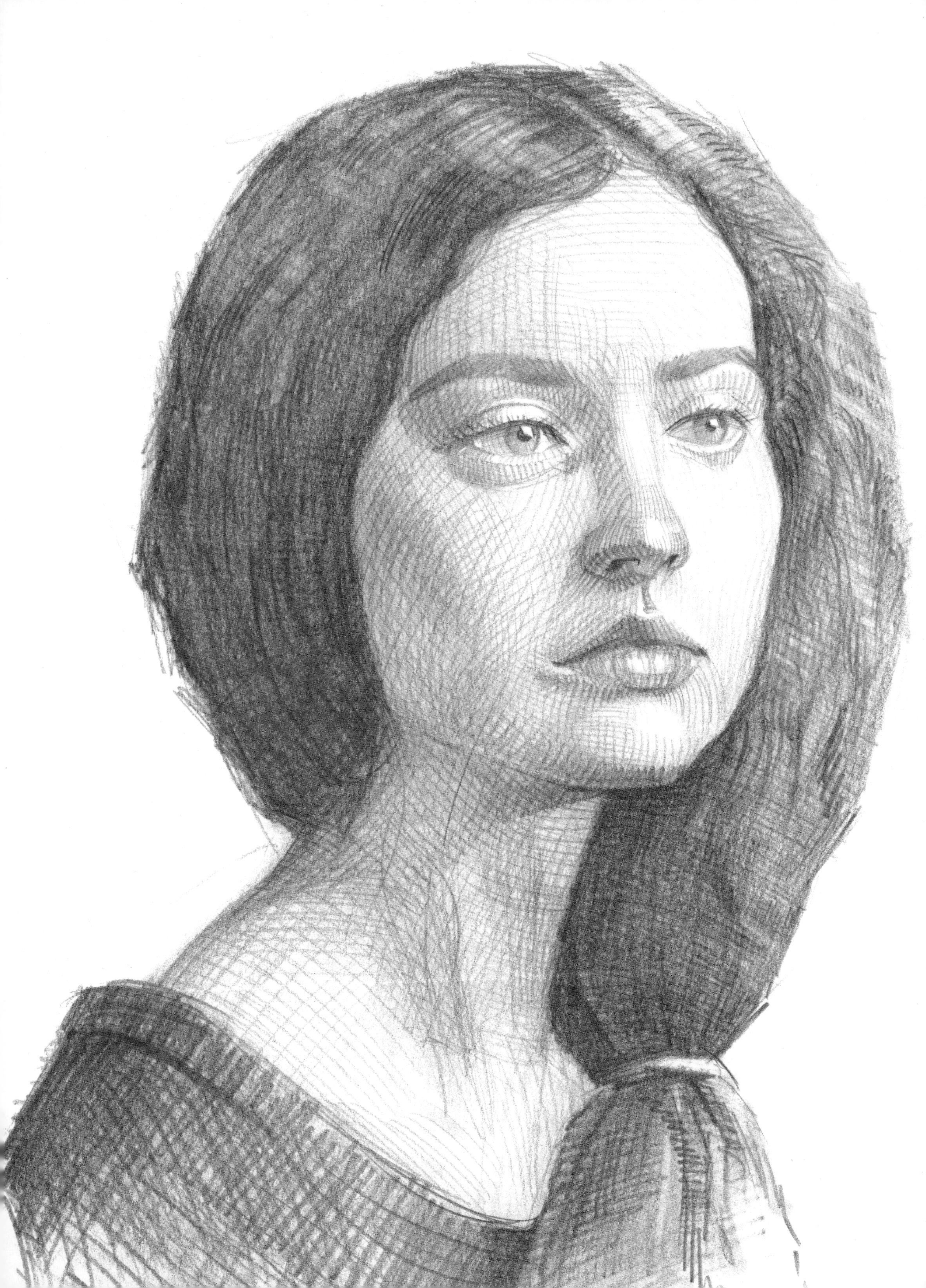

THREE-QUARTER VIEW

In three-quarter view, the model's face is turned, showing only three-quarters of the face, rather than a full profile. This angle is commonly used by portraitists and offers viewers the chance to explore a character of the portrait in more depth.

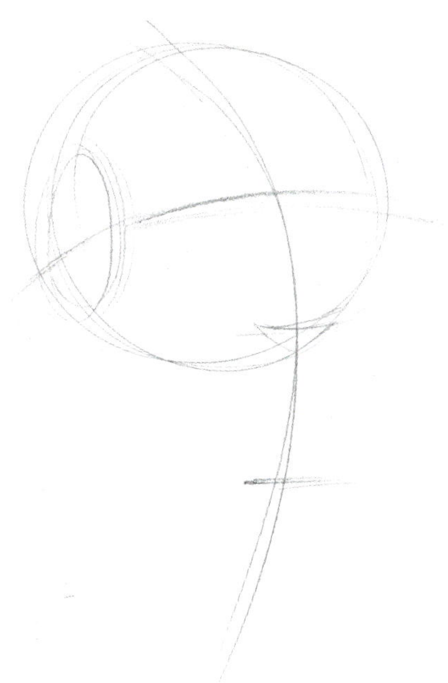

1

2

STEP 1

First, draw a circular shape in half-profile on paper. This forms the basic structure of the head. Draw a guideline in the center of the head. This line will determine the symmetry of the face and mark the location of the eyes.

STEP 2

Next, draw the lower part of the head and the jawline. This determines the basic structure of the face.

Use the center guideline to locate the eyes. Mark the points that correspond to the center and the edges of the eyes. Indicate the location of the nose.

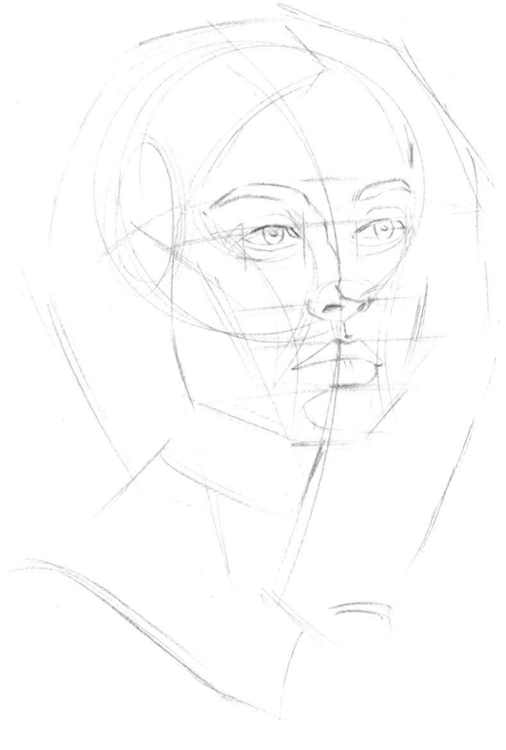

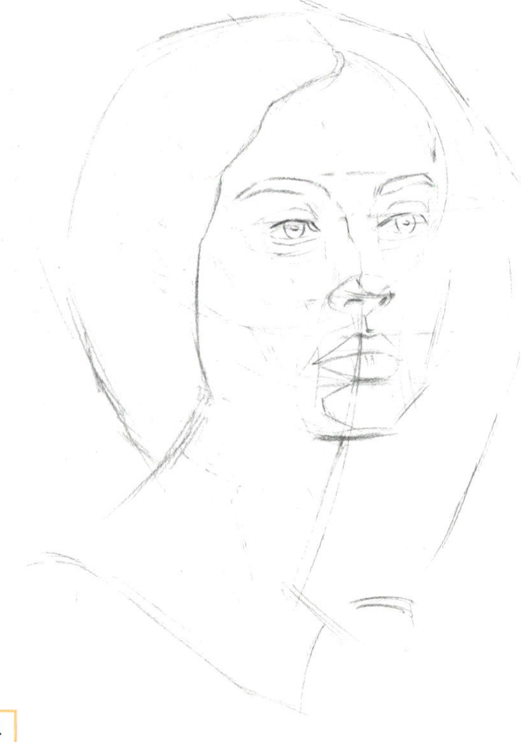

STEP 3

Next, add the details of the eyes. Carefully draw details like eyelids, irises, eye sockets, and eyelashes.

Draw the nose starting under the eyes. Highlight the bridge of the nose and the wings of the nose.

To start drawing the lips, draw a tracing line slightly below the bottom of the first circle you drew for the face. This marks the starting point for the lips. Define the top and bottom of the lips, carefully working out the lip lines and the shape of the lips.

Define the jawline and the jawbones. Determine the roundness of the chin and the jawline to create the profile of the face.

STEP 4

Once you are sure you have placed the elements of the portrait in the correct proportions, you can gently erase these lines with an eraser, as you will no longer need the guidelines.

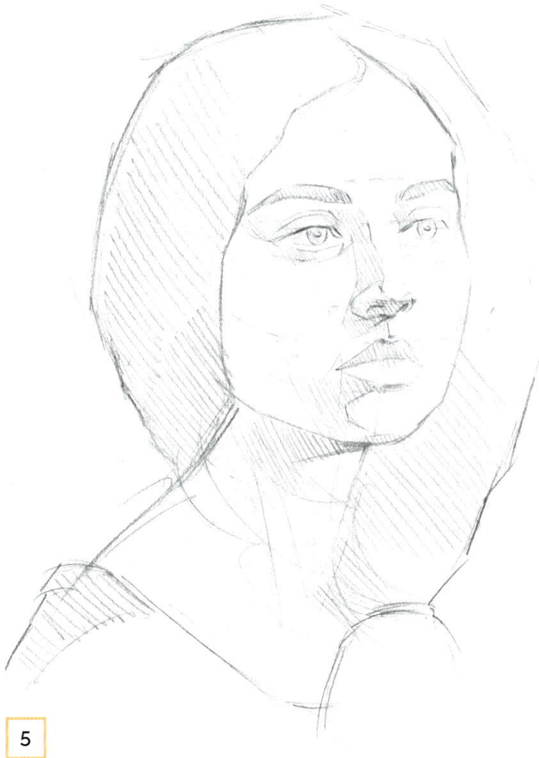

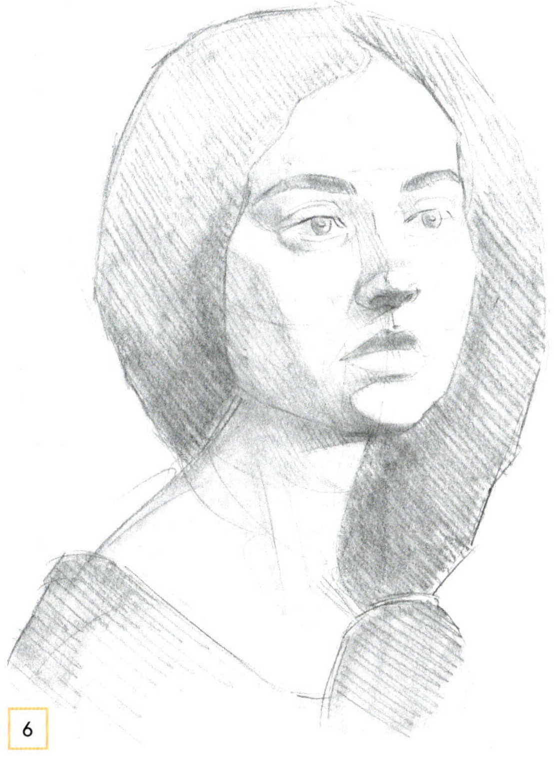

STEP 5

At this stage, identify the dark shadow areas and begin to develop them with light lines. Your portrait will emerge en masse. If you wish, you can diffuse the dark areas using tissue or a blending. While I do not personally use these tools very often (I like to see my lines and marks), I used the technique for demonstration purposes in this portrait. Experiment for yourself to see if you like to use these blending tools.

STEP 6

Then reveal the mass of the hair. Remember that the light reflects from the right side, and both the hair and the right side of the face will have fewer dark tones.

As you develop the hair, you can show the light areas of the hair by making small strokes with an eraser to lift out tone.

Continue hatching the shadowed parts of the portrait: under the chin, under the nose and left side, the left cheek, the eyelid, and a third of the forehead.

BLENDING

You can use blending techniques to soften shadows and combine tones. Using your finger, blending stump, or a tissue, you can make the transitions smoother by softening and gradating different tones in the drawing. You can also achieve a similar effect by using a soft brush in the drawing.

HATCHING

The hatching (shading with lines) technique creates shadows through the use of lines. This technique is commonly used to tone areas using parallel or diagonal lines. You can emphasize tonal differences by intensifying the lines or widening the spaces between them to create shadows. The closer the lines are, the darker the shadow will appear.

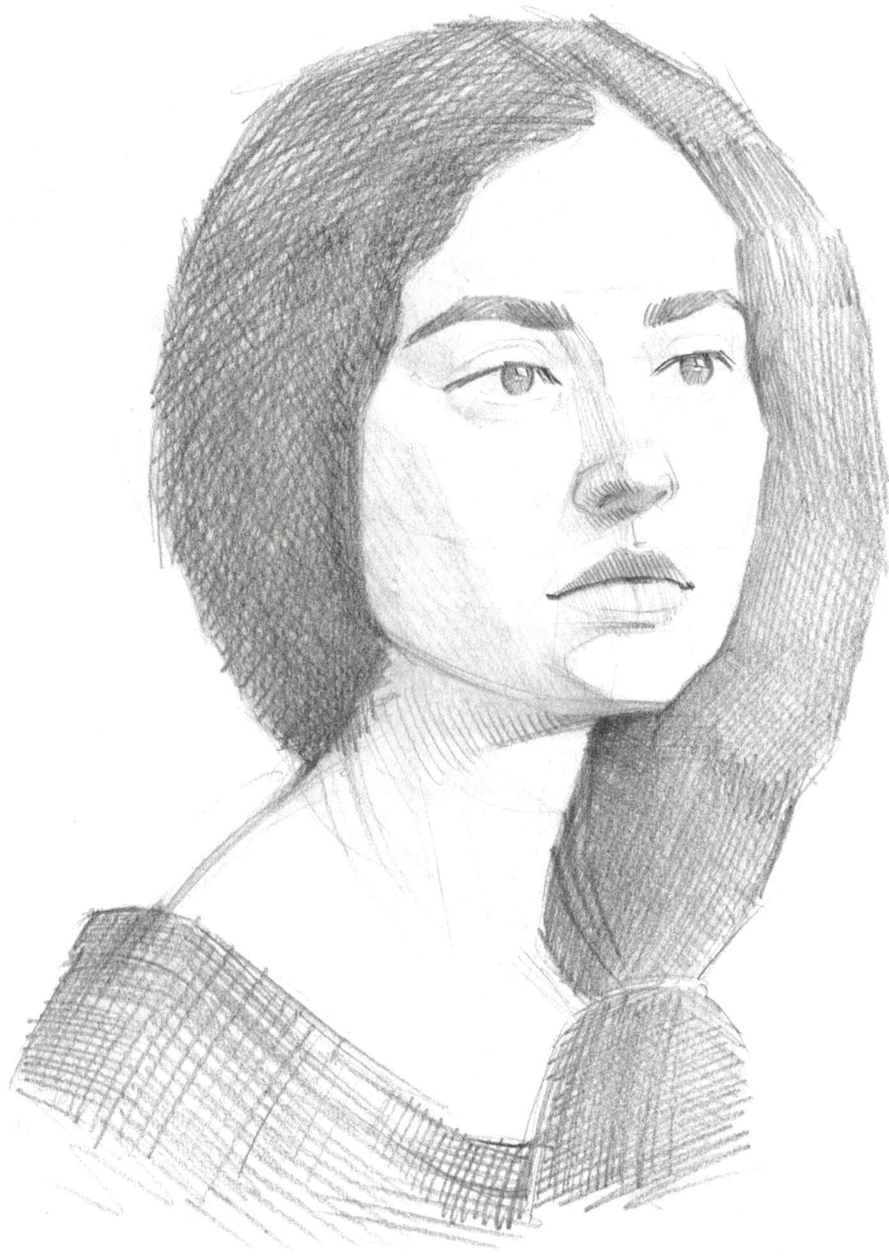

STEP 7

Add some detail to the nose to give it dimension. Make the areas of shadow more prominent with crosshatching. In the areas in the light only cross-hatch once with straight lines to yield softer tones.

CROSSHATCHING

The crosshatching (shading with diagonal lines) technique creates shadows by crossing lines in different directions. This method can be used in combination with hatching to create more intense and deeper shadows. Diagonal lines drawn at different angles create more complex tones and a sense of depth.

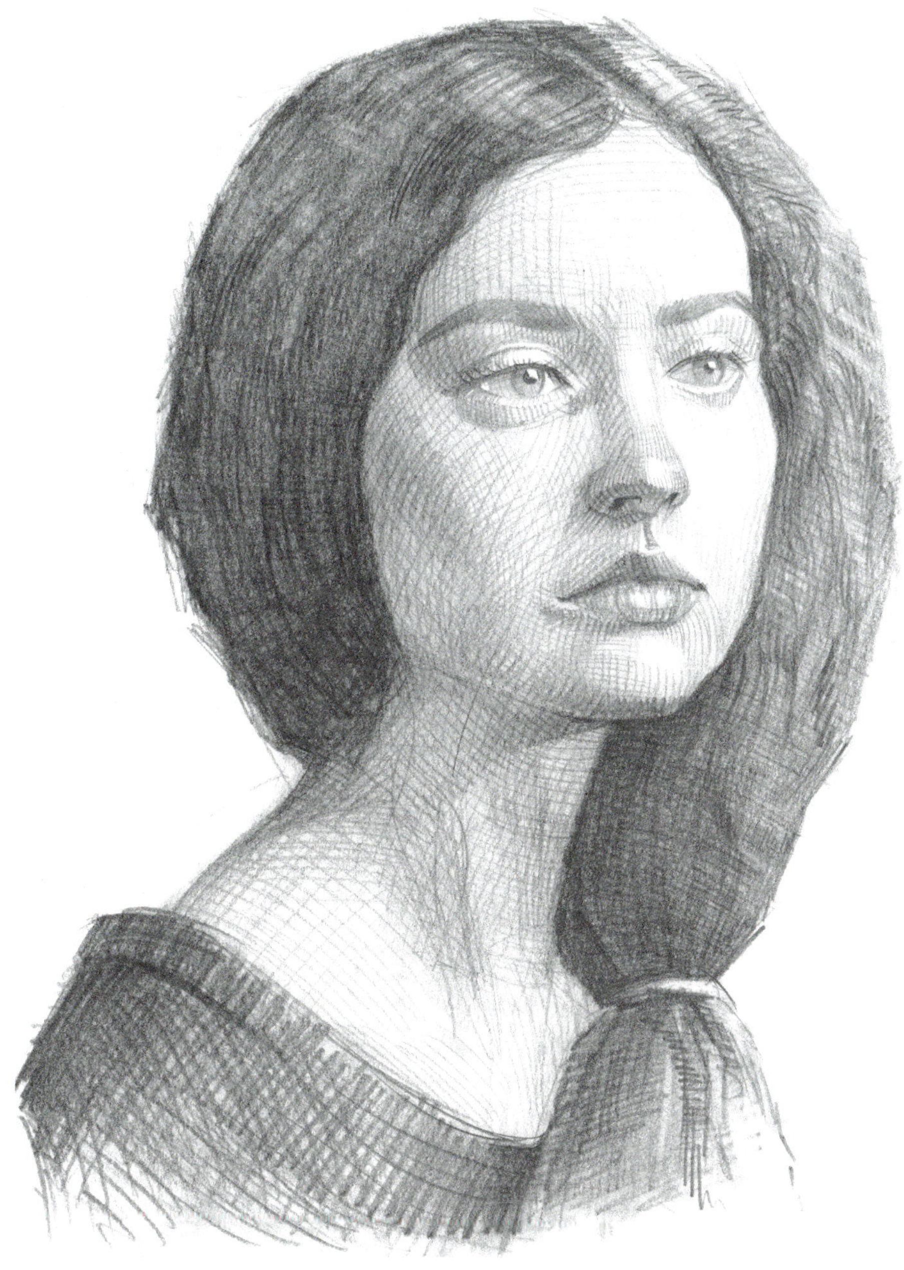

STEP 8

Examine the form and movements of the hair and, with a darker pencil, make small marks in the direction of the hair growth, blending as desired and lifting out tone with an eraser to create highlights.

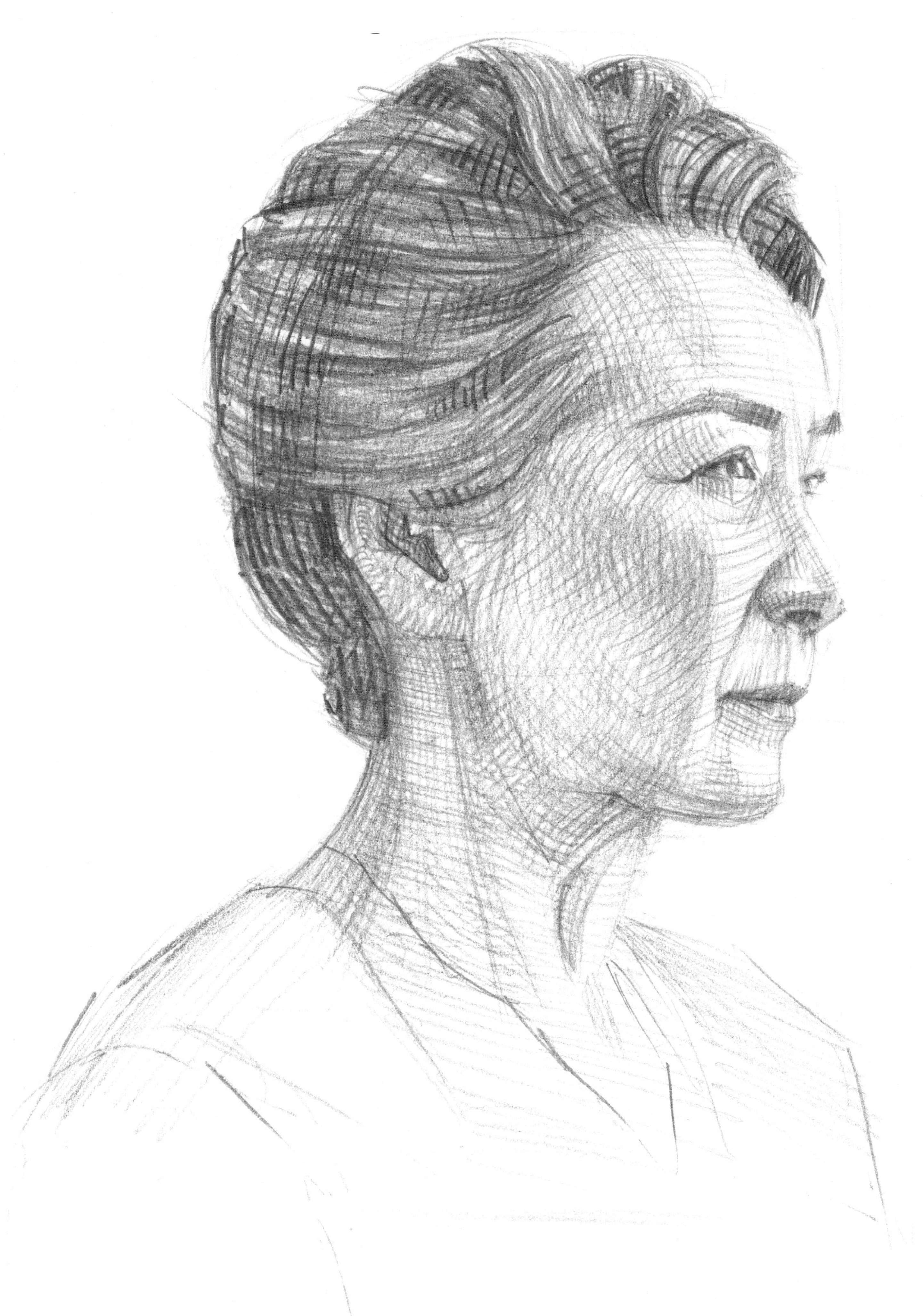

ELDERLY FEATURES IN PROFILE

When viewed from the side the human head is a square equal in width and length. We know that both the height and the width of the head in profile are 3½ times the width of the forehead; the human head is therefore a complete square when viewed in profile.

1

STEP 1

First mark the edges of the paper at equal intervals to position the portrait correctly. Then draw a circle. Add a curved line in whichever direction the head is facing, dividing the circle.

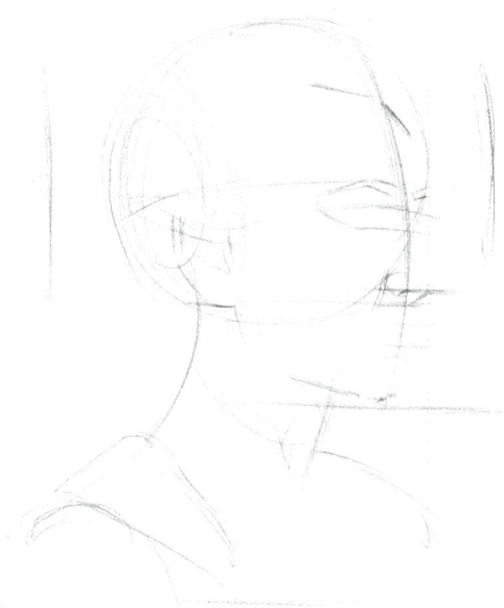

2

STEP 2

Continue to develop the general shapes and lines of the head and neck. By dividing the head module into thirds, you'll get many indication points that will determine the profile angle.

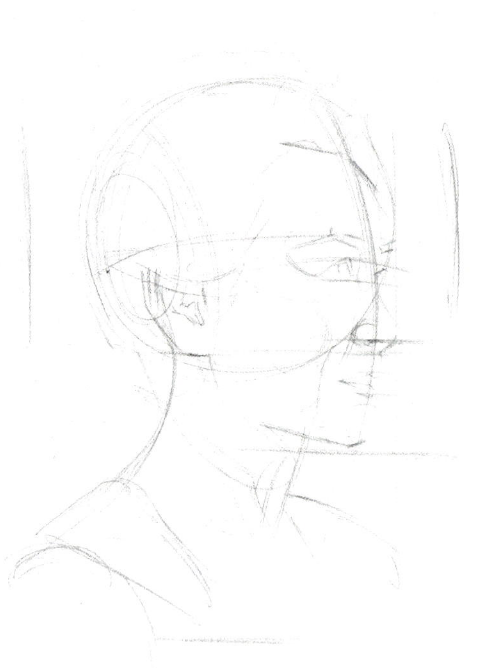

3

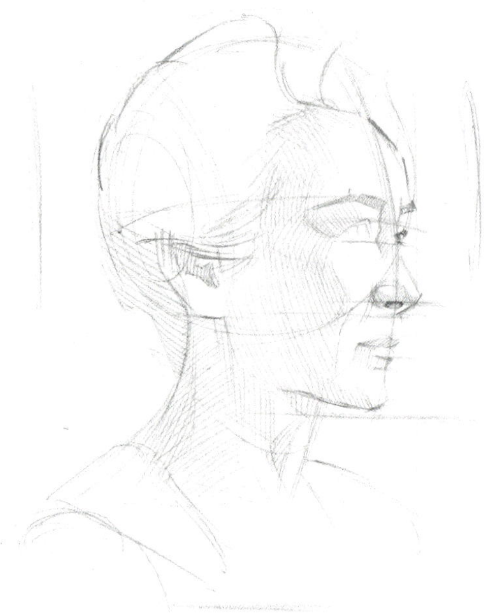

4

STEP 3

Now you can finalize the placement of the eyebrows, eyes, nose, mouth, and other features.

Observe the facial elements and neck connections. What you need to notice here is that the eyes are located below the line where you divided the circle in half in step 1. The lower part of the circle is the lower part of the nose. The bottom of the last section under the circle is the point where you should draw the chin.

STEP 4

At this stage, refine the portrait from guidelines, adding more precise lines. Identify the areas of light and shadow. Begin shading the shadowed parts with fine lines, without applying too much pressure. It's very important to observe the light-shadowed areas before proceeding to toning.

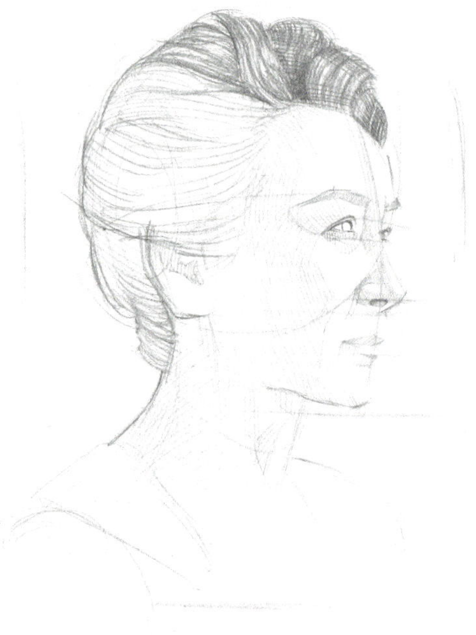

5

STEP 5

Carefully begin to add shading and detail in the irises, eyelids, eyelashes, nostrils, lips, and other details.

Examine the movement of the hair, and begin to stroke in shading, emphasizing the wavy areas by moving your pencil in the direction of hair growth.

As you work, highlight the light parts of the hair with an eraser.

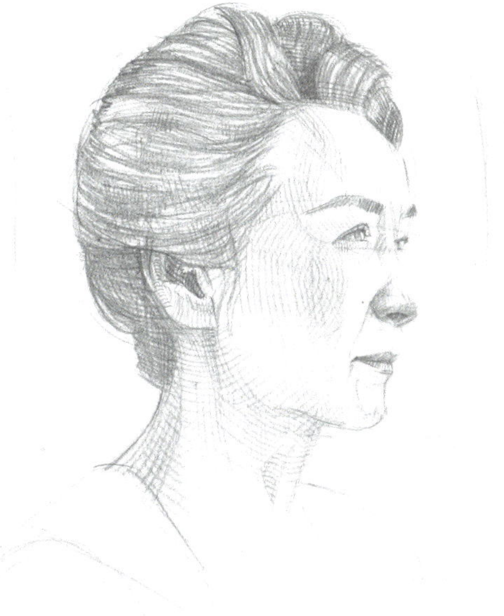

6

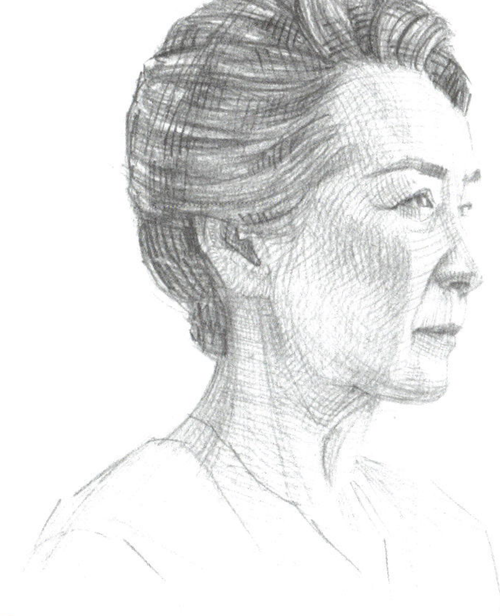

7

STEP 6

Since behind the ear is in the darkest shadow, apply more frequent strokes to create the dark tone.

As you continue to darken the shadows to build volume, pay attention to the light source; in this portrait the light is reflected from the right side.

Use shading techniques, such as hatching or crosshatching to emphasize the shadows and tones of the hair. Create the volume and form of the face by carefully adding shadows.

Continue shading the neck with crosshatching. The direction in which you draw the hatch marks here depends on your ability to think in three dimensions. Sweep the cheekbone with curved lines. Add shadows under the ears and chin.

STEP 7

Continue to develop the tones in your portrait with hatch marks, deepening the areas of shadow with more lines close together, and revealing the shape of the face and its features by curving your lines on the more rounded features.

Review your drawing carefully and make corrections if necessary. Use an eraser to remove excess lines and further enhance the details.

FACIAL CHARACTERISTICS IN THE ELDERLY

Before you start drawing facial features, here are some tips you should know for portraits of the elderly:

- The bone structure in the temples becomes more pronounced.
- The eye socket and the eye itself, in general, collapse more; therefore, the bones above the eye socket protrude more.
- Bags and wrinkles form around the eyes.
- As the cheeks sag or collapse, the cheekbones become more prominent.
- Nose bones become more prominent.
- Lips become thinner.
- Bags and sagging skin appear on the chin and neck.

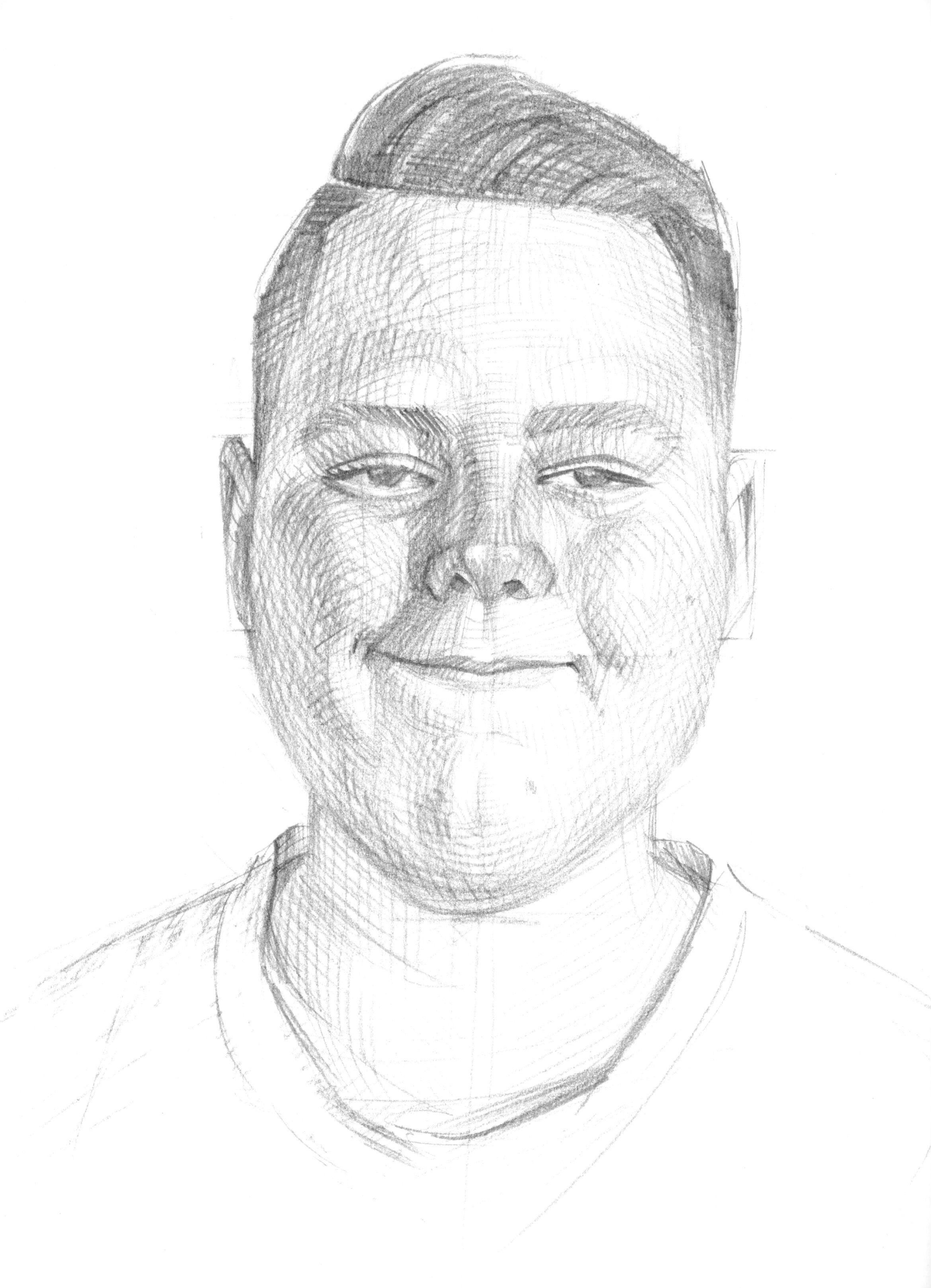

CHEERFUL FACIAL EXPRESSION

The child in the reference photo for this portrait is smiling with a closed mouth, a cheerful facial expression. This type of expression causes some notable changes in the facial features, so pay close attention as you draw.

When drawing a laughing expression, it is important to take note of details and maintain the naturalness of the expression. Studying and observing the expression will help you create a more realistic and expressive portrait of laughter.

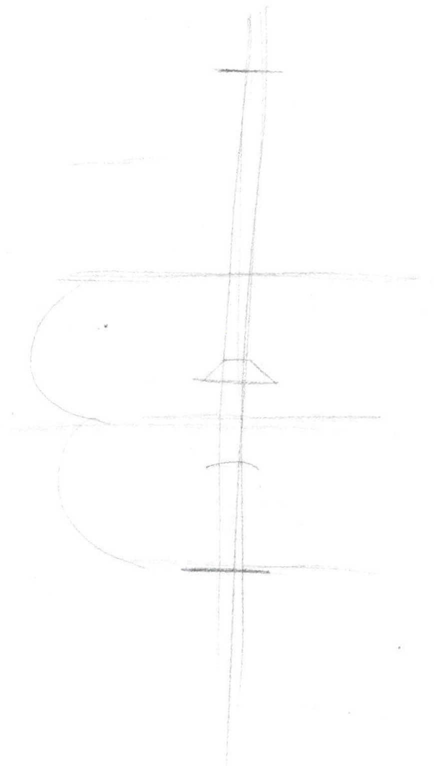

STEP 1

On paper, outline the drawing area and lightly create framing lines.

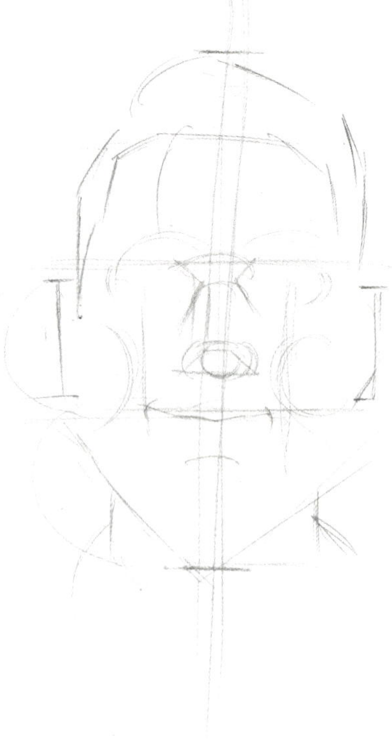

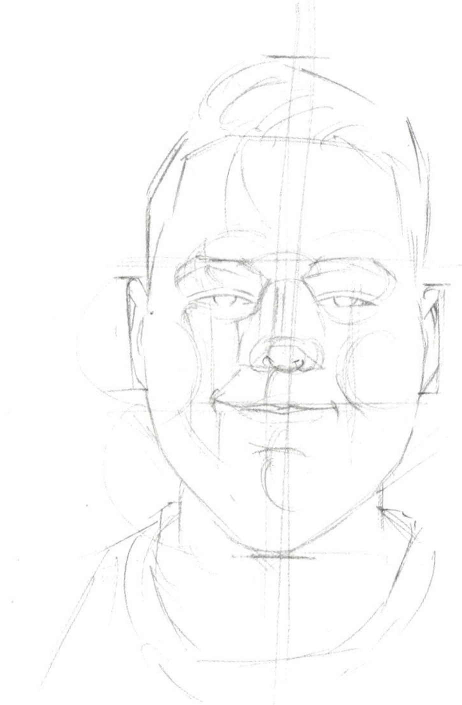

STEP 2

Determine the basic shape of the head. This person has a round face. Next, determine the location of the eyes and ears, which are usually near the center of the face.

Since we are working from a frontal view, the upper part of the ear is equal to the eyebrow line, and the lower part often lies somewhere in the middle of the lip and nose. Use survey lines to locate them accurately. Use simple shapes (circles and triangles) and vertical and horizontal axis lines to mark the features. Remember, in the sketching stage you don't need precise lines; you just need to do the research and find the right lines.

STEP 3

Determine the width and height of the eyes and then add the irises and eyelids. The eyes often play an important role in a laughing expression. The eyelids may be lifted upward and the eyes partially or completely closed. In a raised eyelid position like this, the iris and pupil usually appear smaller.

The nose is wide and full. For a round-faced child, the nose may be bigger, but you must pay attention to one thing: A laughing expression like this is usually characterized by wider and rounder facial features. So use softer and curved lines when drawing the facial features.

In a laughing expression, the lips are often curled. The lips may curve upward, and some or all of the teeth may be visible. The upper lip may be more upturned than the lower lip.

The nose is usually turned upward. The wings of the nose may widen, and the nostrils may become more prominent. The cheeks are often puffy and turned up as well.

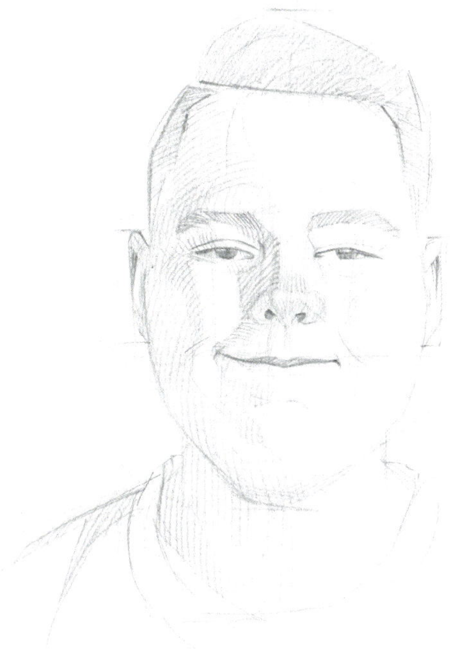

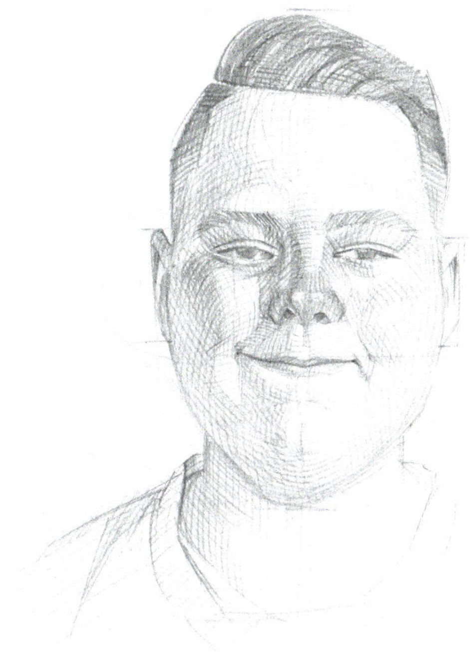

4

5

STEP 4

Use shading to emphasize the cheerful laughing expression. You can emphasize this expression even more by shading areas such as the lines under the eyes, the lines of the nose, and around the lips.

Draw layers of hair, starting close to the child's hairline and moving toward the skull. These layers reflect the volume and fullness of the hair.

STEP 5

Detail the shadowed areas with crosshatching. In the parts that are in the light, make fewer, nondiagonal strokes in one direction.

STEP 6

Examine your drawing carefully and make sure it accurately reflects the expression of laughter. If necessary, improve the expression by adjusting the expression of the eyes, the curve of the lips, or other details.

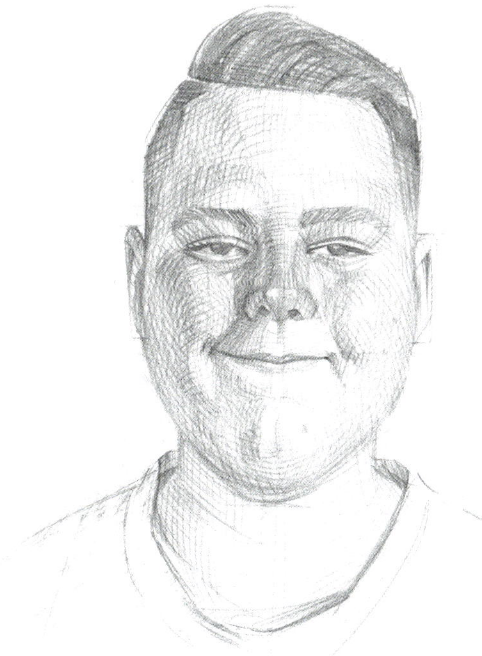

6

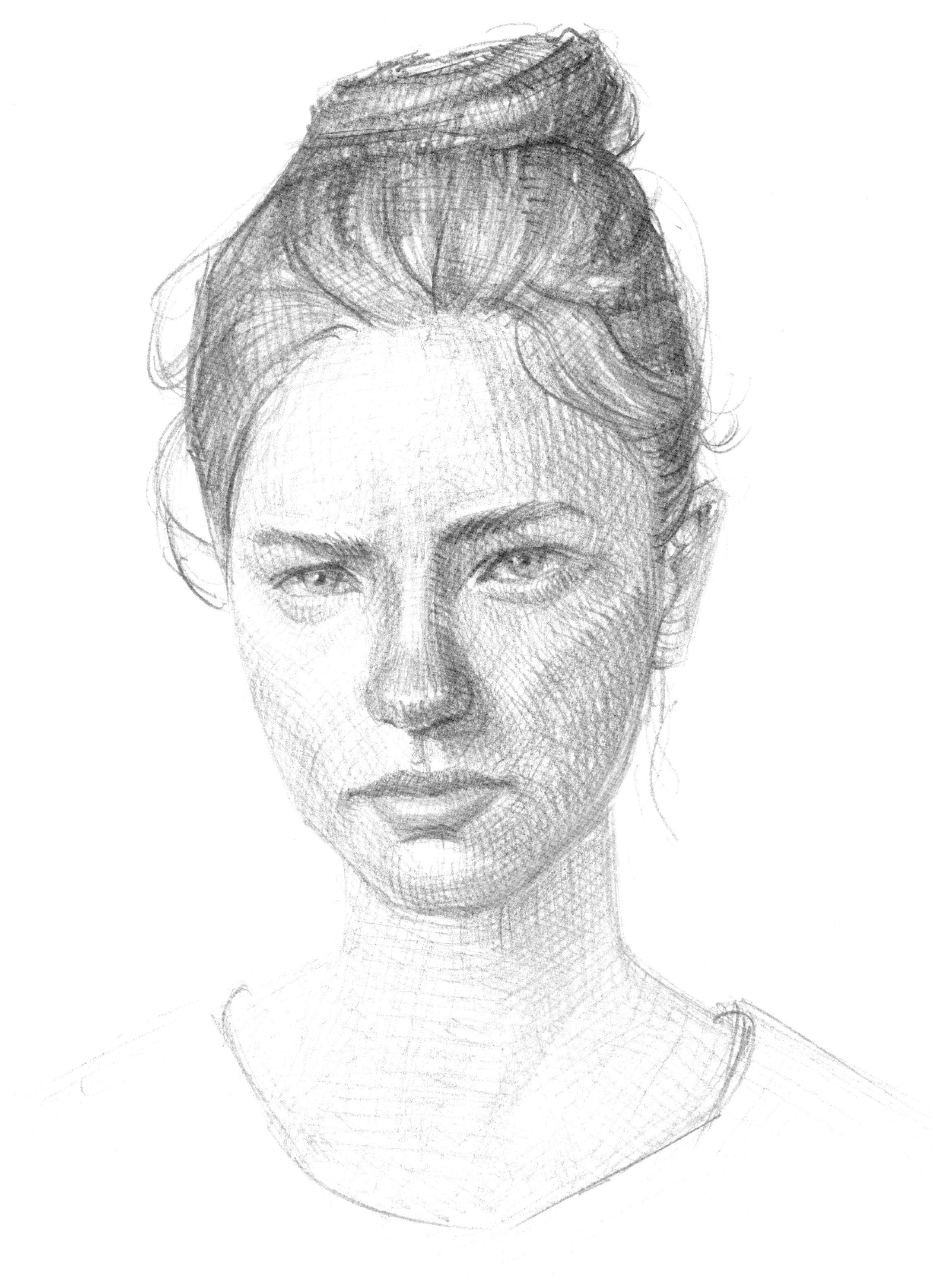

SERIOUS FACIAL EXPRESSION

Facial expressions in portraits significantly affect the emotional and aesthetic quality of the portrait. The eyes are one of the most important elements that determine the emotional expression of the portrait. The size and shape of the eyes, the position of the eyebrows, and the openness, or lack thereof, of the eyes significantly affect the expression of the portrait.

The posture of the eyebrows is also important. Curled or raised eyebrows can create more attention or an emotional expression, while straight eyebrows suggest a calmer expression.

The shape, width, and curve of the lips also reflect emotional expression. The direction of the lip curl and the lip opening can express different emotions such as happiness, sadness, or surprise.

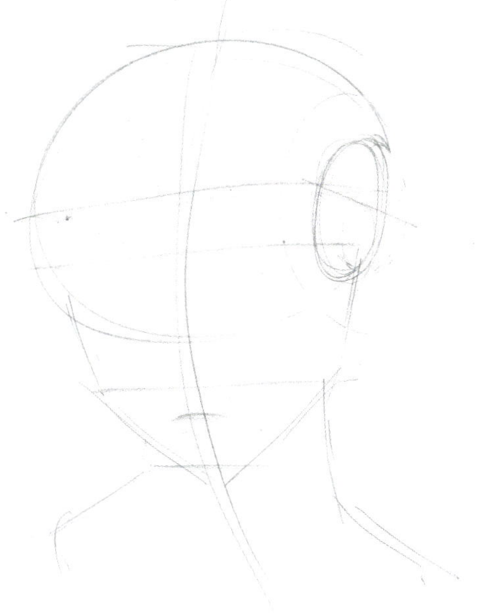

STEP 1

Start by drawing a circle. Draw a perpendicular line with a slight slope in the direction the model is facing. Divide the circle in half and add another line in the middle of the bottom half of the circle. In total you have three equal parts: The bottom part is where you will draw the lower part of the chin; below the horizontal line at the center of the circle you'll draw the eyebrows and eyes.

1

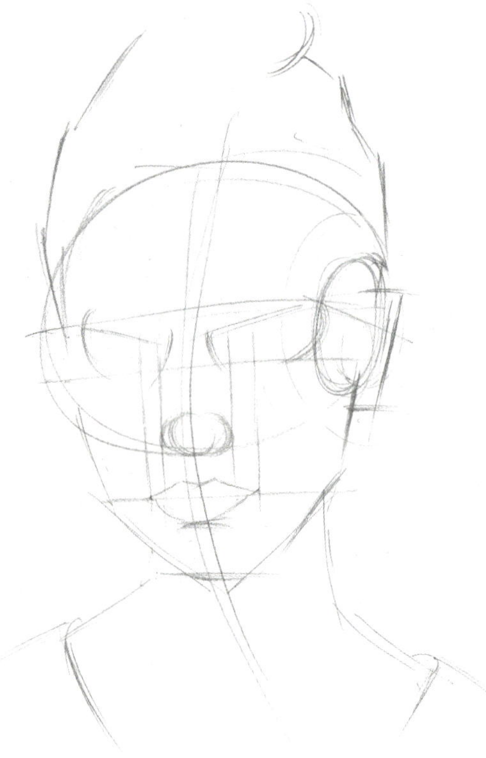

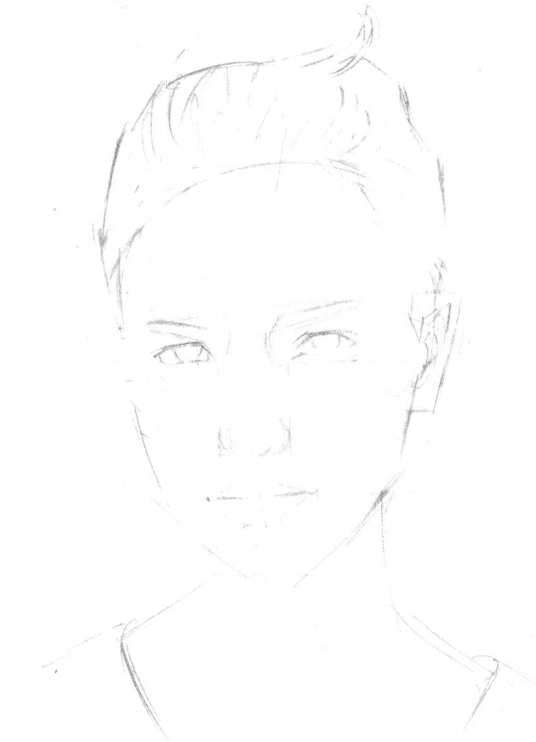

2

STEP 2

Roughly locate the eyes, nose, ear, and lips, using your guidelines from step 1. Block in the overall shape of the hair and the neckline of the shirt.

STEP 3

Carefully determine the shape and expression of the eyes. The size and direction of the pupils can set the emotional tone of the drawing, so pay close attention to your reference photo. Begin to refine the ears, and erase your guidelines as you no longer need them.

STEP 4

As you begin to refine the facial features, pay attention to how much the lips curve and the openness of the mouth. While the lips curl upward in a smiling expression and downward in an unhappy or dissatisfied expression, in this portrait the lips are in a more neutral position, with a slight downward curve.

Block in the darker tones of the hair and begin to add shadow on the darkest areas of the face with light hatch marks.

3

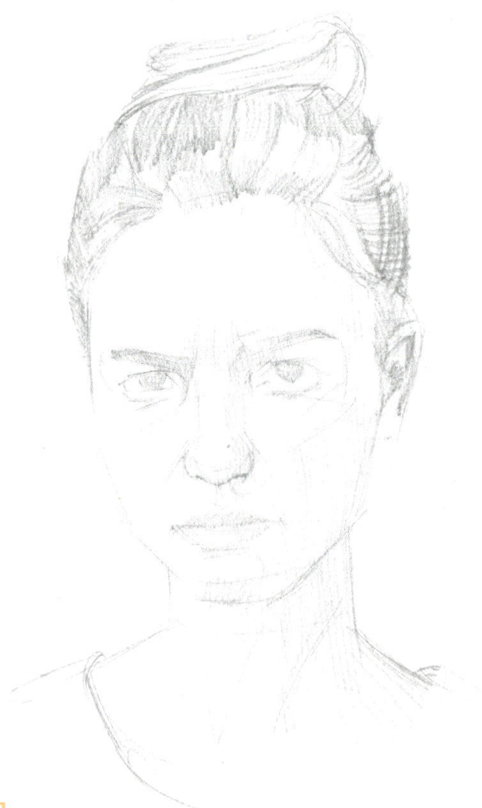

4

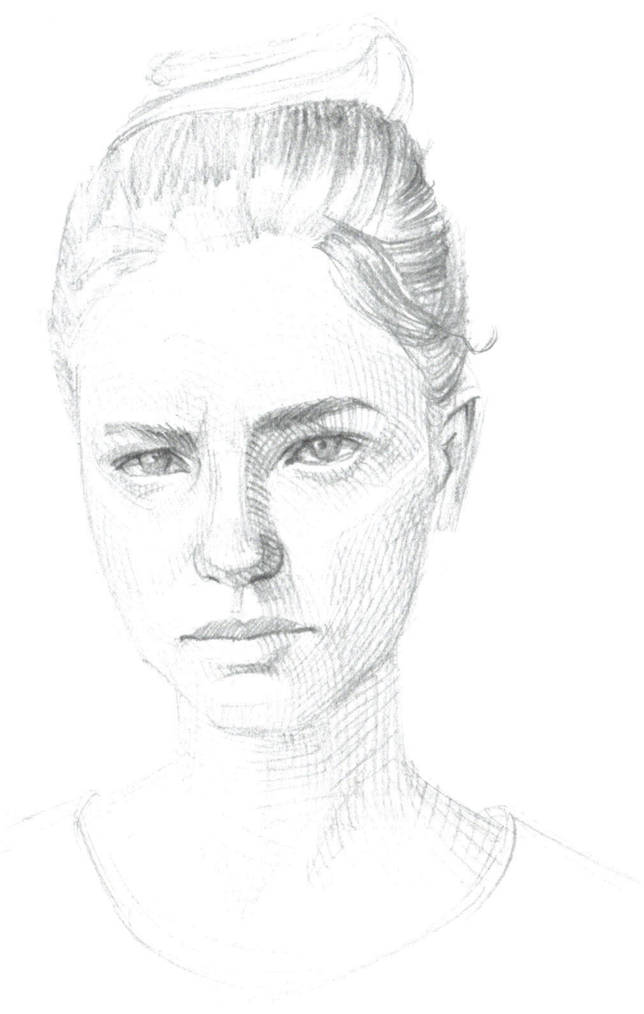

5

STEP 5

Continue to use an eraser to erase any excess lines, and use light hatching with your pencil to suggest areas of light and shadow.

The eyes are one of the focal points of your portrait, so pay special attention to the eye details. Determine the location and details of the irises, eyelids, and eyelashes, and start drawing the details around the eyes. Define the outline of the eyes and add the pupils.

Define the form of the cheeks and chin. Define the facial features with soft lines and shadows. Emphasize the volume and form of the facial features with shadows to begin creating a three-dimensional look.

Accentuate the shadows under the cheeks and define the jawline. Check the symmetry of the face and make adjustments as needed.

Identify the areas furthest from the light source, which do not receive direct light. These areas are usually the back, or nooks and crannies, of the object. Add shadows and tones using shading techniques. Accentuate the shadows under the eyes and nostrils and around the lips.

TIP: Eyebrows are another important element that determine facial expression. The shape, lift, or evenness of the eyebrows can reflect a person's emotional state. Tense, raised eyebrows are often associated with emotions such as confusion or anxiety, while straighter eyebrows often reflect calmness or happiness.

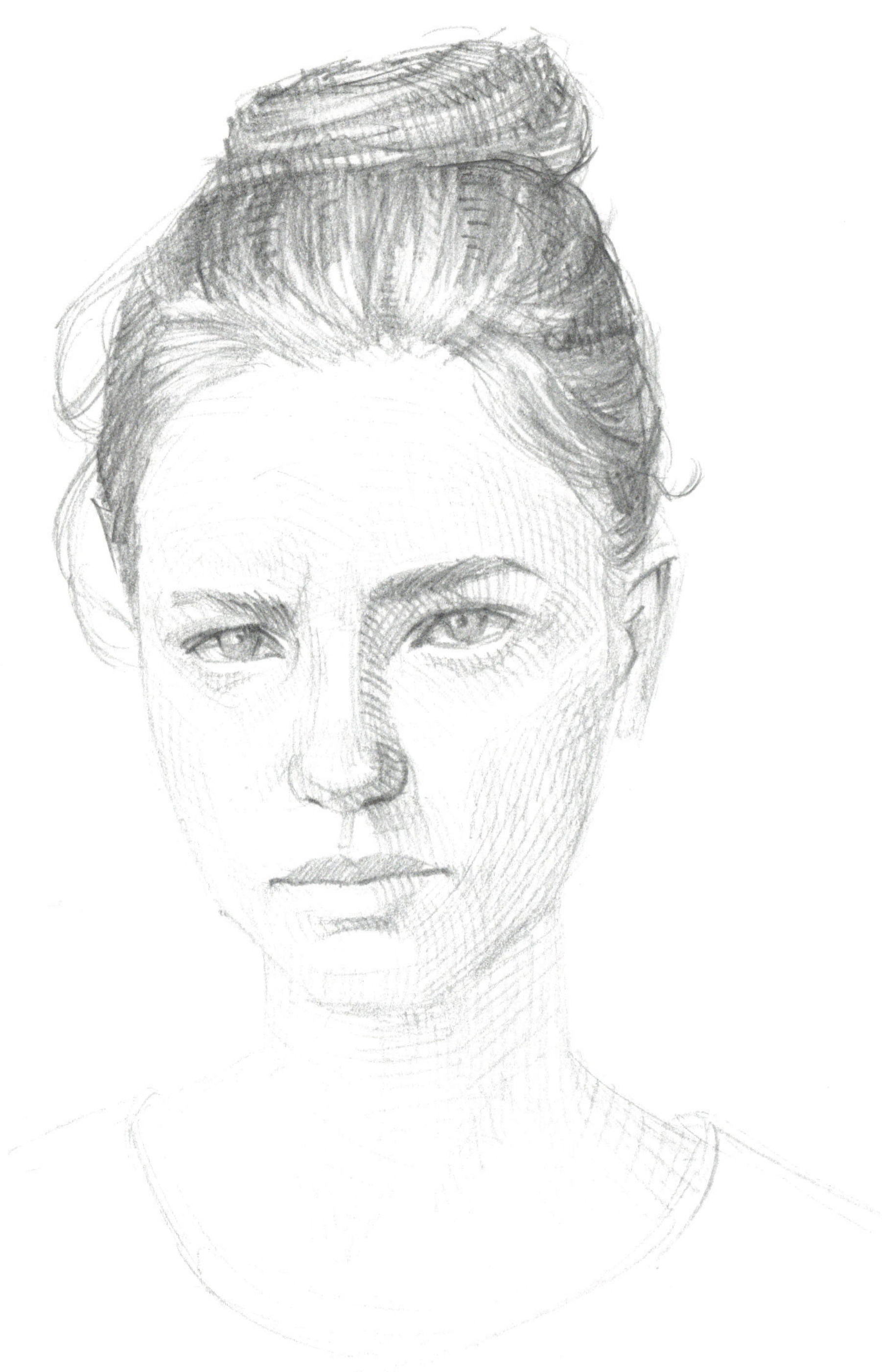

STEP 6

Shade the lower parts of the hair with darker shades and highlight the upper parts with lighter shades. Create the natural texture and pattern of the hair using hatching or crosshatching. Use streaks of different intensities to define the hair strands.

To enhance the movement and naturalness of the hair, add movement lines that suggest the hair is gently moving with the wind.

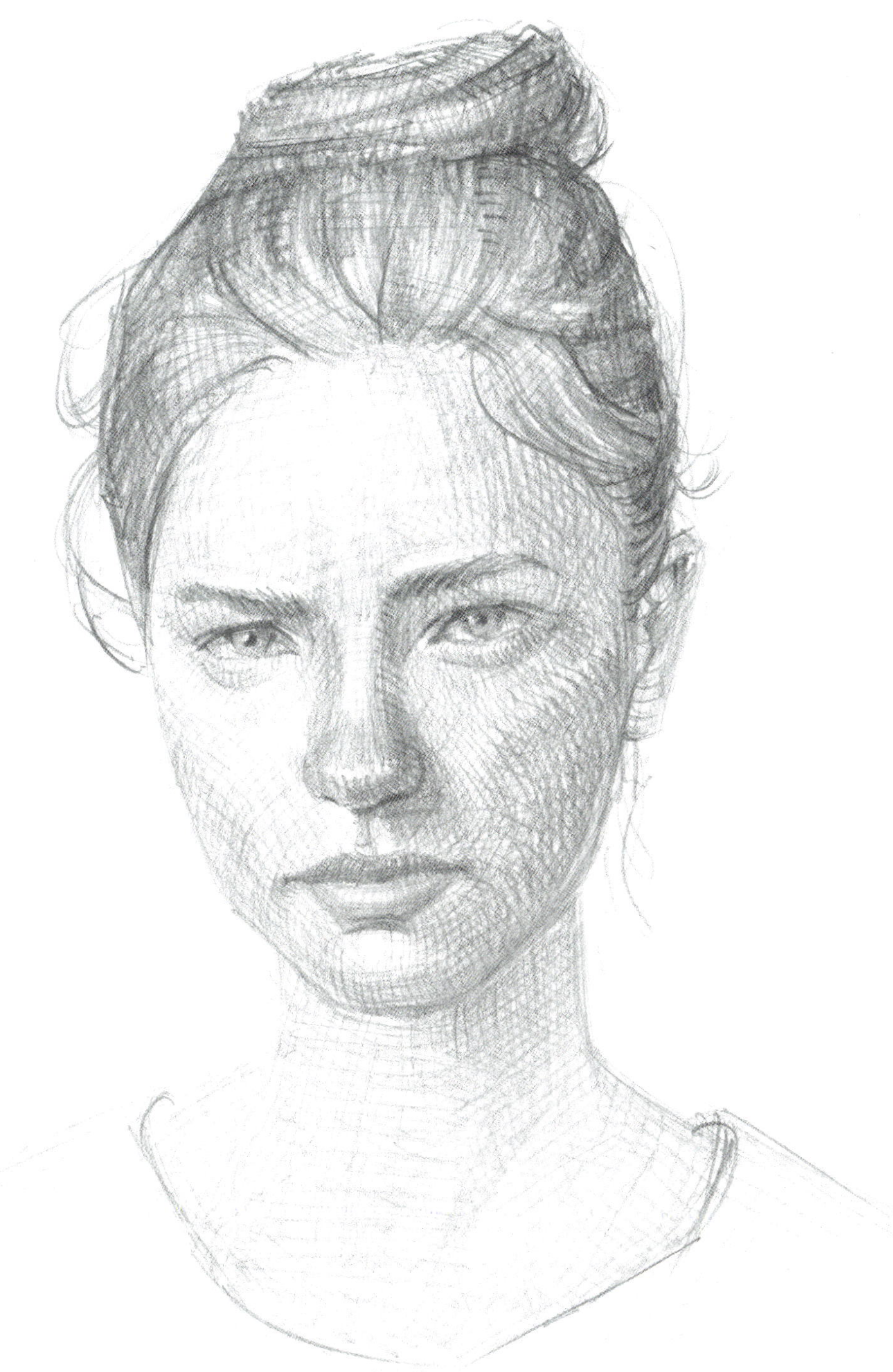

STEP 7

Adjust the movement and shape of the hair in harmony with the other elements in the drawing to emphasize the natural flow and volume of the hair.

Highlight the shaded areas in the portrait with more frequent pencil strokes. Use crosshatching to make the shadows under the lips and the nose more dense.

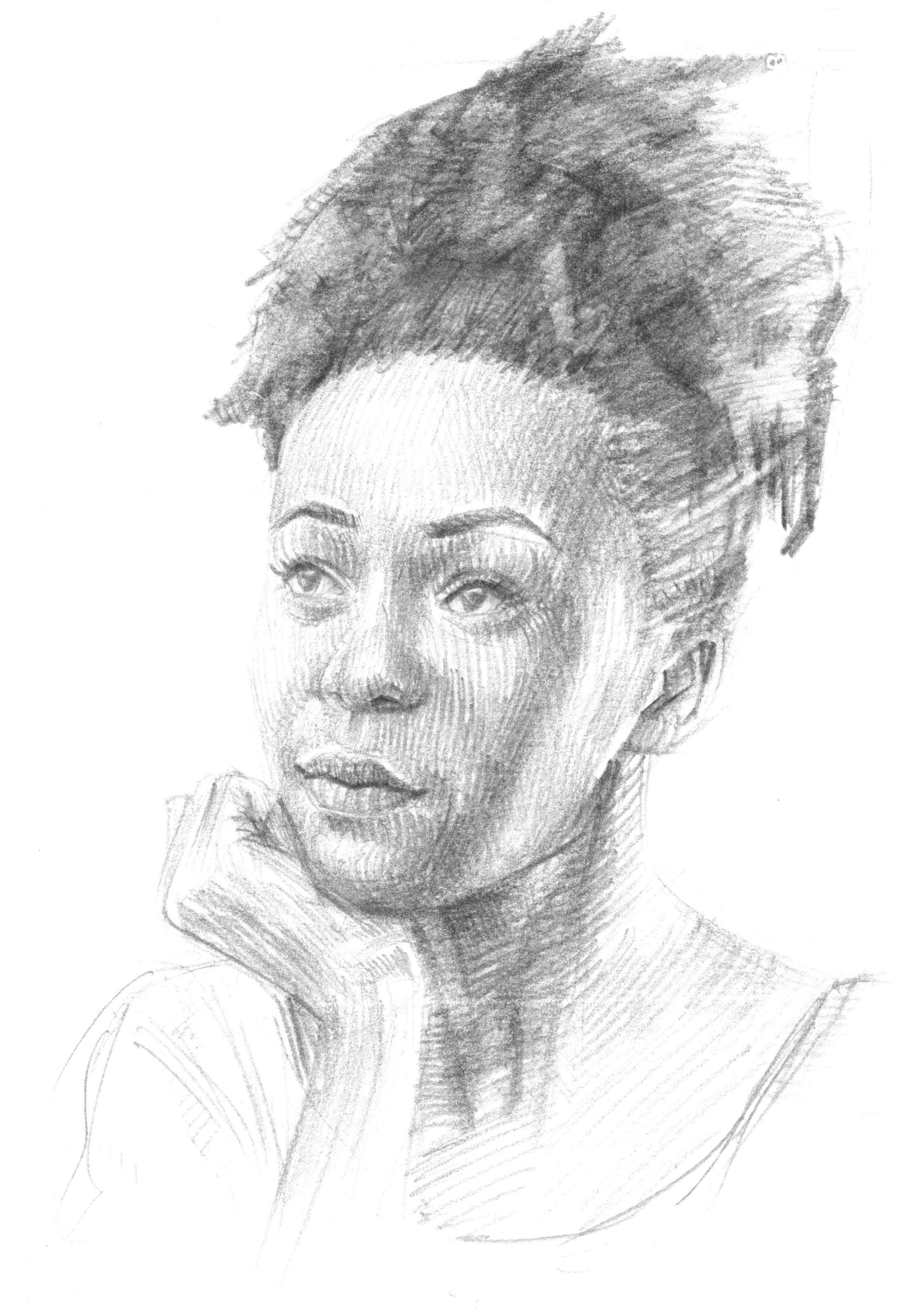

PROJECT 9

PENSIVE WOMAN

When we examine male and female heads, we see very little difference in proportion. But there are still differences in the facial features. A female face tends to be made up of soft lines and rounded or curved shapes, while male features are more angular.

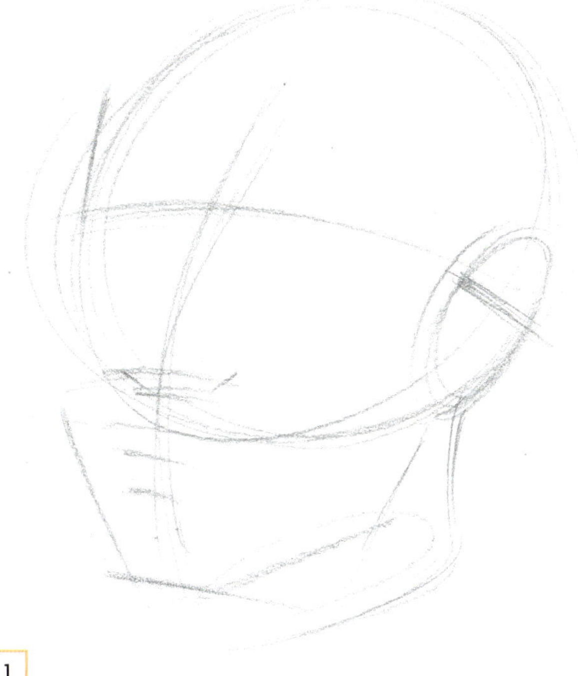

1

STEP 1

For this three-quarter portrait start with a circle and divide it with a curve in the direction the model is facing. The bottom of the circle is where you will place the nose. Below the line dividing the circle in the middle will be the eyebrows and eyes.

Roughly mark and draw the facial features with your guidelines without applying too much pressure, observing the distance and alignment of the eyebrow to the ear, and the alignment and distance of the eyes to the nose and lips.

TIP: The most important thing during the sketching stage is to observe very well. Continuously make comparisons and take measurements. The whole point is actually to learn to see correctly. By practicing constantly, you will learn to see more accurately, and you will start to notice your mistakes more quickly.

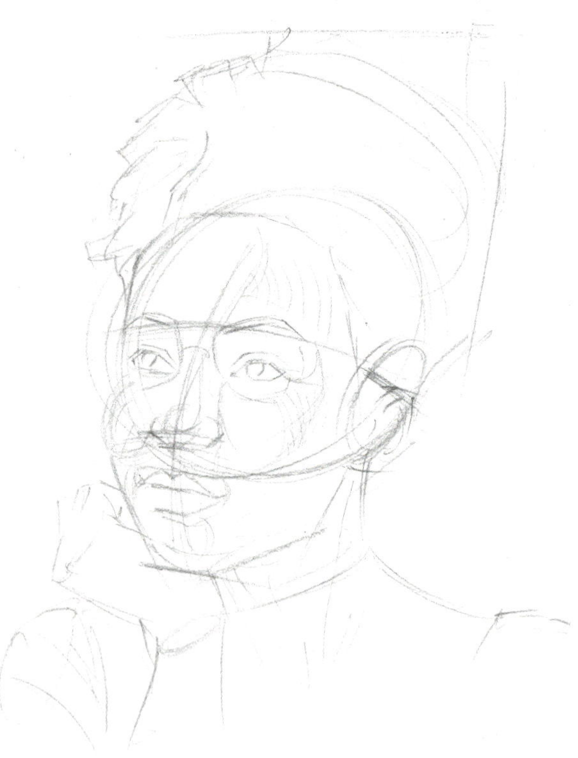

STEP 2

Continue to investigate the position of the hand under the chin and the location of facial elements. Block in the overall shape of the hair.

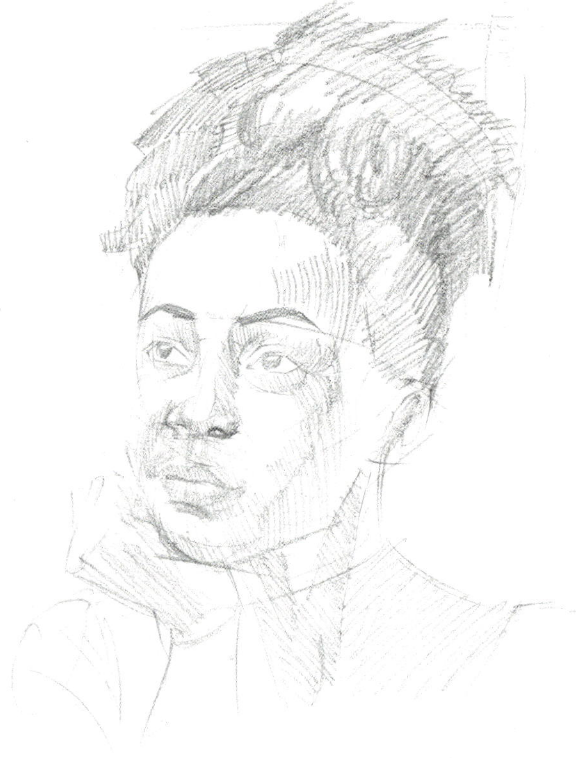

STEP 3

In this portrait, the light source is shining on the face from the left, and the right side is in shadow. Begin to add shading without applying too much pressure.

Observe the overall mass of the hair, rather than sketching it in strands. Notice the direction and movement of the hair. Give a sense of movement and texture to the hair with loose strokes.

Define the nostrils, the bones of the nose, and the lines of the mouth. The shape and lines of the lips affect the expression of the portrait.

CHARACTERISTICS OF FEMALE FEATURES

- The face is slightly smaller.
- The eyes are a little bigger.
- The eyebrows are a little higher and curved.
- The nose and mouth are smaller.
- The chin is rounder.

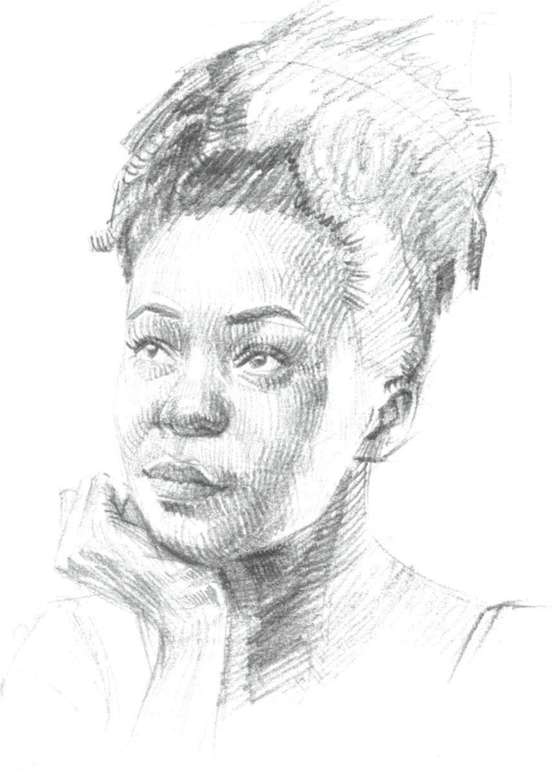

4

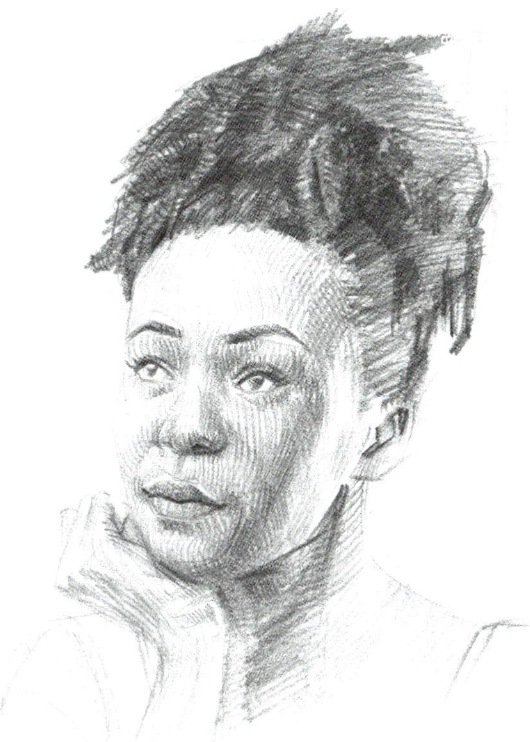

5

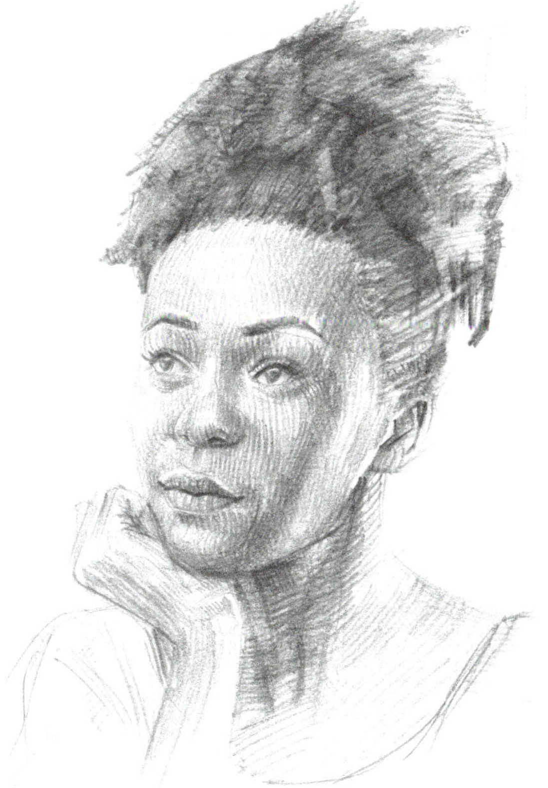

6

STEP 4

Detail the face, taking into account the light and shadow. Notice that my lines are slightly curved and slanted. This is because I think of the portrait in three dimensions. I think about the movement of the cheekbone, and I curve my lines in that direction. Continue to apply shading and build the tonal values with diagonal lines over the areas in shadow, including the lower part of the nose, under the chin, the cheekbone, lower eye socket, and under the lip.

STEP 5

Define the form and thickness of the eyebrows and the brow lines. Continue to develop the tones in the hair, leaving bits of white paper for highlights.

STEP 6

Add sparkle in the eyes, or the details of a smile, to reinforce the emotional expression of the portrait. Adjust the curve of the lips and the position of the eyebrows to emphasize the expression.

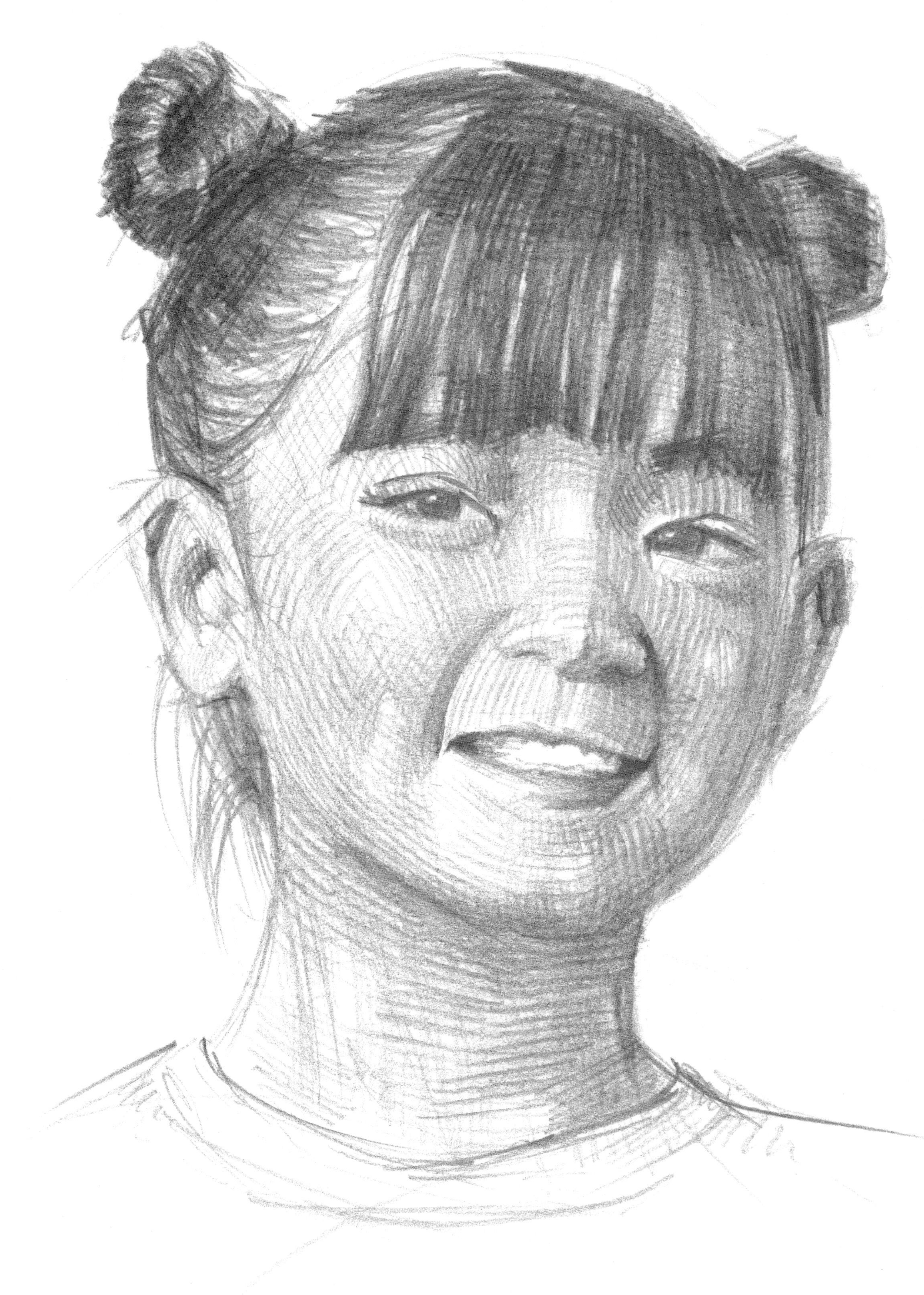

YOUNG GIRL SMILING

Young girls usually have rounder, softer facial features. As is usually the case with babies, the face is smaller and rounder and has more indistinct features. Take care to draw the facial features gently and softly, noting that the cheeks may be fuller, and the chin may be smaller and more rounded.

The model in this portrait is about six years old. While her face still has characteristics of a very young child, her head is also developing and changing. The hair is growing more, particularly at the forehead and temples. The jawbone is more developed, so the face is slightly longer compared to a toddler. The bone structure of the mandible is also more pronounced, and the jawbone is less curved.

STEP 1

Start by drawing a circle. To determine the location of the eyes, draw a horizontal line through the center of the face. This will help you to accurately position the eyes. Draw another horizontal line to mark the bottom of the chin. Block in the shape of the neck and ear, and mark the location of the eyes, mouth, and nose with basic shapes and lines.

Children's noses are usually smaller and flatter than an adult's. The nostrils and bridge of the nose may be smaller. Avoid emphasizing the lines of the nose too much, as this can damage a childish appearance. You can measure the width of the nose just below the eye socket, create the nose sketch by drawing three circles.

1

STEP 2

Block in the general shape of the hair. The eyebrows are usually thinner and more slightly arched, while the eyelids are usually more rounded and indistinct. Keep this in mind as you begin to detail the eyes.

Children's nostrils can often be small and flat. Draw the nostrils under the bridge of the nose at a slight angle. Characterize the tip and wings of the nose, noting that children's nasal tips are often smaller and rounder, and the wings of the nose flatter and less prominent.

The bridge of children's noses is usually flatter and may be less prominent than those of adults. Use a straight and slightly curved line to accentuate the bridge of the nose.

Children's lips are often thinner. Be gentle when emphasizing the lines of the mouth and lips. Draw the lips slightly curved to capture a childish smile. Highlight the upper lip line, which is often thinner and may not have a pronounced curve in children. Starting from the center of the lips, draw a slight upward curve. Define the lower lip line. The lower lip is often fuller, but can also be thin in children. Draw the lower lip line curving slightly upward, and let it intersect slightly with the upper lip.

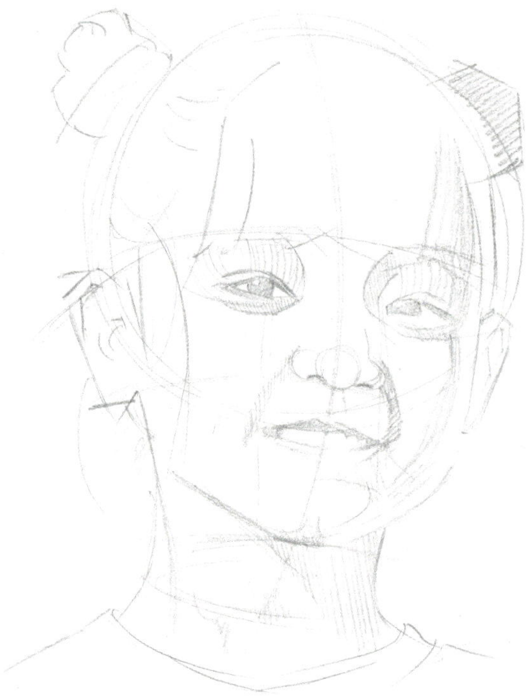

2

TIP: The eyes are important to convey a childlike expression. Girls' eyes are usually bigger and brighter. However, they should not be exaggerated. The iris of the eyes can be larger, but avoid drawing them too big, which can create an exaggerated and unnatural look. Bagging under the eyes may not be evident, and the eyelashes may not be prominent.

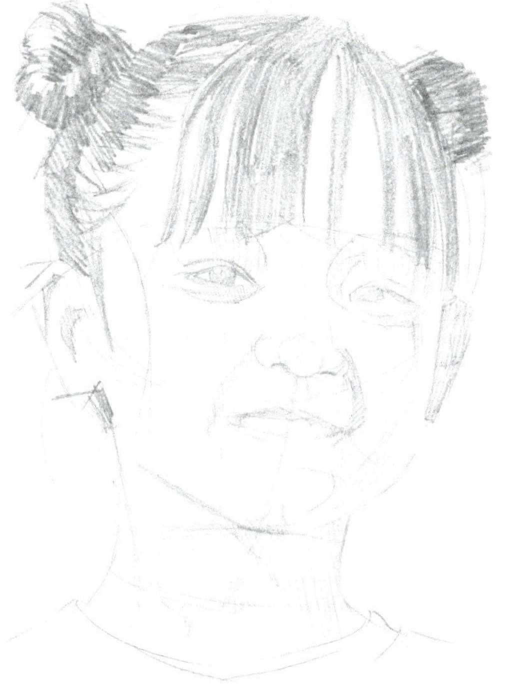

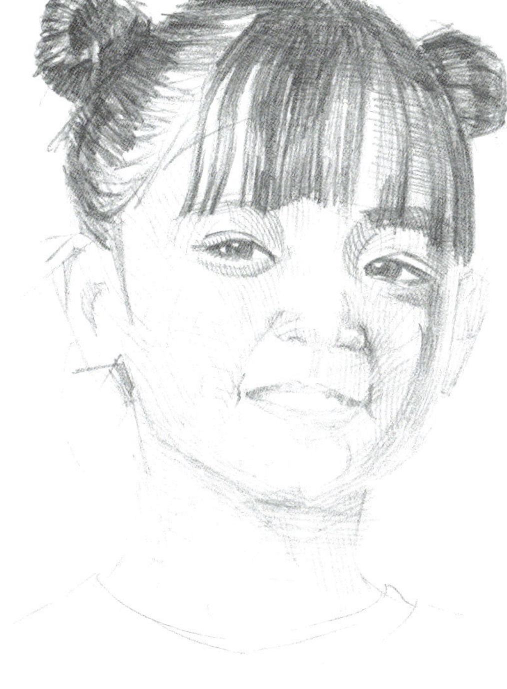

STEP 3

In this portrait, the light source shines on the face from the left. Identify the areas where the shadows fall. The areas under the nose, eyes, lips, and chin are where the shadows are concentrated.

Soft shadows usually occur in the lower parts of the face and in the recesses, while hard shadows usually occur on the sides of the facial features, under the bridge of the nose, and under the eyelids. Using a soft-tipped pencil or shading pen, fill in the shadowed areas you have identified. Slowly apply the shadows according to the direction of the light and blend the tones gently.

Pay attention to detail, and preserve facial contours when applying shadows. Avoid making the shadows too intense or pronounced, as this can reduce the realism of the portrait.

Roughly draw the hair in mass and tonal value. Characterize the movement of the hair and the way it falls. Emphasize the movement and dynamism of the hair.

STEP 4

Add light tones and shadows, taking into account the light and shadows falling on the teeth. This will help emphasize the volume and depth of the teeth.

Skin tones and texture enhance the realism of the portrait. Determine the skin tones correctly and draw the skin's texture with soft and natural strokes that follow the curves of the facial features.

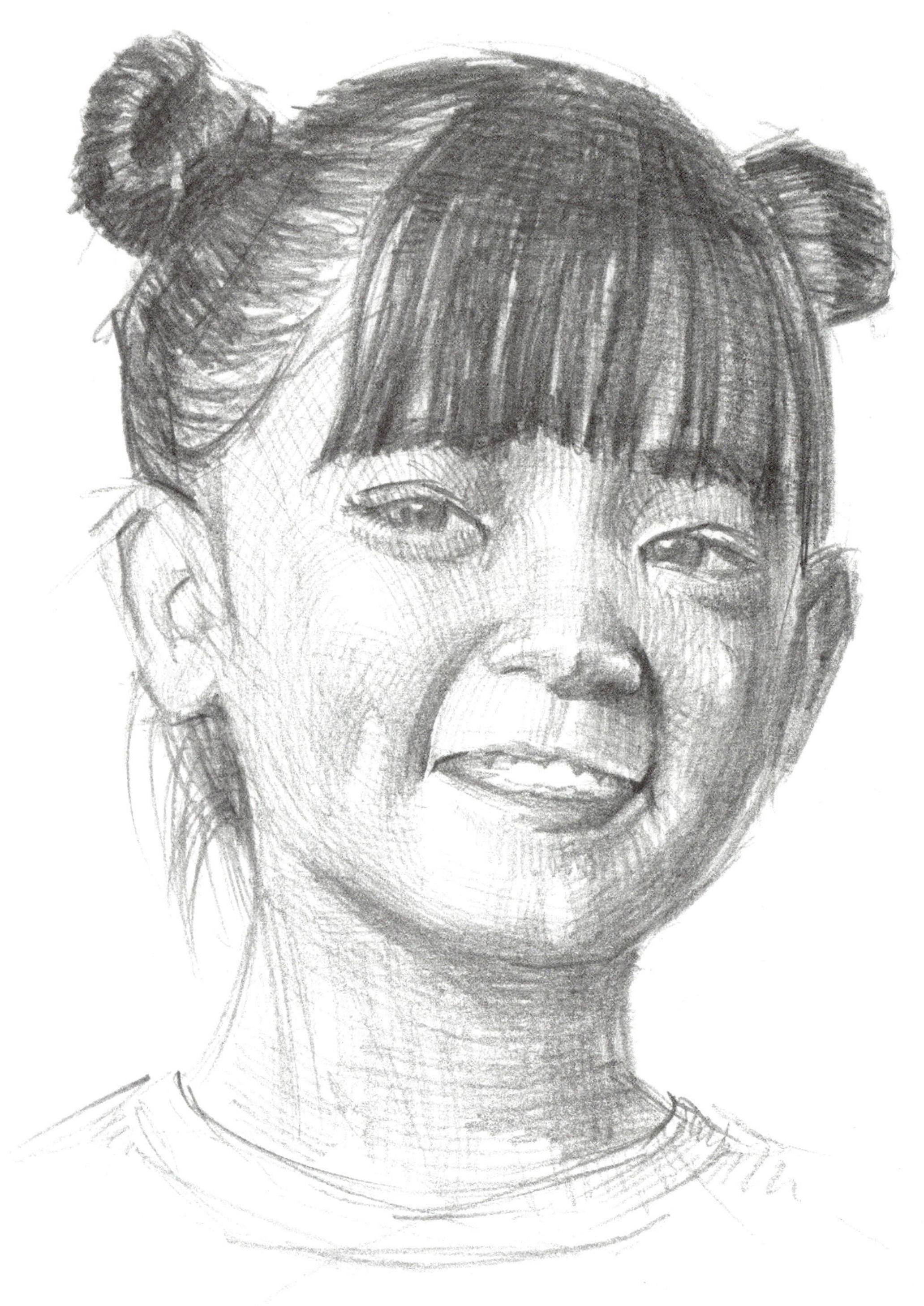

STEP 5

As you deepen the shadows, take care to keep your drawing natural and cute. Try to achieve a childlike look by using soft lines and natural details. Avoid overdoing the details in the drawing and try to keep it simple.

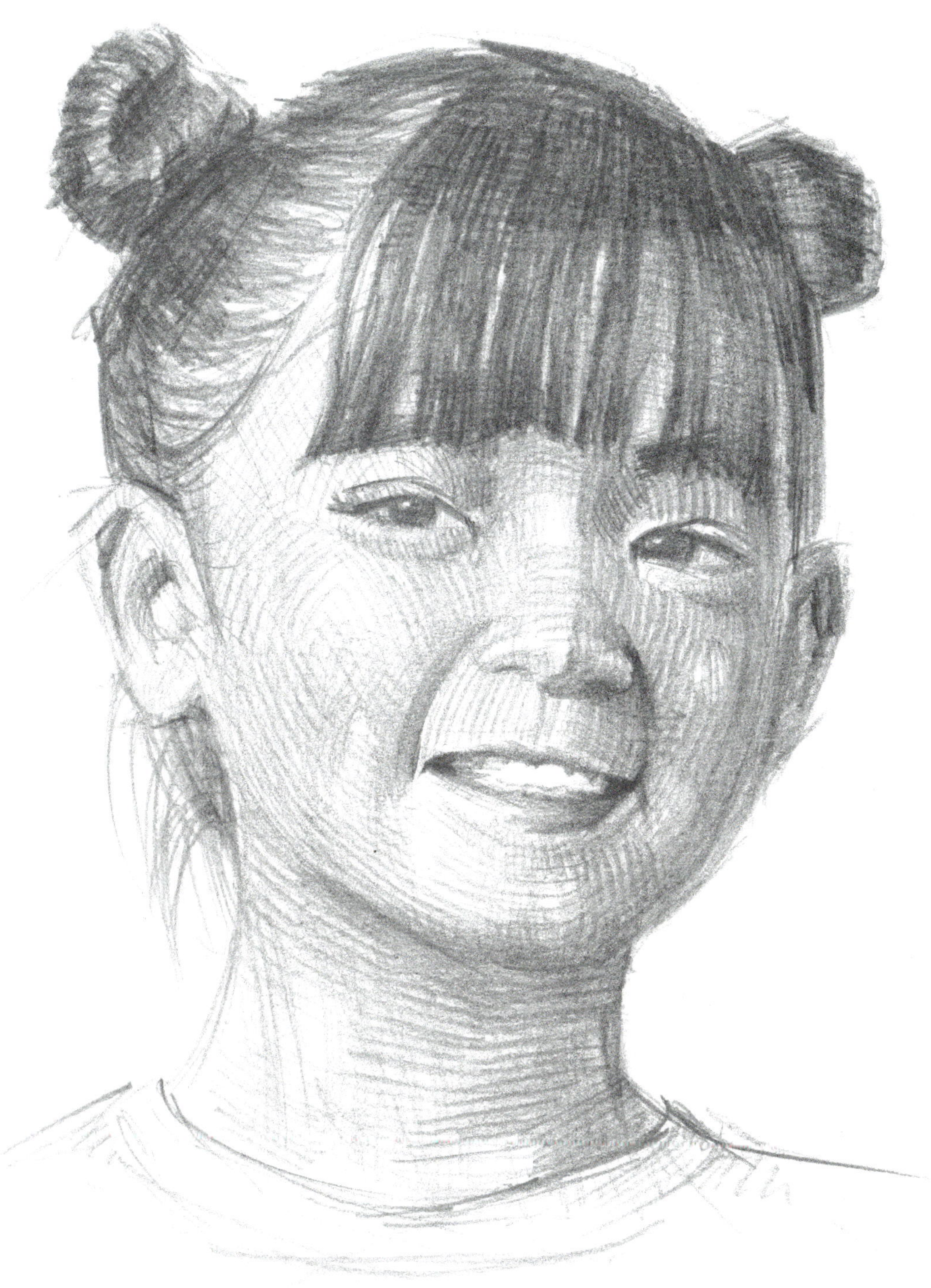

STEP 6

Make the face look more alive and realistic by adding
shine inside the eyes and applying a light gloss over
the lips.

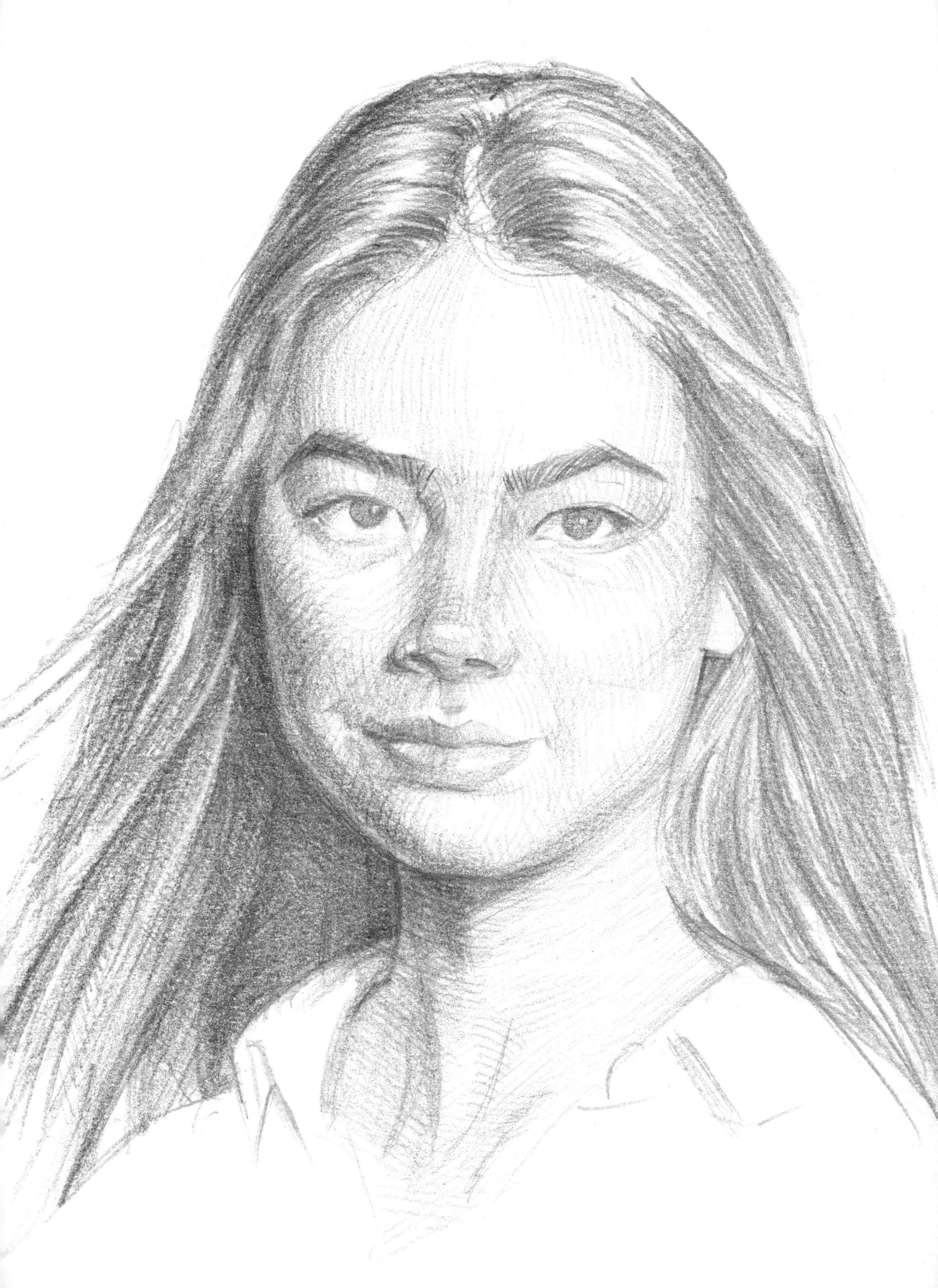

PROJECT 11

LONG HAIR IN THE BREEZE

Long hair may seem intimidating to draw, but the hair-drawing "rules" are the same no matter the length. Remember to start with the general shape of the hair. Observe which way the hair grows and lies, and follow this direction with your pencil strokes to mirror the natural flow of the hair. Draw the hair in sections, rather than trying to sketch individual strands. Work from dark to light, using an eraser to pull out highlights as needed.

STEP 1

Start by drawing a circle for the face, with a line dividing the circle in half. This line marks where the bottom of the eyes are. Use a few simple lines and a circle to sketch the nose, and add another horizontal line to mark the bottom of the chin.

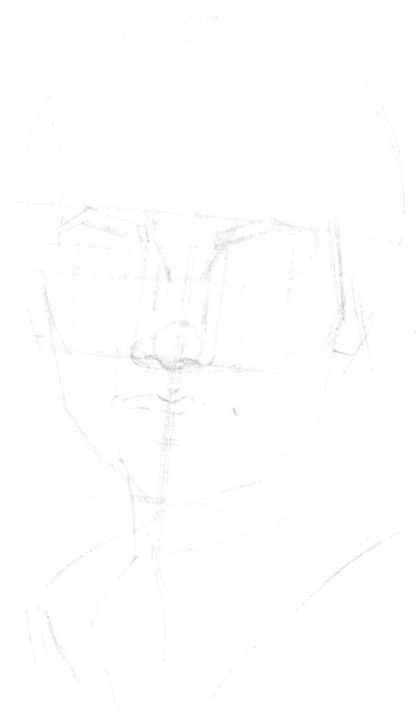

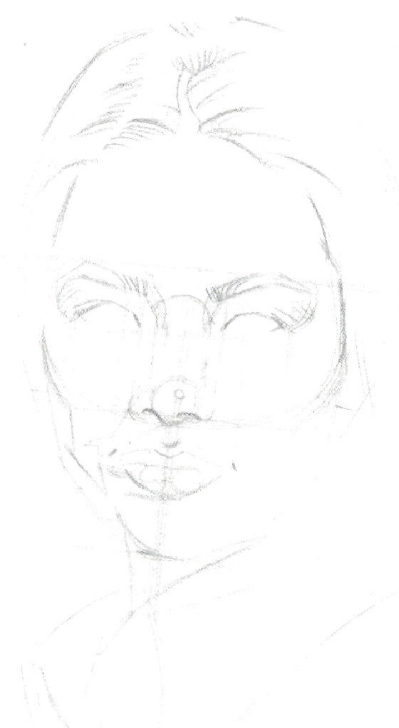

2

3

STEP 2

Draw the bridge of the nose, the nostrils, and the tip of the nose. Consider the side lines of the nose and try to achieve the right proportions.

Determine the general form of the lips and draw the upper and lower lips. Carefully observe the lip lines and the fullness of the lips.

Refine the outline of the face to start shaping the jawline, chin, neck, and shirt. Block in the eyebrows, eyes, and ears with light lines.

STEP 3

The eyes are usually the most striking element of the face. Place them in the center of the face and draw the general form of each eye. Refine the shape of the bottom lip.

Determine the general form and location of the ears. They are usually located in a line starting above the eyes and ending below the nostrils.

Determine the hairline by following the form of the head. Consider the general style and flow of the hair as you begin to sketch it.

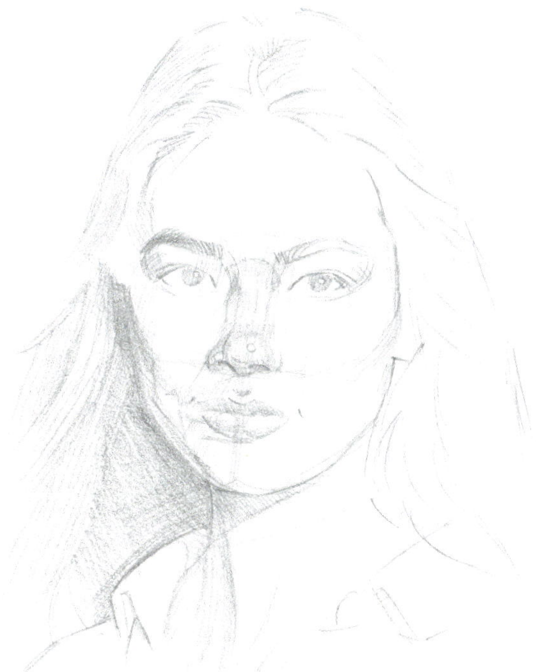

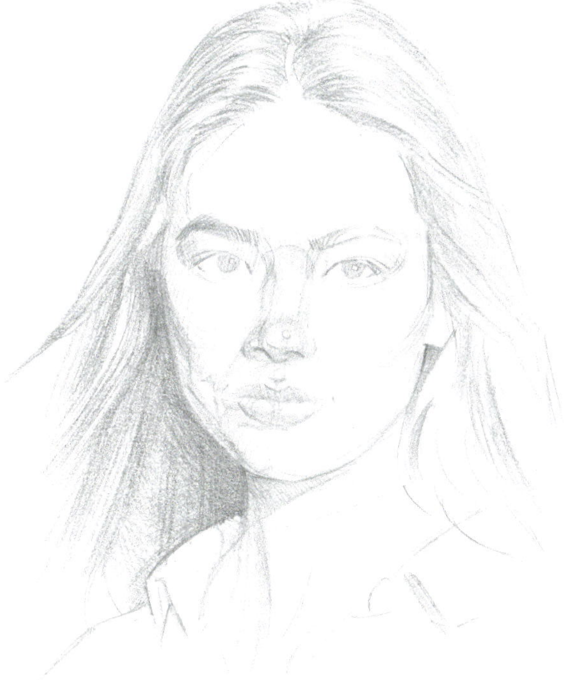

4

5

STEP 4

Add eye details such as the pupil, iris, and eyelashes. Identify the light source to determine which areas of the face are in the light and which are in shadow. Identify the main areas of shadow and light on the face. Typically, the nose, cheeks, and under the chin and the forehead are shadow areas, while under the eyes, on the forehead, on the nose, and on the lips are light areas. Identify the main shadows with a light shading.

STEP 5

Gradually intensify the shadows and make smooth transitions between shadows to correct gradations and create tonal contrast. Erase your initial guidelines as you no longer need them and are confident in the proportions and placement of the facial features.

Continue to develop the values of the hair. Her long hair is moving in the wind; keep your strokes loose and free to mimic this natural movement, pressing harder at the top of each stroke and lifting off the paper as you near the end to create natural-looking hair.

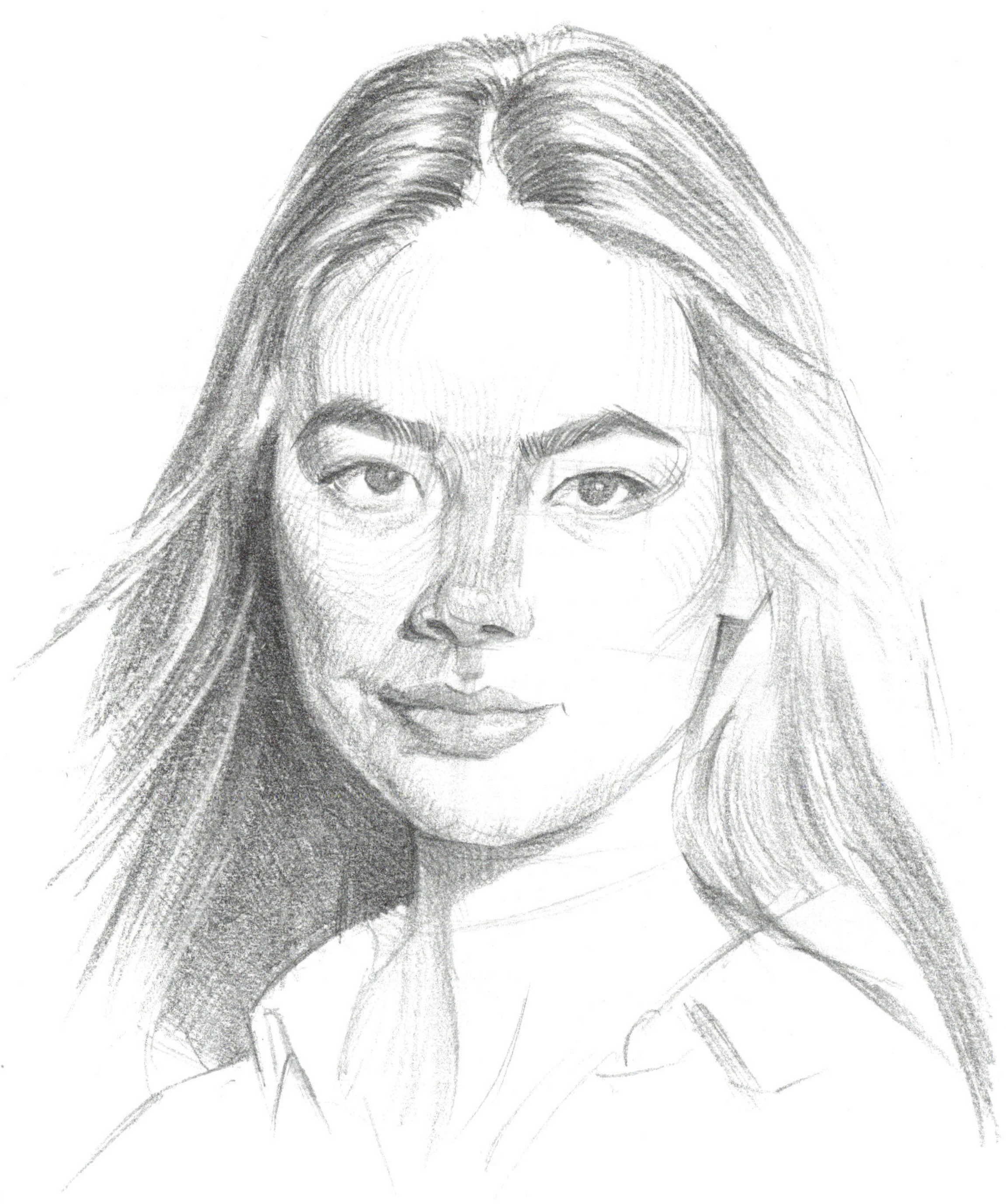

STEP 6

Add more pronounced shadows to areas such as
the chin and under the lips and nose. Add depth
to the eyelids by creating shadows under the eyes.

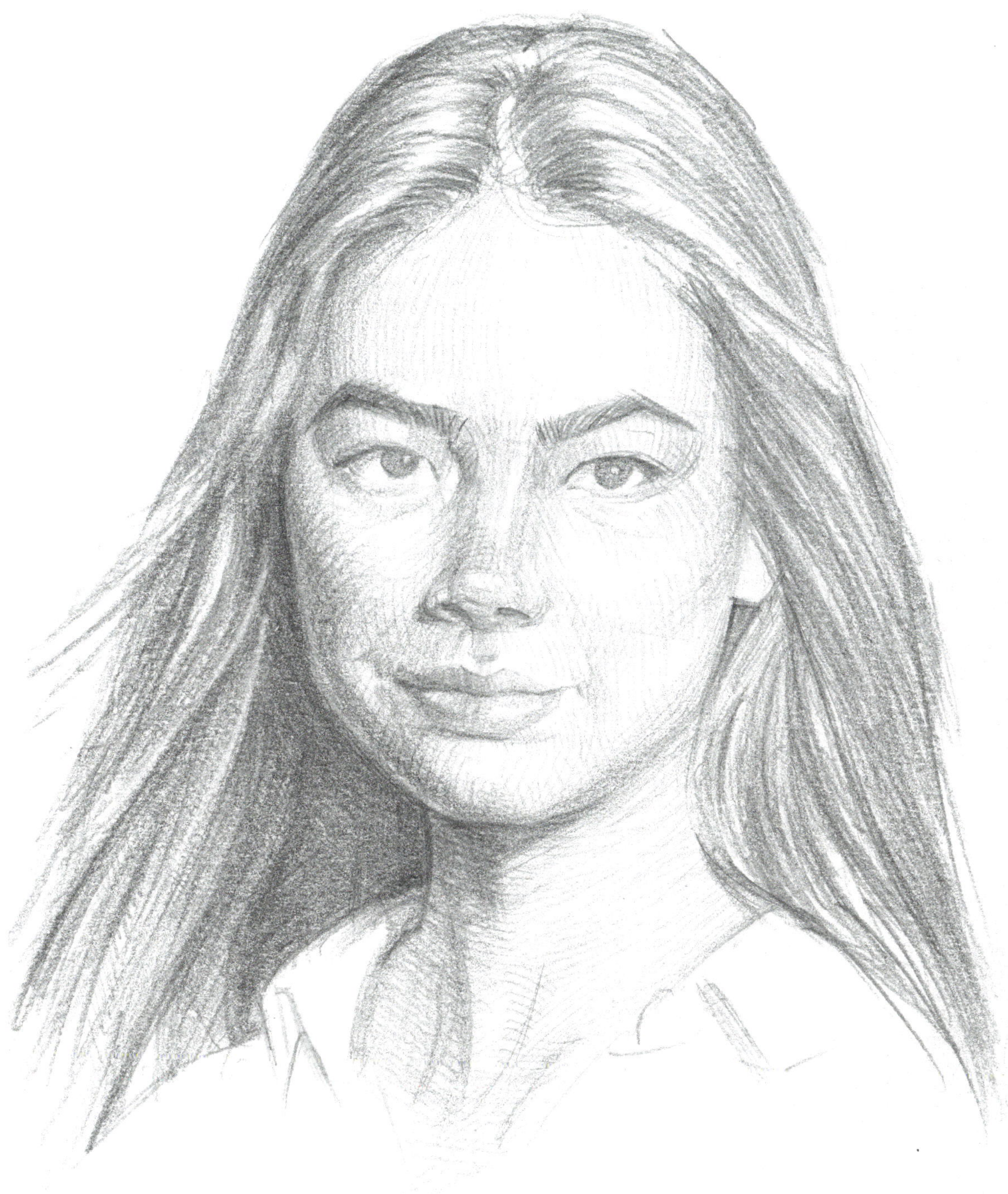

7

STEP 7

Hair often creates shadows that fall over the face. Add shadows following the hairline, taking into account the form of the hair.

Emphasize the gradations of shadow, especially in detailed areas such as the eyes, nostrils, and lip lines. Make the portrait more realistic and detailed by shading fine details.

Emphasize the volume and texture of the hair by following the form of the hair and adding shadows to the strands. You can also shade clothing or other detailed areas to finalize your portrait.

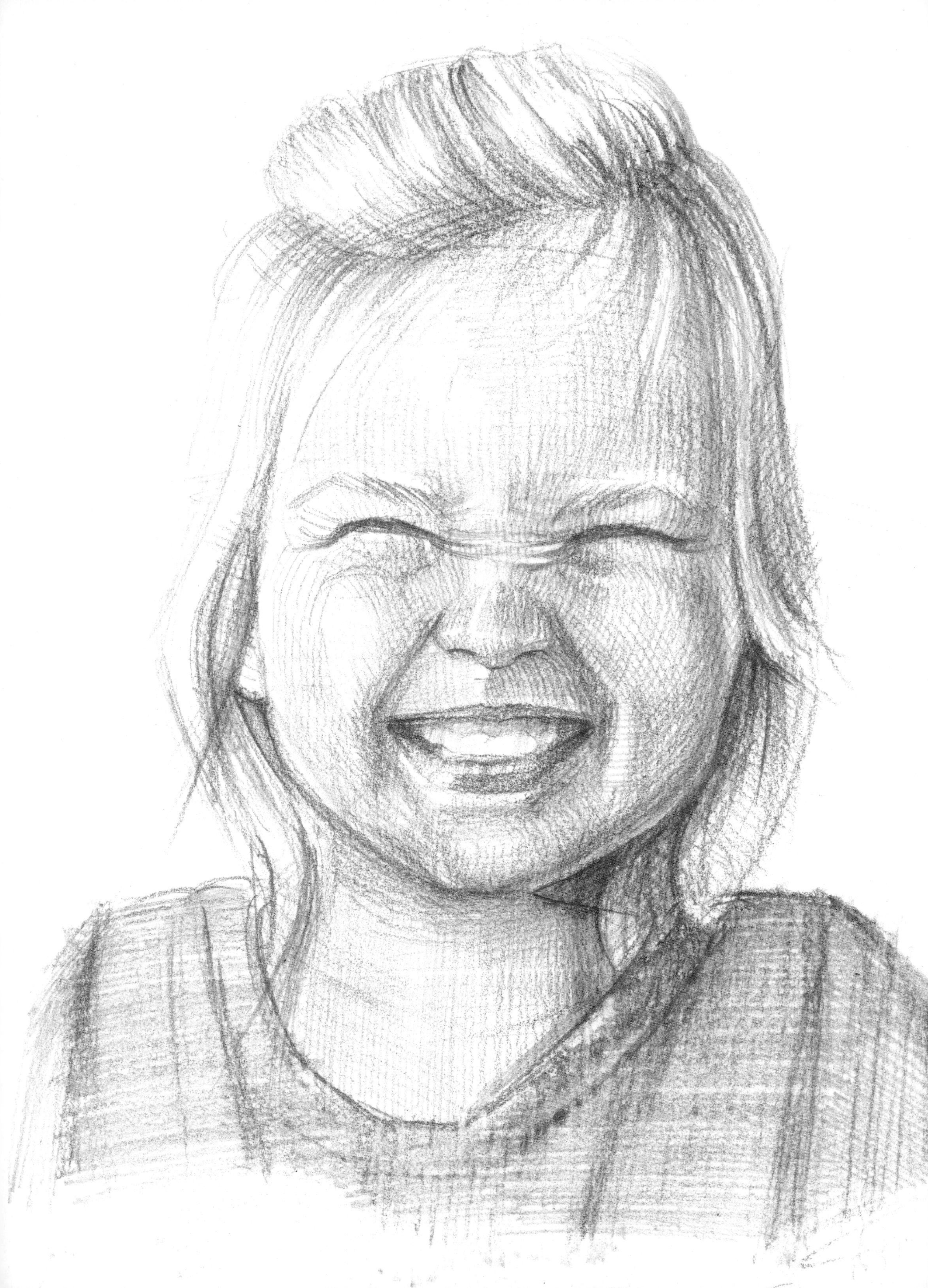

PROJECT 12

LAUGHING CHILD

This portrait is great practice for drawing both children and laughing facial features. When drawing a smiling expression, note that the mouth is usually open and the lips are curled. Conversely, the mouth may be more closed and the lips pulled down in a sad expression. The shape of the lips and lip lines determine the expression.

Eyebrows also greatly influence facial expressions. The shape and position of the eyebrows determine many emotions: happy, confused, worried, or angry. For a happy expression, the eyebrows are usually raised upward, while in a sad expression the eyebrows are drawn downward.

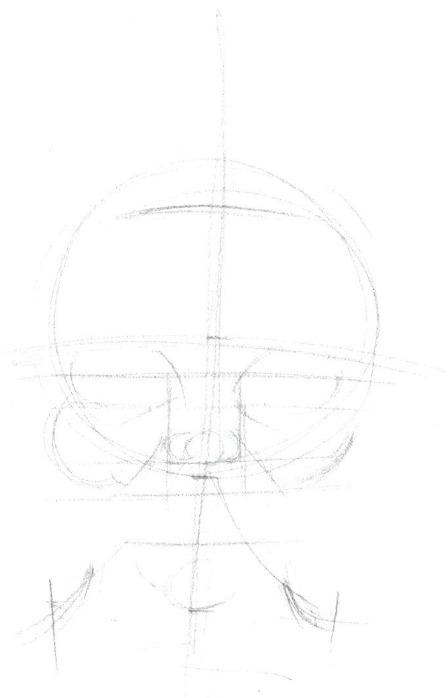

STEP 1

Start with a circle for the face, drawing a vertical line through it to divide the face in half. Add a horizontal line to help place the eyes, and use loose strokes to outline the neck.

Determine the general contours of the child's face, initially creating the overall form of the face with light and loose lines. Use simple shapes to place the eyes, nose, and ear.

TIP: Remember that children's faces are often softer and more innocent looking. Be careful not to overemphasize wrinkles around the eyes, eyebrows, or other details. Less detail can create a more innocent look.

1

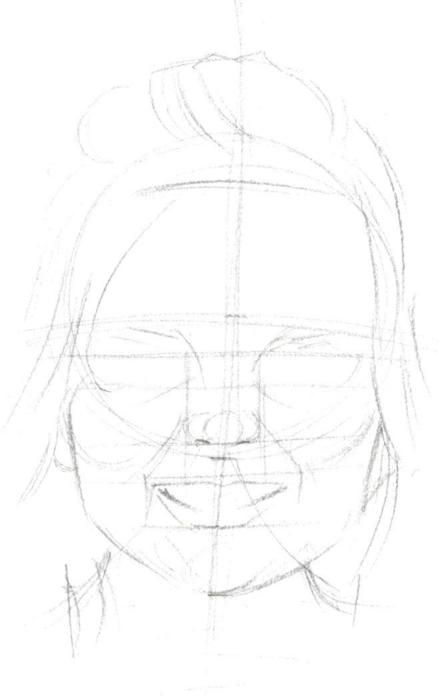

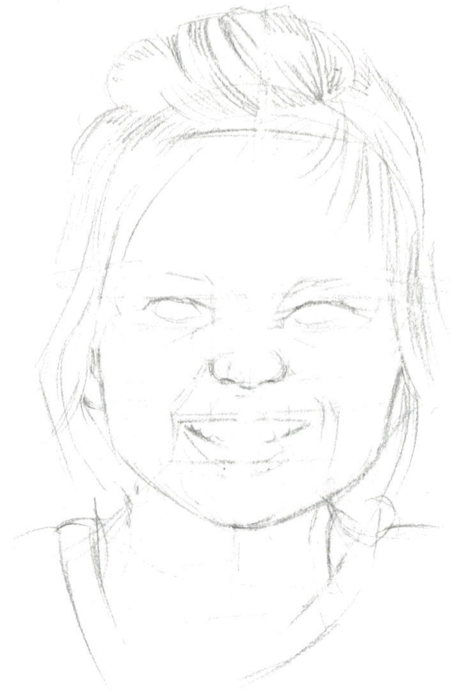

2

3

STEP 2

Refine the outline of the face, sketching in the jawline and chin. Determine the smiling shape of the mouth and draw the general form of the lips. Carefully indicate the wrinkles and folds around the mouth with simple lines. Block in the general shape of the hair.

STEP 3

Begin to detail the eyes and eyebrows, as well as the wrinkle lines on the face created by the smiling expression. Add more pencil strokes in the hair to start creating the hair detail.

Once you are happy with the overall proportions of the portrait, you can erase the guidelines.

TIP: Children's faces are often fuller and more disproportionate than those of adults. Determine the position of the eyes, nose, and lips correctly, but adjust them in accordance with the child's age and face shape.

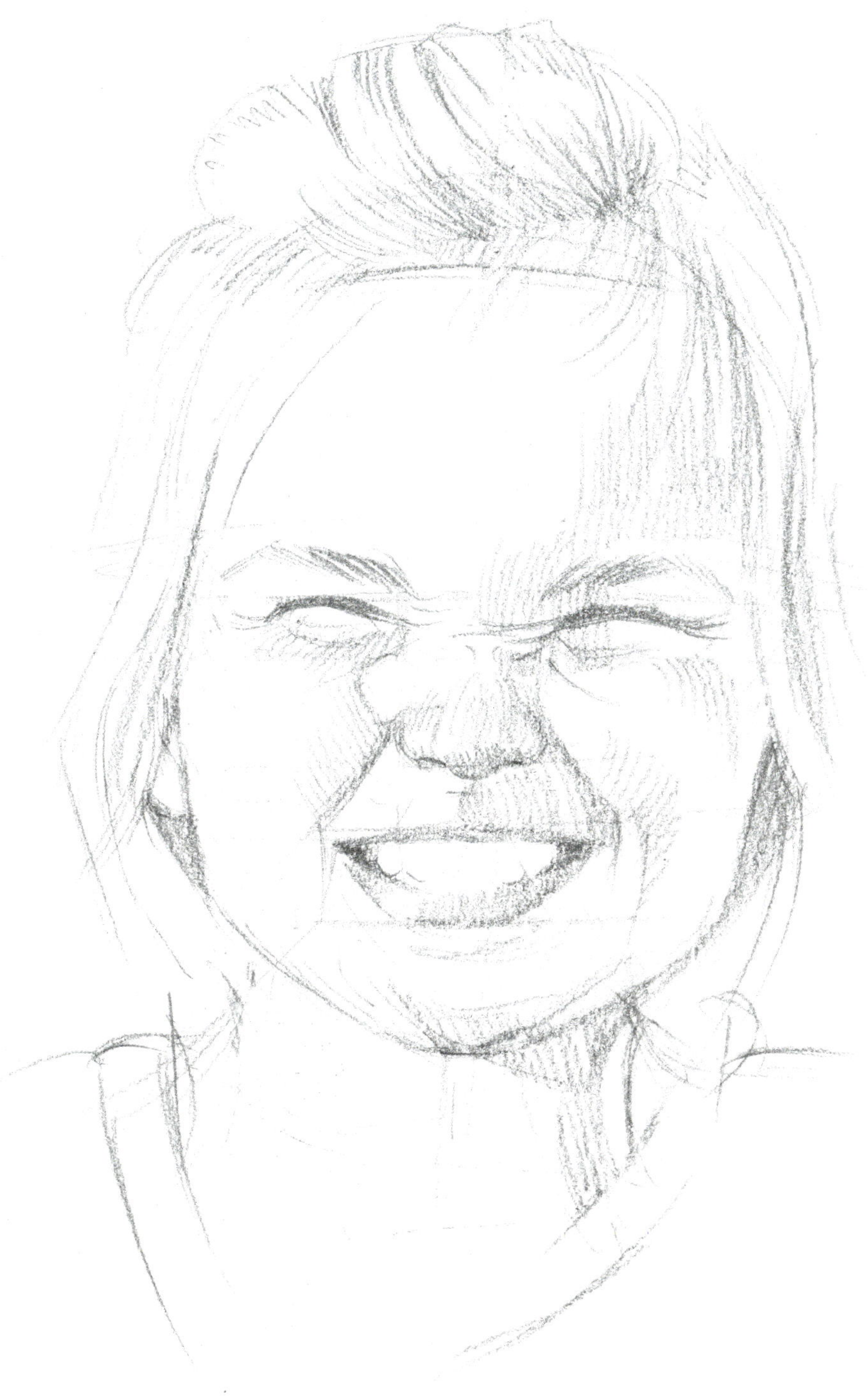

4

STEP 4

If you are inspired by a real person or using a photo reference, carefully study the person's expression as you refine and add detail to the facial features. Observe which muscles are active, which areas are moving and how, and which parts of the face are changing. In this portrait, notice how the eyes are barely visible in this expression, as the face scrunches in joy.

Other details that complement the facial expression, such as the jawline or the shape of the cheeks, should also be taken into account.

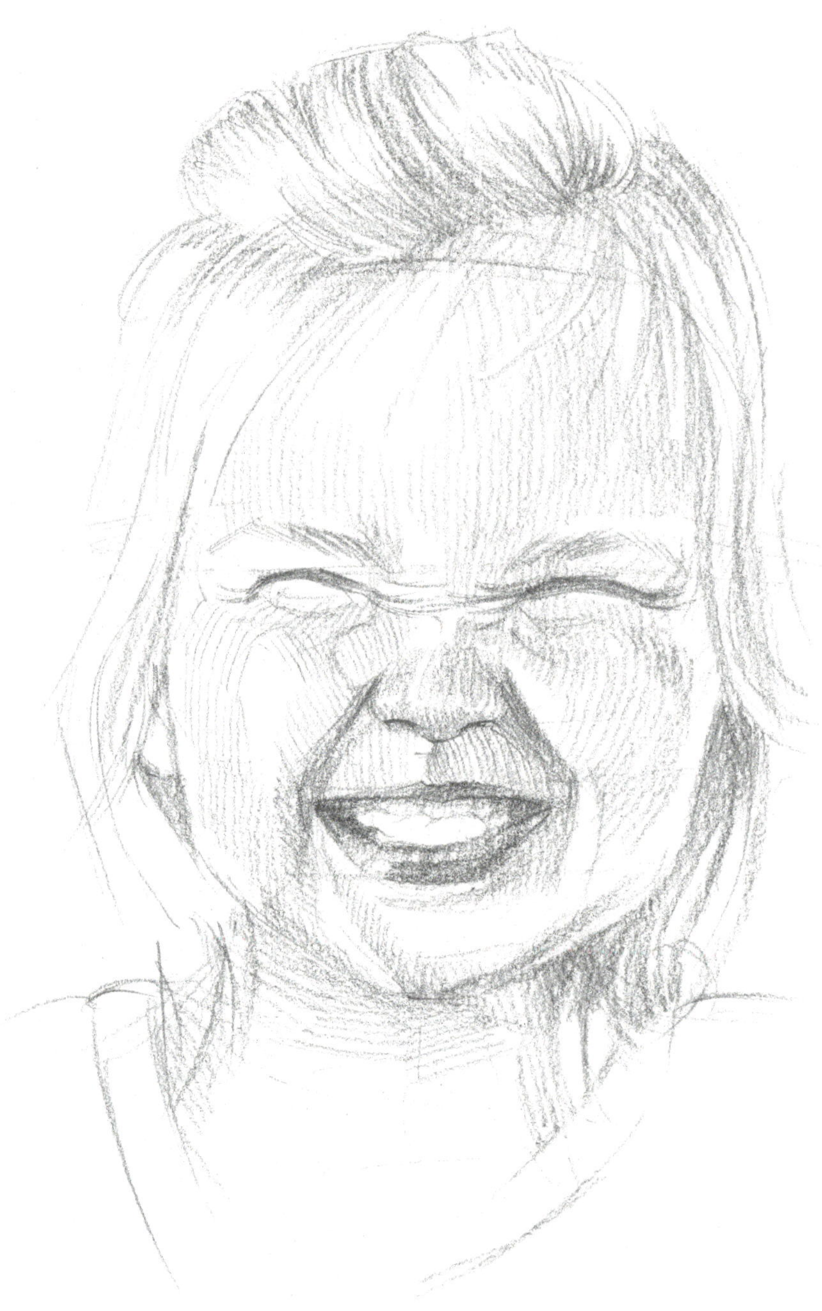

5

STEP 5

Determine the light source and identify shadowy and bright areas on the face. Create a sense of depth and volume in the face by carefully defining the shadows and creating smooth transitions. Pay close attention to the deeply shadowed areas created by this laughing expression, such as the lines around the mouth and eyes. Determine your skin tones and work in different shades and lines to reflect the natural texture and patterns in the skin. Hatch with lines in the right direction, following the shapes of the facial features. Intensify the shadowy parts with your lines. Begin to add detail and shading to the shirt, and add more detail in the hair.

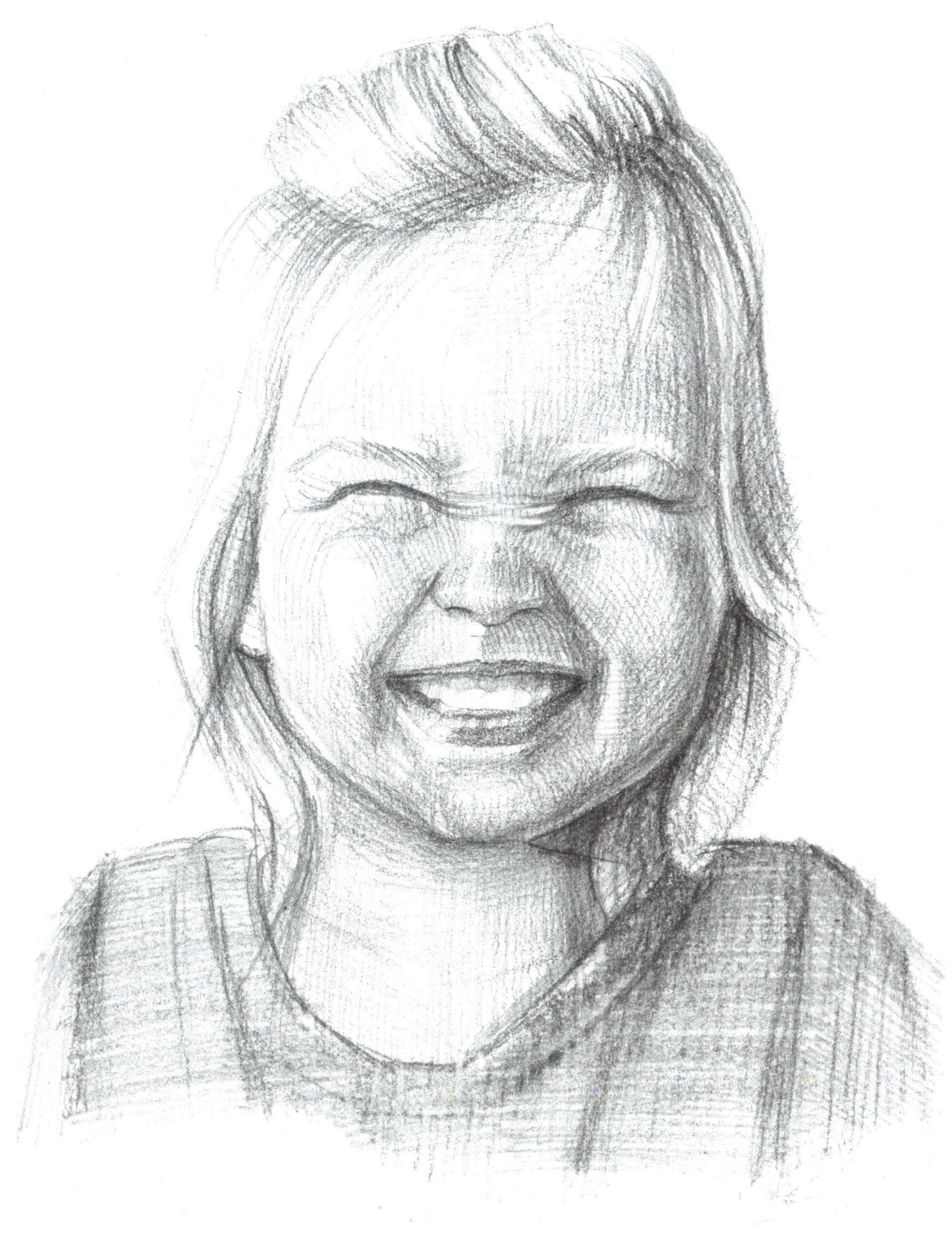

STEP 6

Deepen the shadows in the hair and face even more
as you finalize your portrait. Pass through the drawing
to add small details to the skin to make your drawing
more realistic, but remember not to overdo the details.
Keep it simple to maintain the childish features.

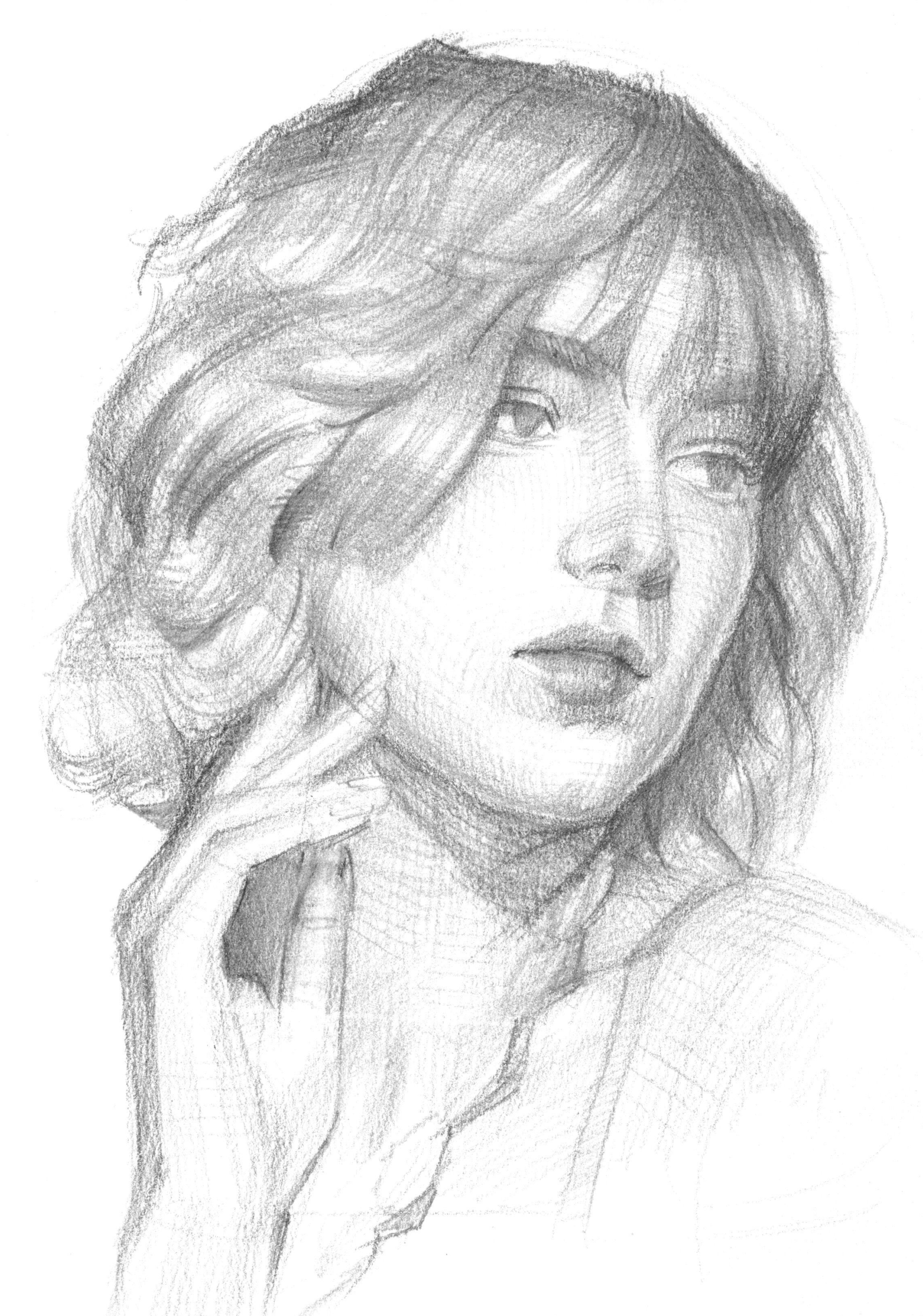

INCLUDING HANDS IN PORTRAITURE

Including a hand, or both hands, in a portrait brings a new level of interest and can convey more emotion. Hands may seem complex at first, but when you apply the same principles as for drawing the face and work step by step, you may find them easier to draw than you think.

Baselines are simple, usually linear lines drawn to determine the general shape of an object or a figure. Basic lines form the building blocks of a drawing or painting and help you determine the overall composition before you start adding more complex details. When it comes to adding hands into your portrait drawing, treat them the same way you do the rest of the face and look for the shapes that make up the hand.

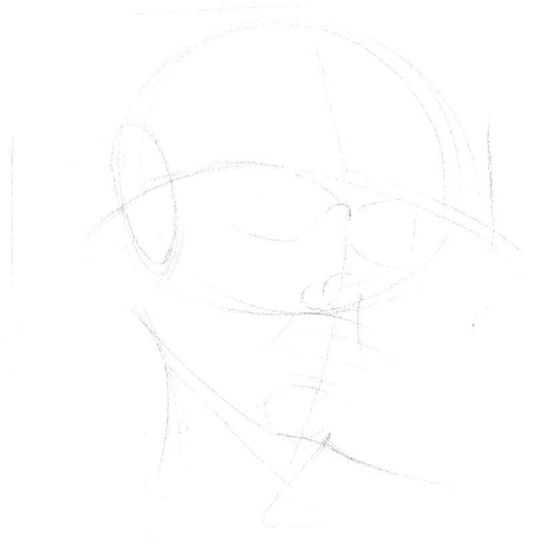

1

STEP 1

Use a sharp pen or pencil that is easily erasable to draw the basic lines. Determine the general shape of the face and start with simple geometric shapes and lines. In this case you can use an oval to represent the face. Draw a curved vertical line along the oval in the direction the model is facing, and divide the oval horizontally to mark the top of the eyes.

Mark the location of the eyes. The top or midpoint of the face is usually used to determine the starting point of the eyes. Next, determine the lower part of the eyes and the distance between them.

Below the eyes, mark the location of the nose and mouth. The nose is usually at the lower level of the eyes and the starting point of the nose usually extends to the inner edges of the eyes.

STEP 2

Study the position of the hand and sketch it in with simple lines, not worrying about any detail at this point. Continue to develop the shape of the mouth, and make simple lines to mark where the hair falls over the face.

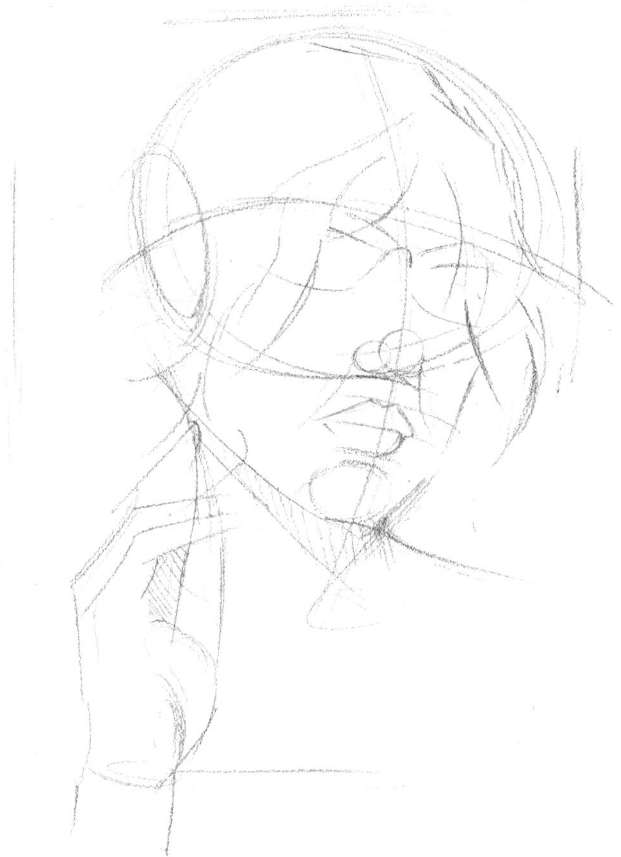

STEP 3

Add eye details, including the pupils, irises, and eyelids. Create the shape of the hair and hatch the shaded parts with thin lines. Add light hatching in the darkest shadows in the face as well, to mark the darkest values.

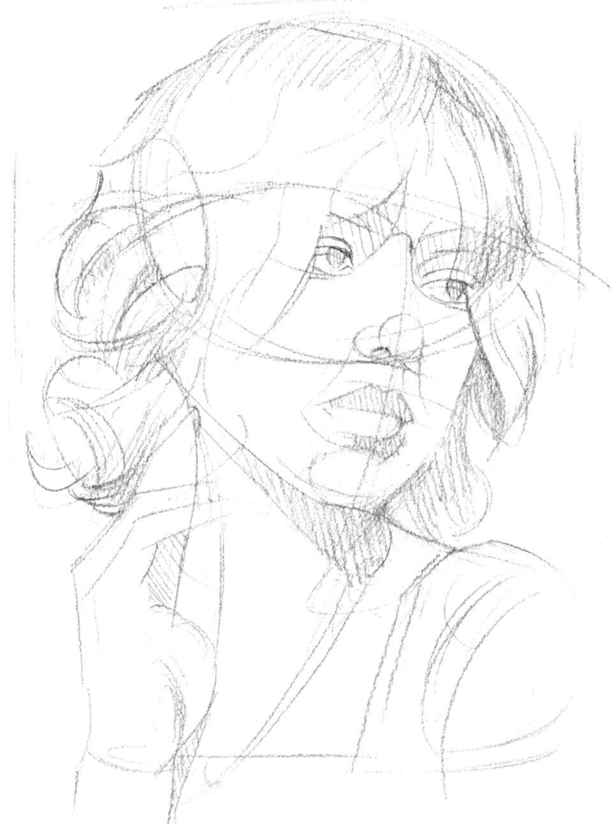

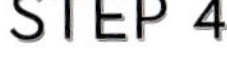

STEP 4

Erase your guidelines as you feel confident in the placement of the features and begin to add detail. To draw the nose, clearly outline the bridge of the nose, the nostrils, and the wings. Shade the lower part of the nose wings.

Draw the upper and lower curves of the lips, then mark the location of the teeth and tongue. Shade the upper part of the lip so that it is in shadow.

Determine the starting point, the high point, and the end point of the eyebrows, and draw them over the eyes.

Add more hatching in the area of dark shadow on the neck, and continue to add dark strokes in the hair to refine its shape.

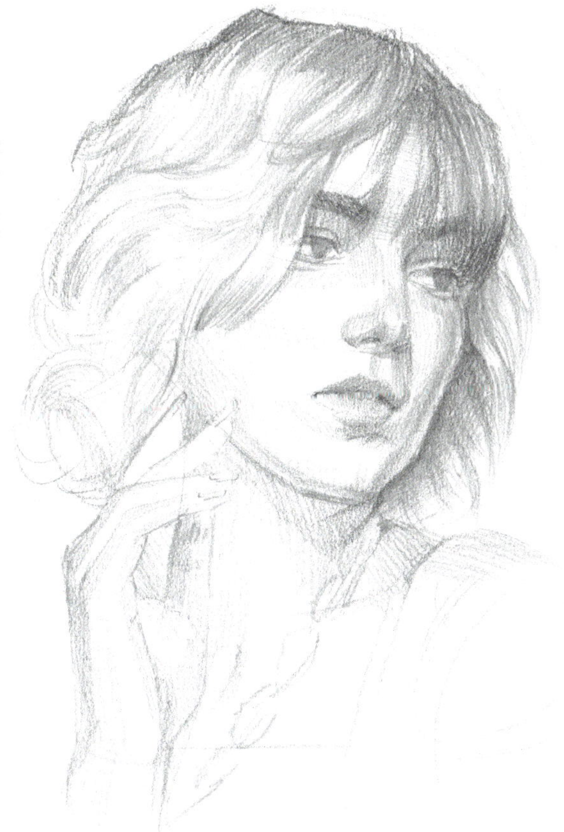

STEP 5

Use shadows to emphasize facial features and add depth. Add shadows under the eyes, on the sides of the nostrils, under the lips, and in other areas of the face.

When drawing the hair, move your pencil in the direction and flow of the hair growth. Draw the mass of the hair with curved and angled lines.

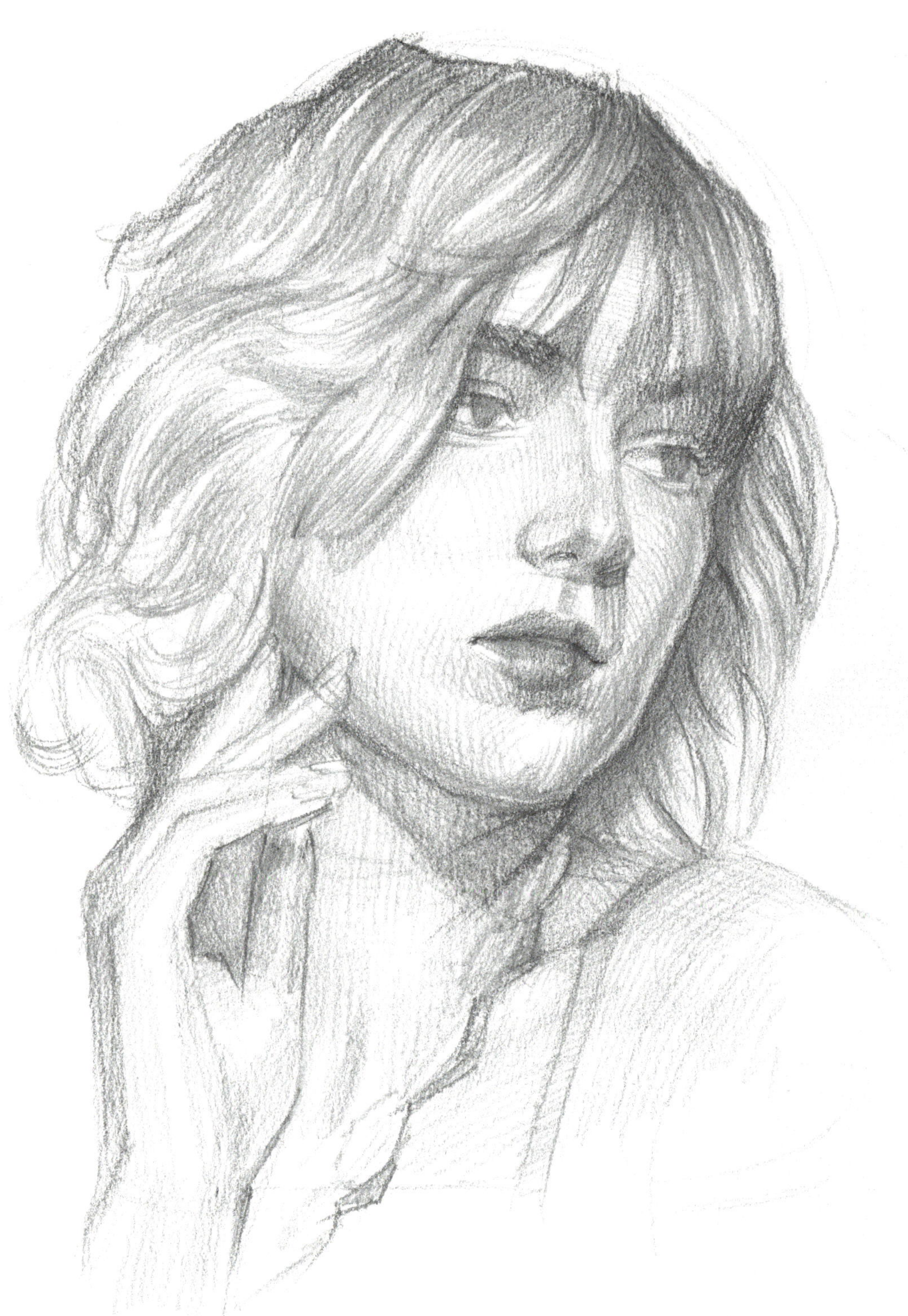

STEP 6

Since the light source reflects on the face from the
left, apply the darkest tones on the right side, including under the chin, where the face covers the hair,
and the shadow cast by the hand. Add detail in the
portrait with short, curved lines, thinking in the right
direction and in three dimensions.

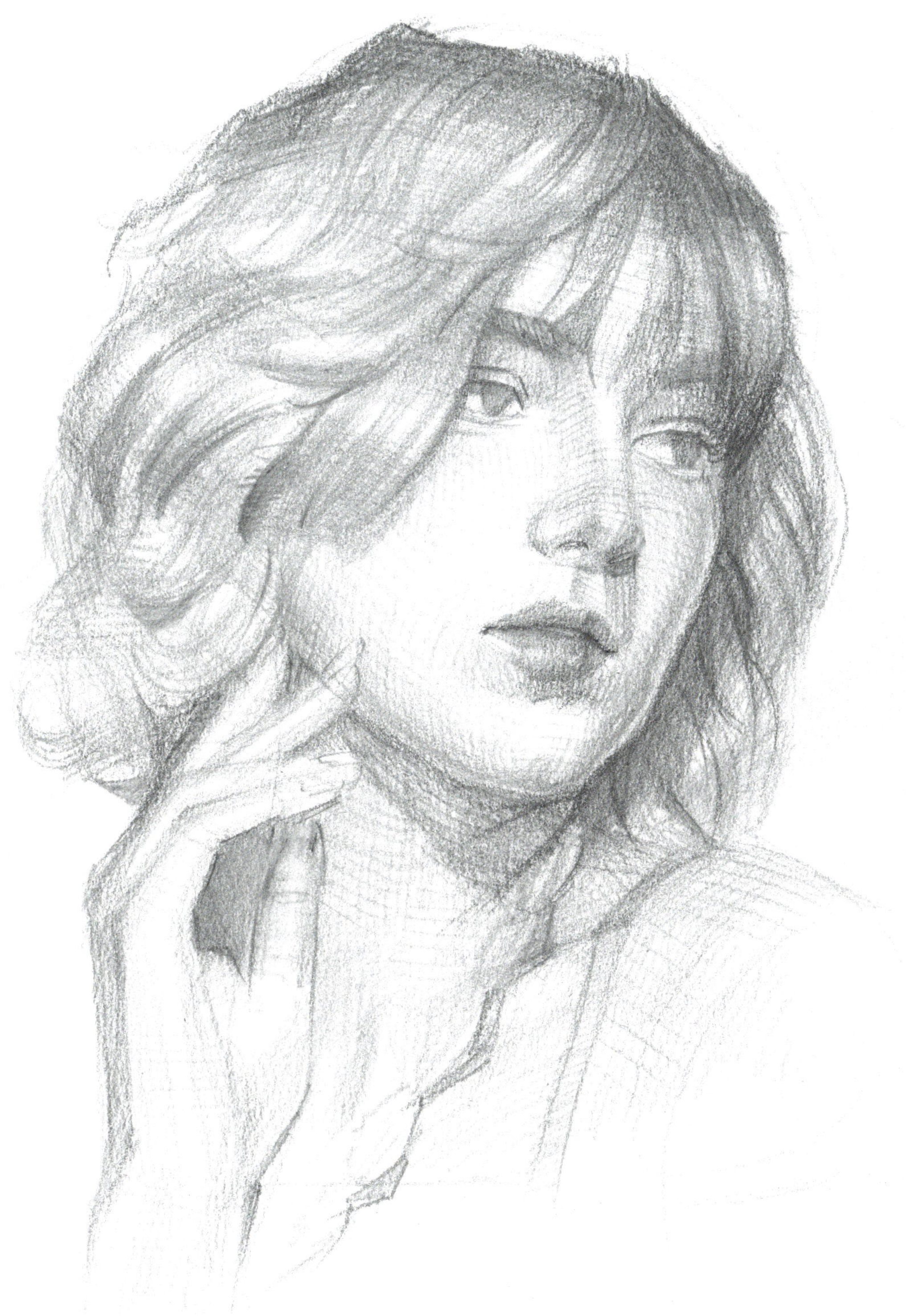

STEP 7

Examine each area of your drawing carefully and correct any details that are missing or need to be corrected. Especially check prominent areas, such as facial features, shadows, and lighting effects.

By adding more detail in some areas, you can make your drawing look more realistic and expressive. In particular, you can enhance your character by emphasizing small details on the face, such as wrinkles or veins.

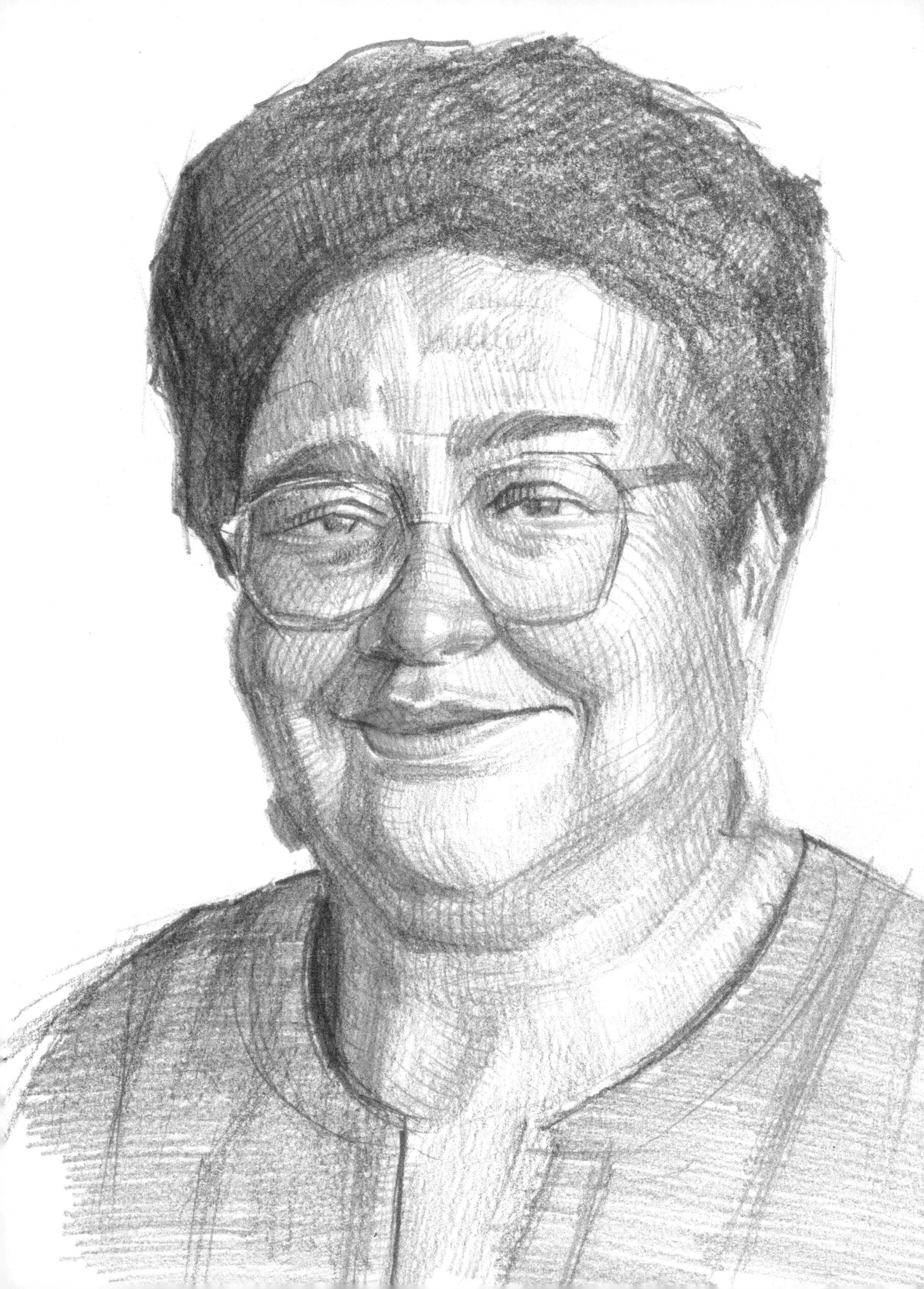

PROJECT 14

DRAWING GLASSES

When drawing glasses on a face, it's important to understand the anatomy and structure of both the glasses and the face. You still need to draw the face and its proportions accurately, so it's important to do this before adding the glasses. Begin your portrait like any other, without thinking about the glasses at all.

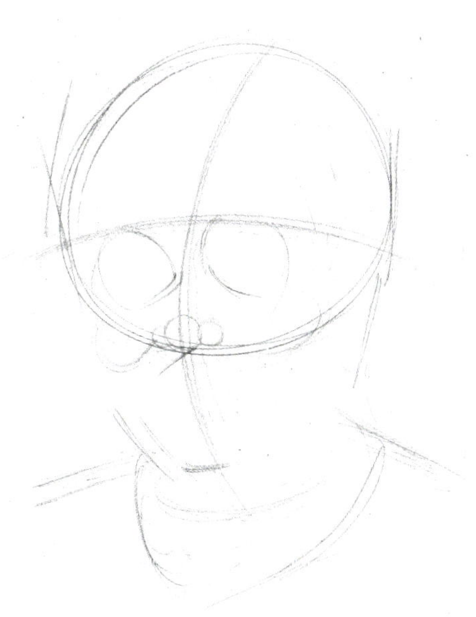

1

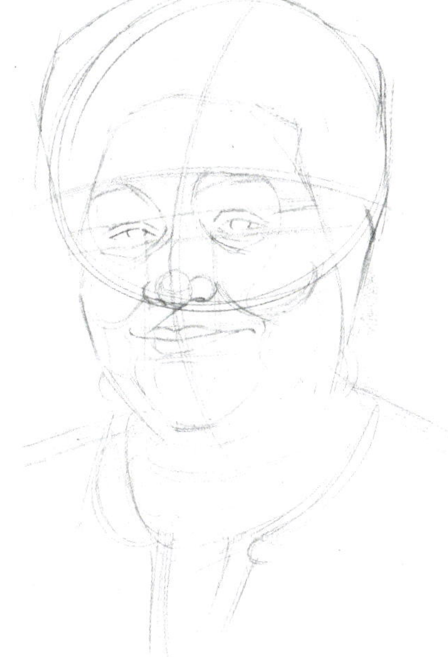

2

STEP 1

First, use large geometric shapes to establish the general outline of the portrait and to provide a starting point for capturing the overall form of the head and face. Add smaller geometric shapes to represent facial features, placing these shapes in the right proportions and positions.

STEP 2

Once you have established the basic outlines, make your portrait more realistic by filling the geometric shapes with details. Add iris and pupil details inside the eyes, emphasize the details of the nose, and draw the outline of the lips for the mouth. As you work, strive to maintain the correct proportions and positions with the help of your initial geometric shapes. Add simple lines to mark the shirt as well.

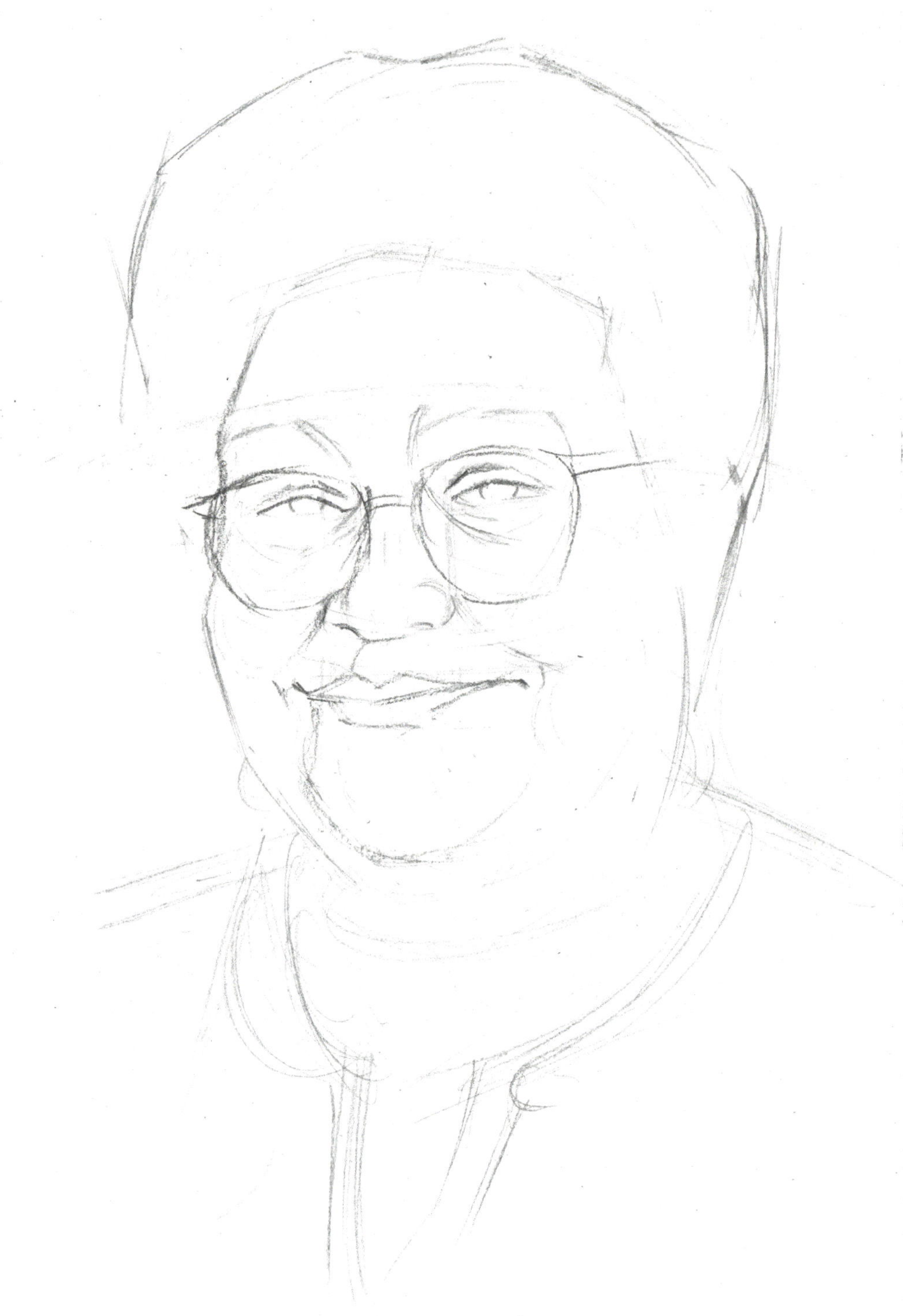

STEP 3

Once you're happy with the placement of the facial features erase your initial guidelines. Add the outline of the glasses and begin to refine the details of the features.

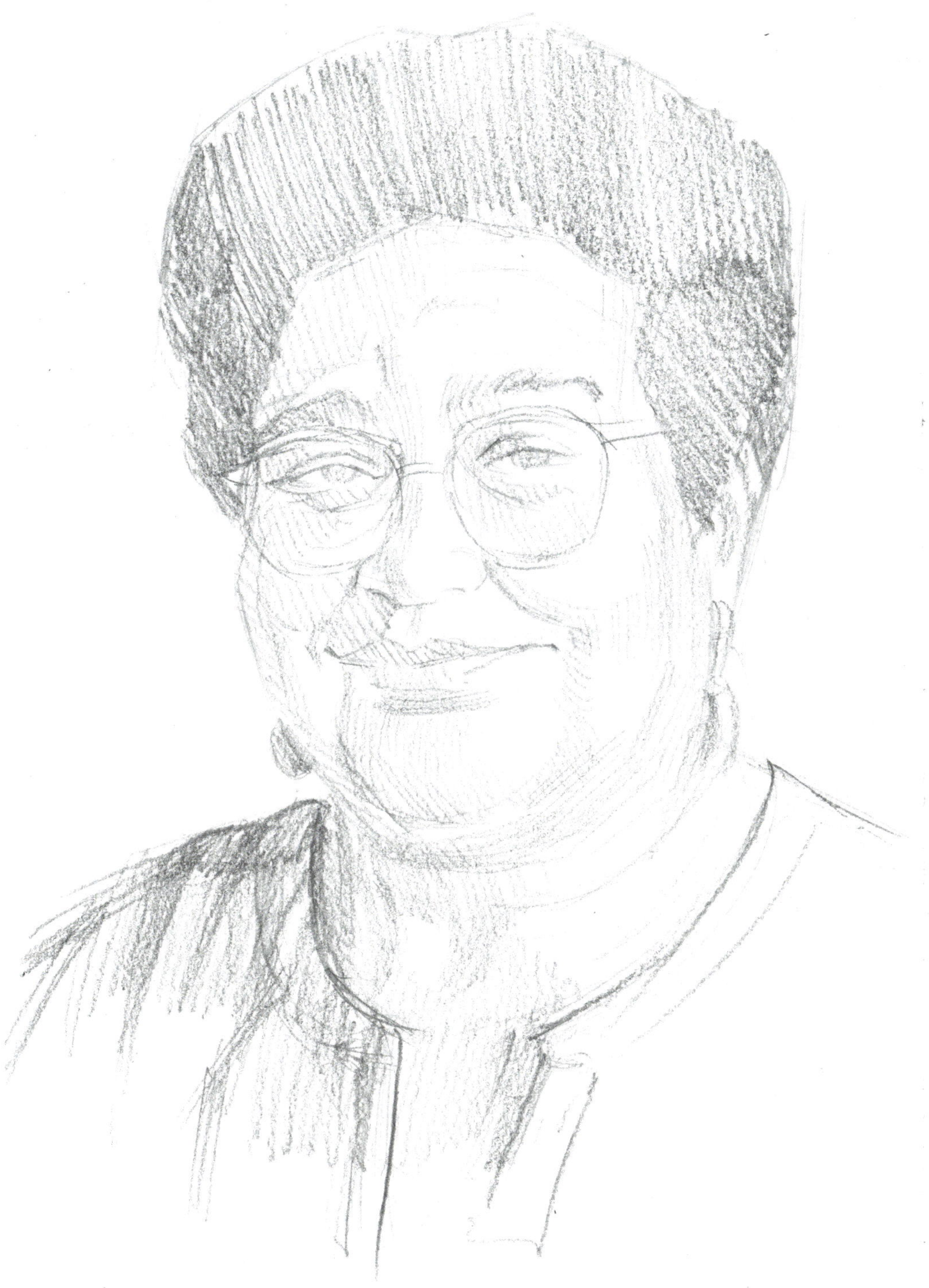

STEP 4

Shade your portrait to give it depth and make it look more realistic. Use geometric shapes to define shadows and light. In this portrait, the light source is shining on the face from the right. The hair is darker in tone than the face. Pay close attention to the tonal values, or you will end up with a portrait that is gray with the same shades throughout. Increase the volume of your portrait by adding shadows under the eyes, on the sides of the nose, and under the lips. Also, add fine lines and textures to enhance details.

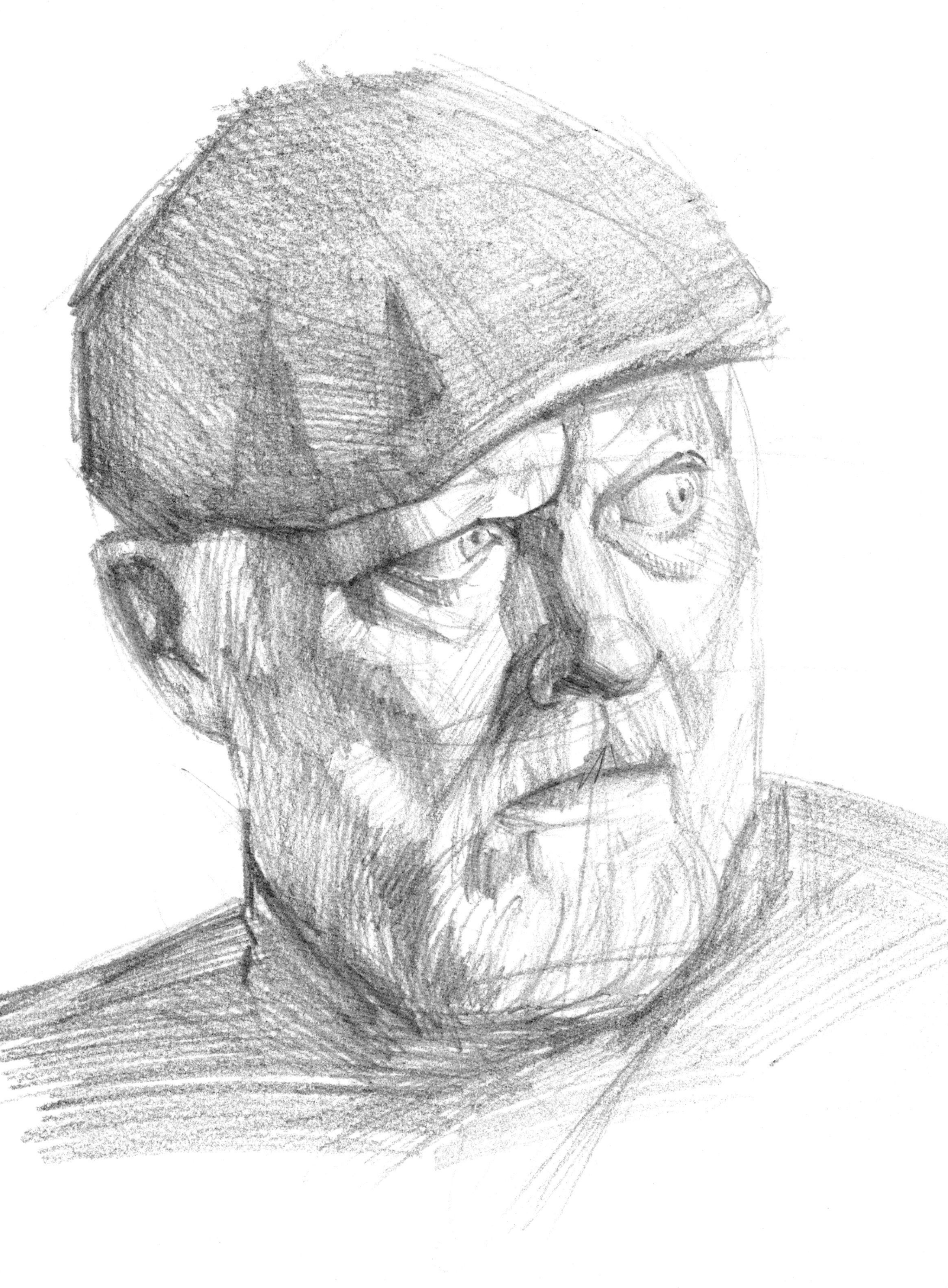

ELDERLY MAN IN A HAT

Older people have distinctive facial features. It is important to include these features in your drawing. For example, wrinkles, sagging skin, age spots and other signs of aging will add character to your drawing.

Other signs of aging can include details such as drooping ears, a prominent jawline and tooth loss. Express these characteristics in the drawing in the correct proportions and appropriate shapes to create a successful elderly portrait.

STEP 1

Initially, define the general outline of the elderly portrait. Draw lightly with a pencil to determine the contour of the head and the general shape of the face, using basic shapes to mark the eyes, nose, mouth, and ear.

1

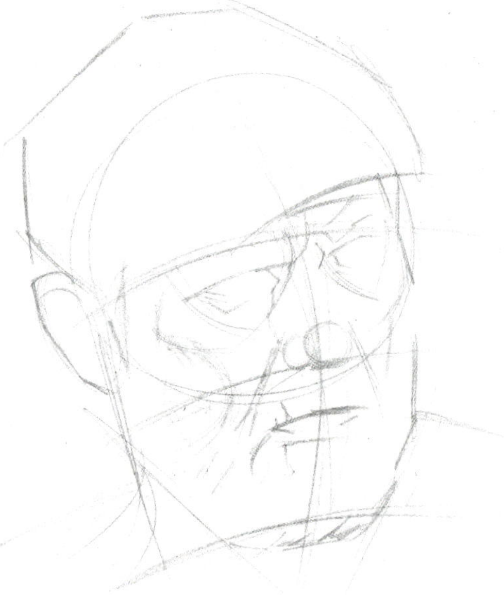

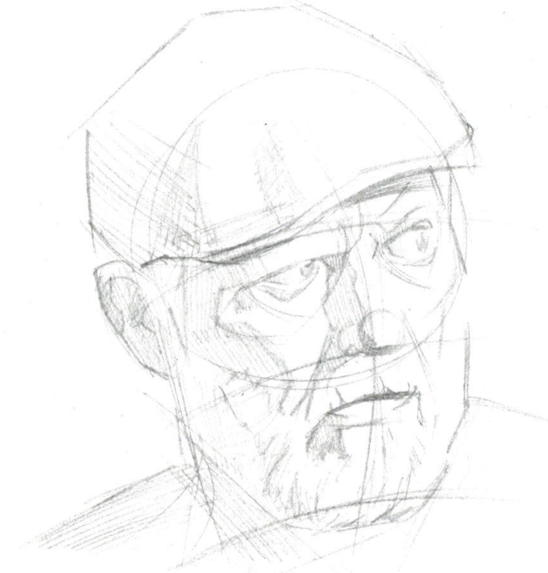

2

3

STEP 2

Refine the shapes of the facial features a bit more, and block in the shape of the hat. Add a few simple lines to locate the darkest shadows to the left of the eye and nose.

STEP 3

Begin to hatch in some of the shading, beginning with light lines. One of the most obvious signs of aging is wrinkles. There may be wrinkles around the eyes, on the forehead, around the nose, and around the mouth. Use these wrinkles in the drawing to give the impression of old age. You can achieve a realistic look by adding wrinkles in smooth and thin lines.

STEP 4

Add detail in and around the eyes. The eyes can change significantly with age. Eyelids may sag, bags may form under the eyes, and wrinkles around the eyes may become more pronounced. Express these changes in your drawing with shadows and lines around the eyes. Make the bags and wrinkles under the eyes prominent.

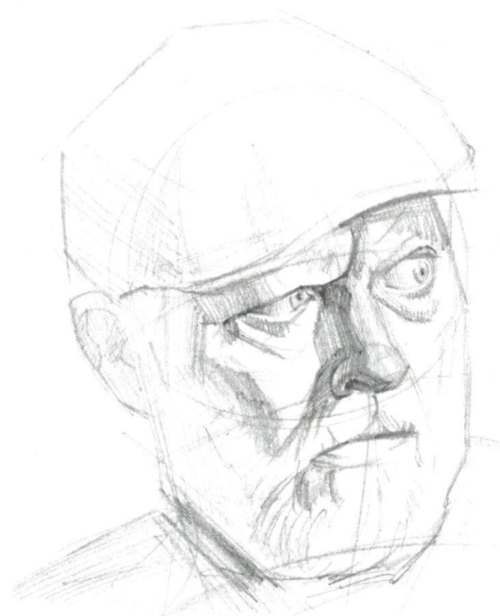

4

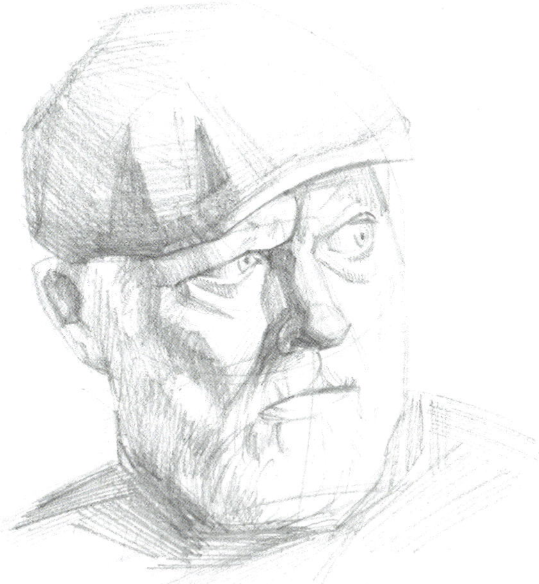

5

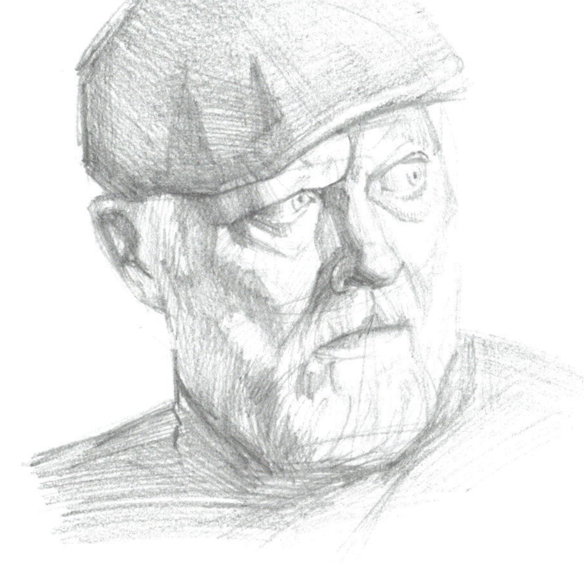

6

STEP 5

The skin of an older person is usually more saggy and wrinkled. The skin may have prominent veins, blemishes, and age spots. Emphasize the effects of aging by adding these details on the skin. You can express the skin texture with light lines or dots in the drawing. A person's hair and beard often turn gray or white as they age. Express the color of the hair and beard in this way to reinforce the effect of old age.

Use hatching and crosshatching to add shadow and texture to the hat.

STEP 6

An older person's skin is often more saggy, especially in the cheek and neck areas. Make this sagging effect evident in the drawing by using light shadows under the facial features, on the jawline, and on the neck.

TIP: Symmetry is important when drawing a portrait. Regularly check whether both sides of the face are symmetrical. For example, after determining the position of one eye, make sure that the other eye is aligned and the same size.

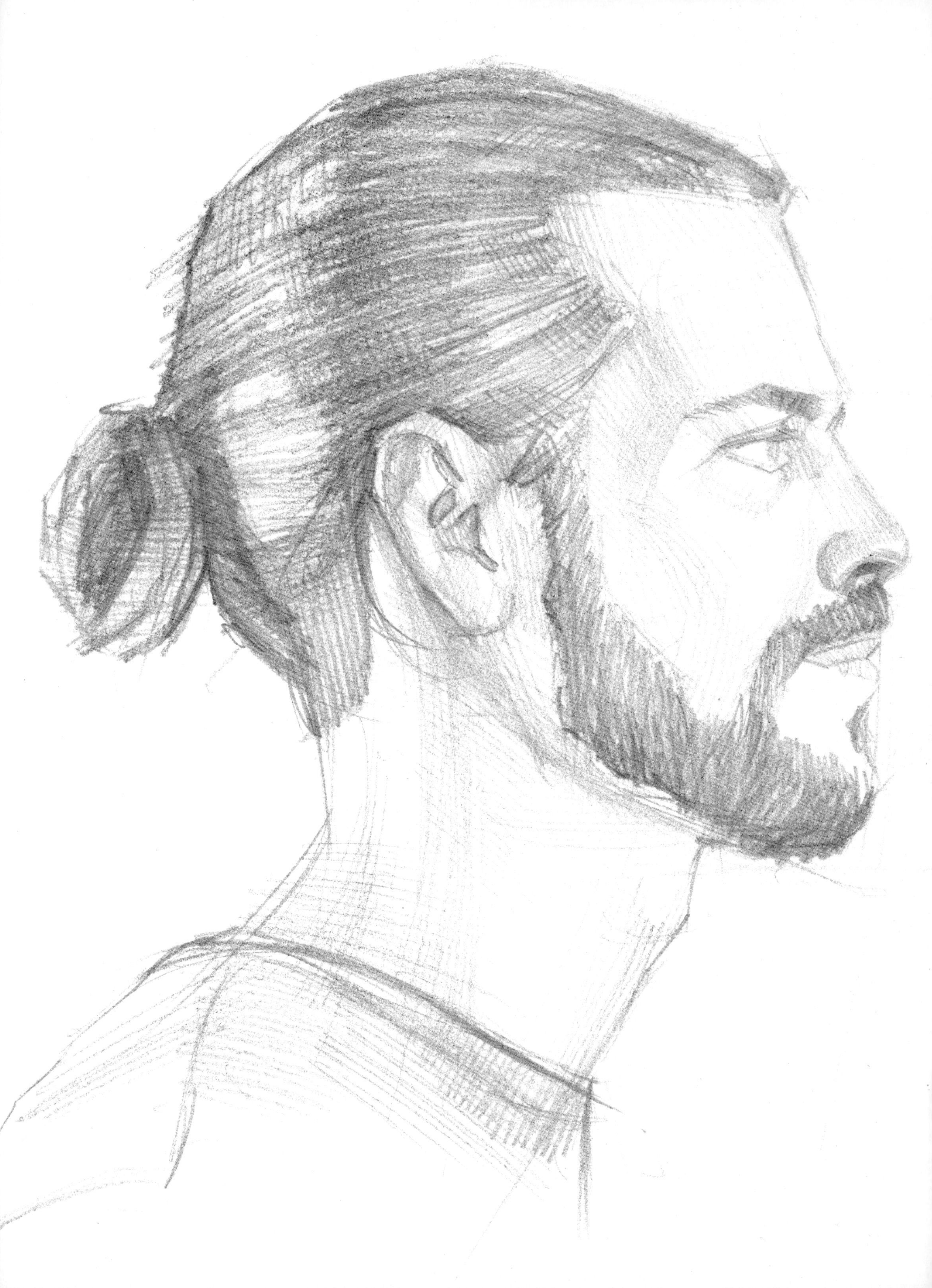

MAN IN PROFILE

Drawing a portrait in side profile requires accurately capturing the character's facial features and profile. All the facial features are different from that angle—you can only see one eye, the nose has a strong line, and only half of the mouth is visible—but the approach is the same. You'll still begin with simple shapes and lines, dividing the head into thirds to find the placement of the features.

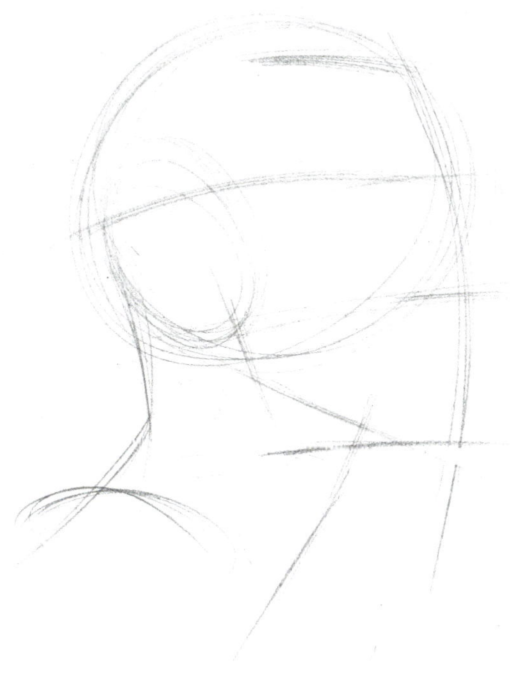

1

STEP 1

First, determine the overall length of the head on your paper. This will help you determine how large your drawing will be and where to place other features of the face.

Determine the proportions by dividing the overall length of the head into three sections. Consider specific proportions, such as the distance from the top of the eyes to the beginning of the eyebrows, the distance from the beginning of the eyebrows to the beginning of the nose, and the distance from the beginning of the nose to the bottom of the chin.

Start lightly drawing the side profile of the head. Determine the starting point and then outline the back of the head, the forehead, the bridge of the nose, the lower part of the chin and the neckline.

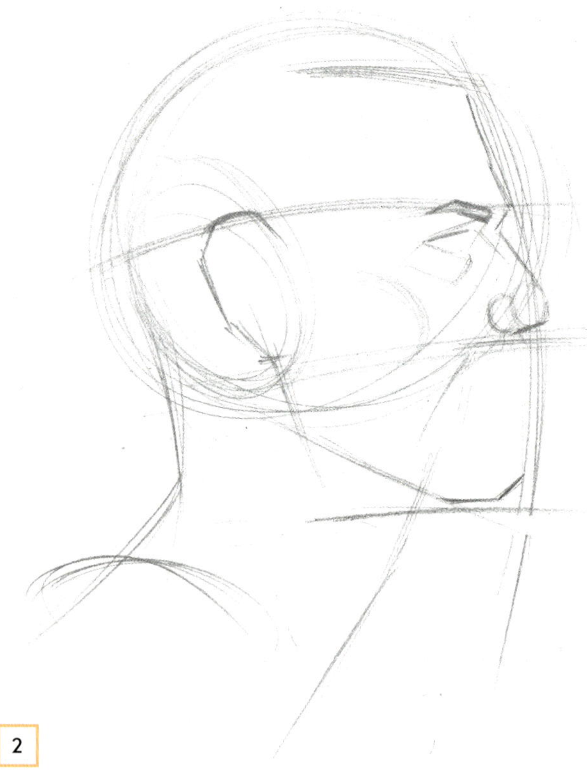

2

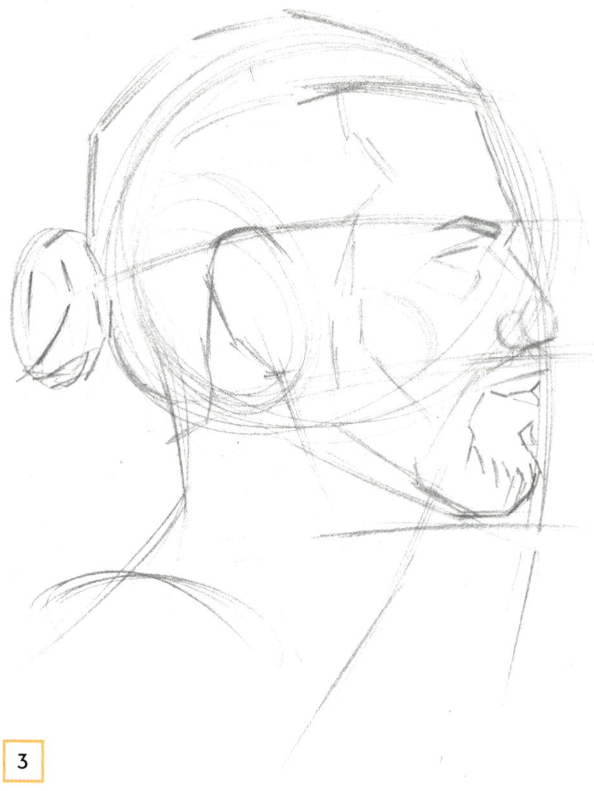

3

STEP 2

Locate the eyes. The eyes are usually placed in the center of the face.

Define the contours of the nose and mouth and place them in the correct proportions. The nose and mouth usually start below the eyes and extend toward the chin.

Define the jawline and draw the lower part of the chin in the correct proportions. Next, mark the position of the ear and draw it in. The ears usually start at the top of the eyes and extend to the bottom of the nose.

STEP 3

Continue to refine the shapes of the facial features. As you work, you can accurately determine the proportions by designating certain points on the face as control points. For example, use the distances from the inner edges of the eyes to the beginning of the nose, from the beginning of the nose to the beginning of the mouth, and from the beginning of the mouth to the bottom of the chin as control points.

TIP: Some artists use pencil marks to determine the main proportions of the face before starting a portrait drawing. For example, you can more accurately determine the proportions and placement of the eye by marking the start and end points of the eyes with a pencil.

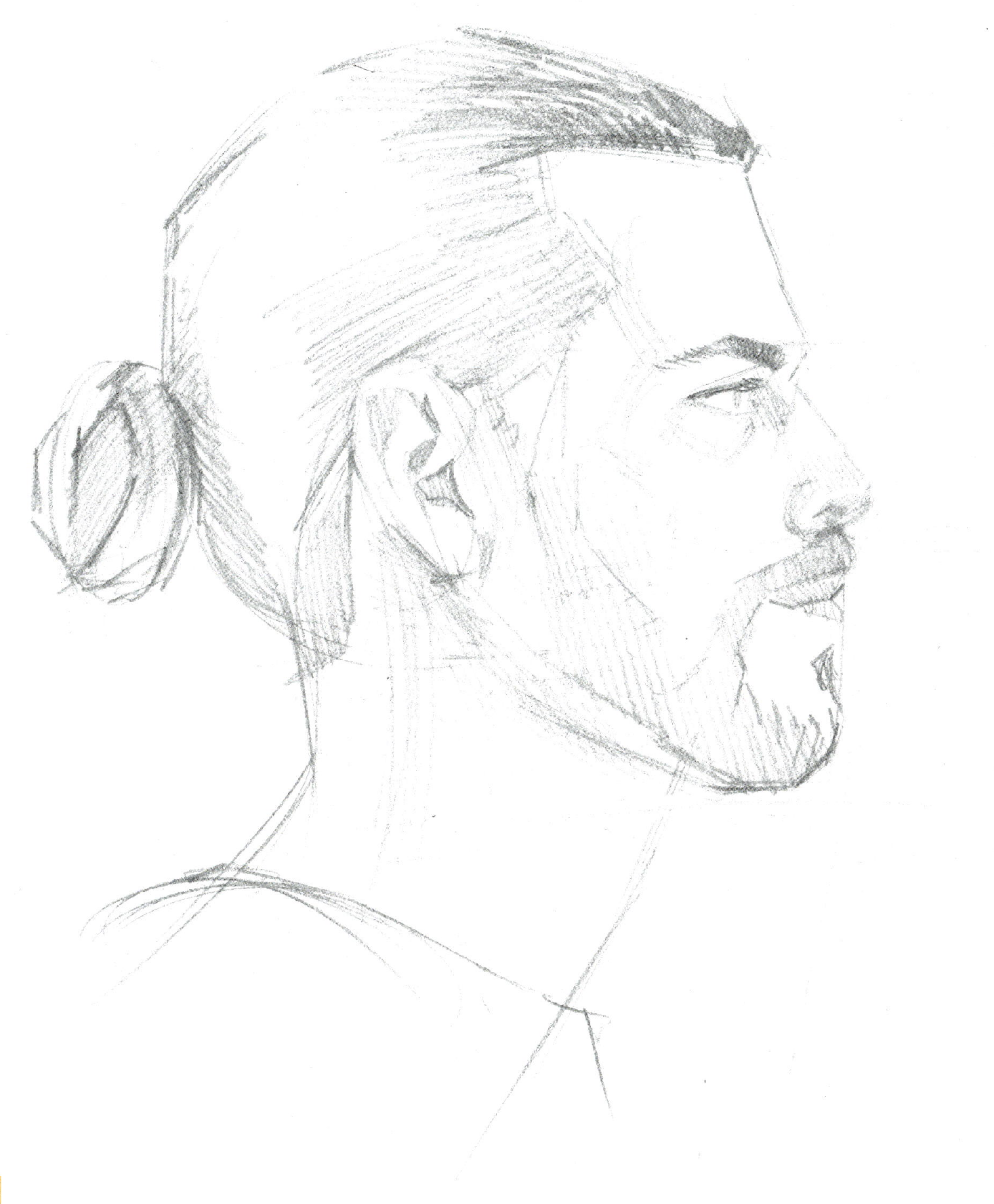

STEP 4

If you are sure you have drawn the proportions correctly, you can get rid of the extra lines. Erase the guidelines to reveal the general outline of the portrait.

I often start by adding shadows to the hair, eyebrows, and beard. Unless you are drawing light shades of hair, it usually is darker in tone than the face. Pay attention to the tonal values in the portrait so there is differentiation.

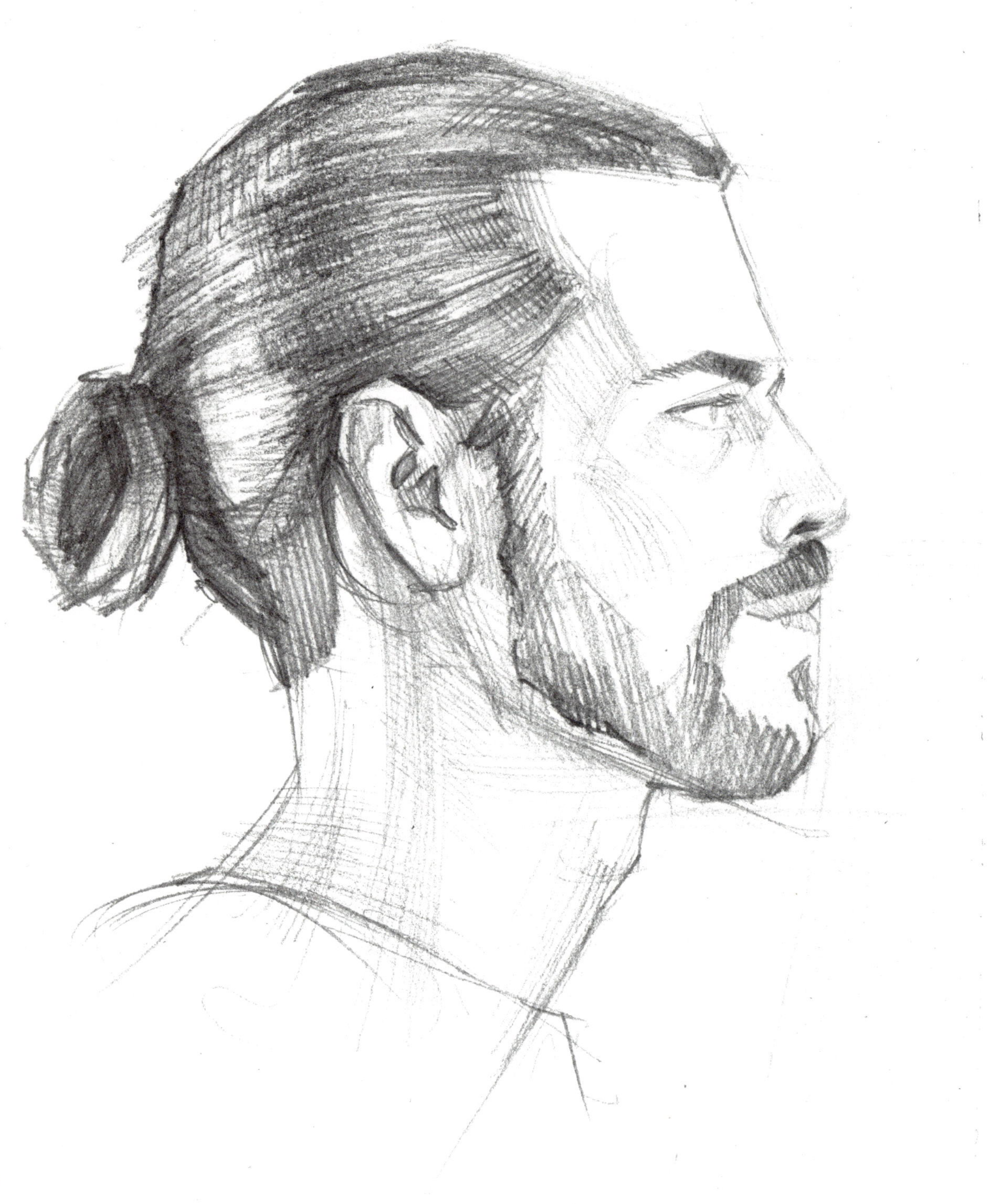

STEP 5

In this portrait, the hair and beard have darker tones than the face. Pay attention to the values as you add hatching and crosshatching to develop shading in the face to ensure the darkest values are in the hair and beard.

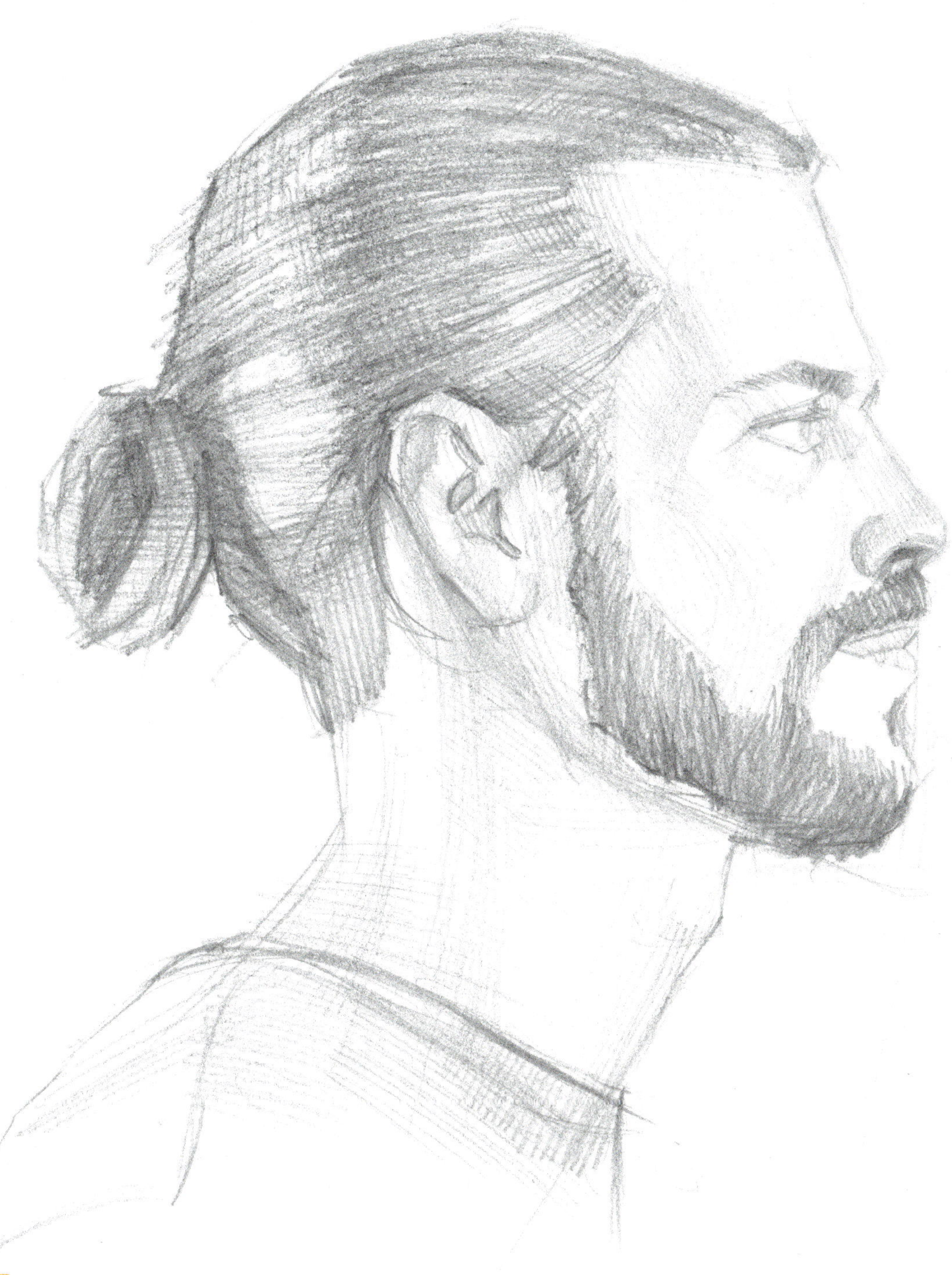

STEP 6

When adding shadows, observe the movement of the hair and beard. Make strokes in that direction. The same goes for the face. Don't think of a reference portrait as a photo print—imagine the person is in front of you. The areas of the face that receive light are usually the parts in front, while the dark parts are the places with depth, such as under the lips, chin, nose, and eyes, and inside the ears.

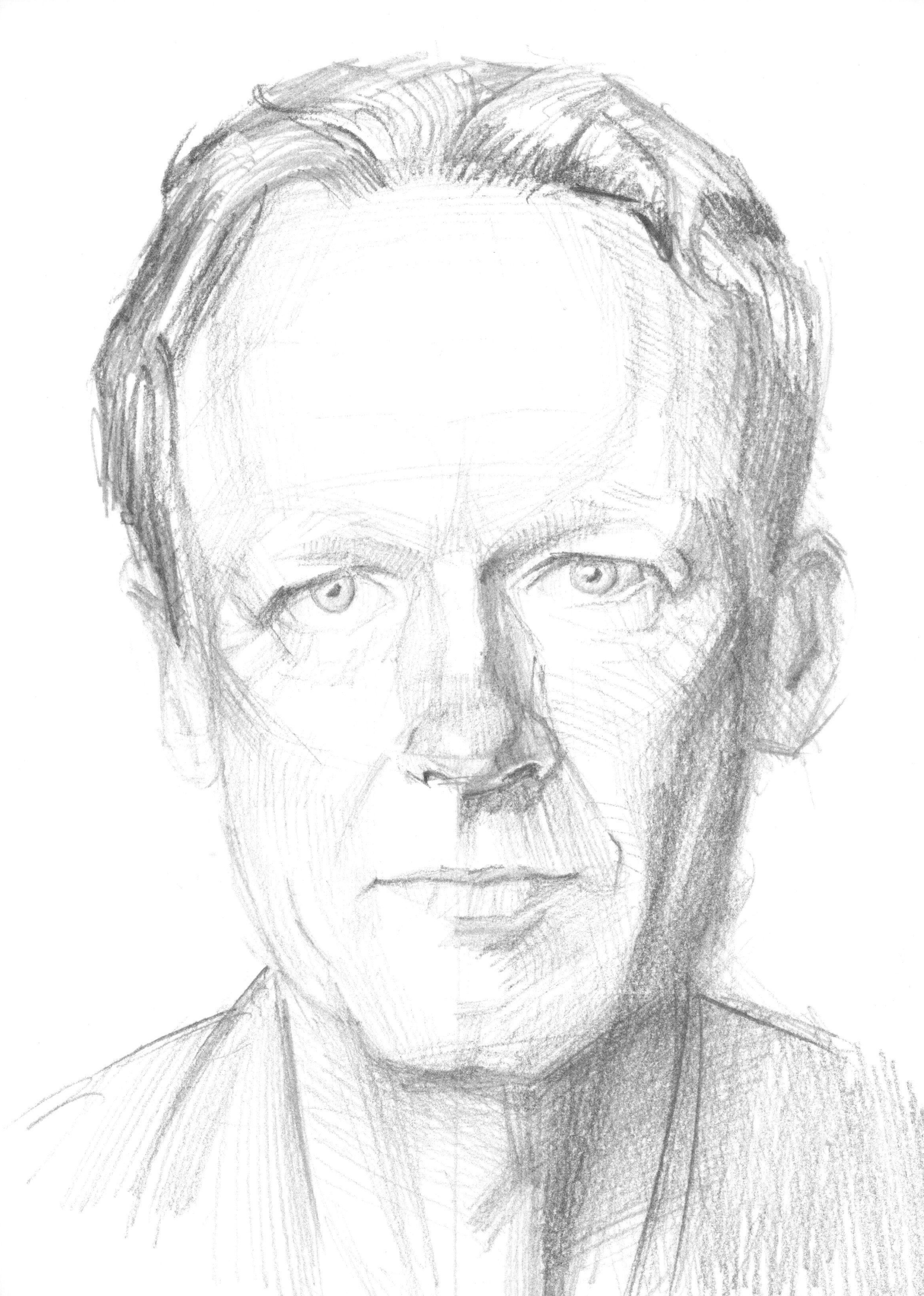

MIDDLE-AGED FEATURES

The face and its features gradually change over time as a person ages. The face of a middle-aged person won't typically be as heavily wrinkled or sagging as an elderly person, but it may appear softer and fleshier. Some sagging in the cheeks may occur, especially around the jawline, and there may be more creases and wrinkles around the eyes and mouth.

Pay close attention to the hair as well. Hair on a middle-aged person may start to change in color as the hair begins to gray or turn white, and the hairline may be receding, revealing a higher forehead.

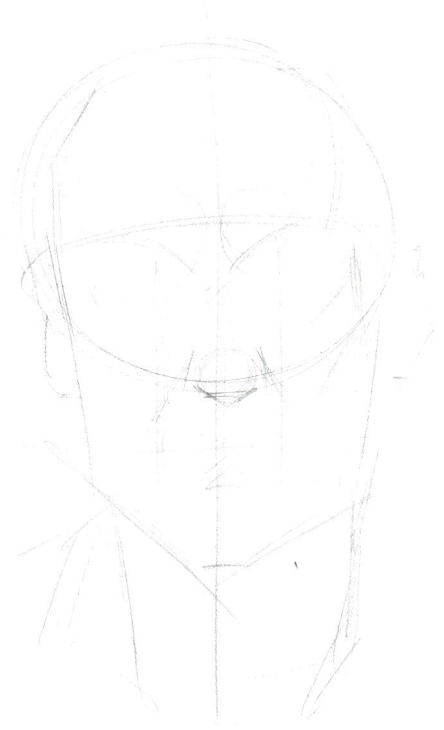

STEP 1

Start by sketching the shape of the face with basic shapes and lines. Draw a circle for the face, and add a vertical line to divide it in half. Use horizontal lines to mark where the eyes, nose, and mouth will be placed to help you determine the symmetry and proportions of the face. You can also use horizontal lines to mark specific points, such as the beginning of the eyebrows, the top of the nose, and the bottom of the mouth.

You can use vertical lines to evenly divide the two sides of the face or mark specific points, such as the inner edges of the eyebrows, the two sides of the nose, and the outer edges of the mouth.

STEP 2

To correctly determine the proportions of the face, identify the starting points of the eyes, nose, and mouth. The eyes fall halfway around the circle you drew, the nose is under the eyes, and the mouth is between the nose and the chin. By identifying these points, you can accurately adjust the proportions of the face.

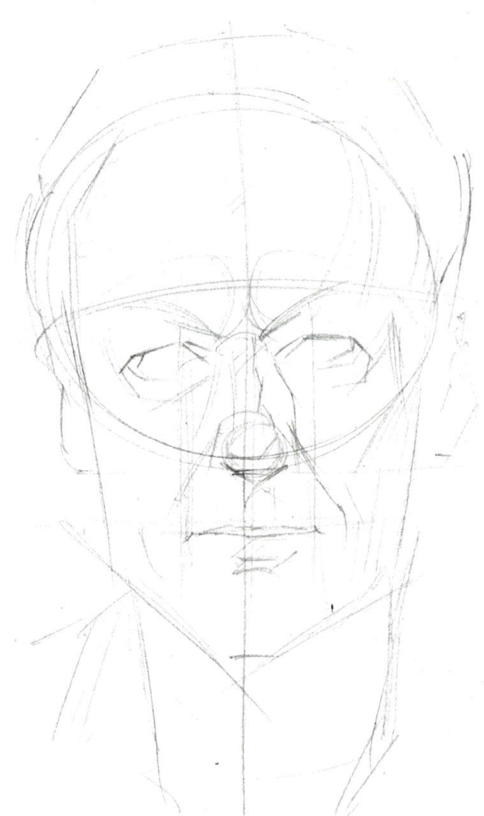

STEP 3

When shading, it is important to first identify the light source to determine the direction from which light falls on the objects in your drawing. This will determine how shadows and highlights are created.

In this portrait, the right side should be shaded with darker tones, because the left side is flooded with light. You do not need to think in detail at this stage. Just go over the right lines and identify the areas to shade.

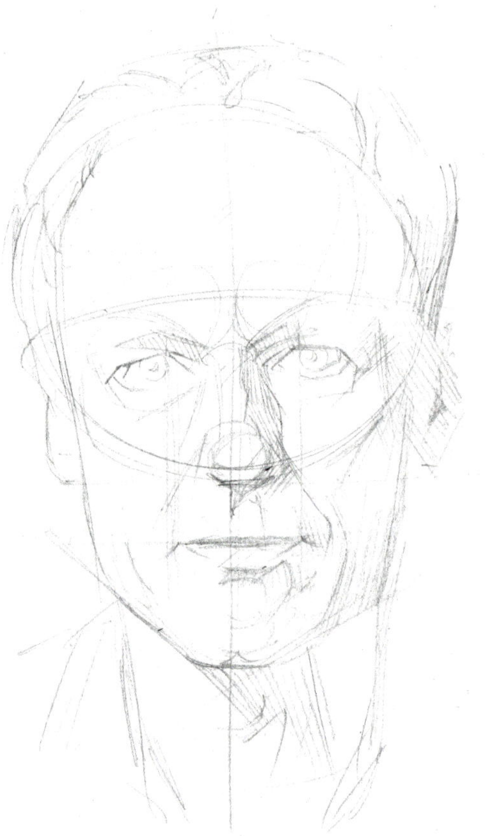

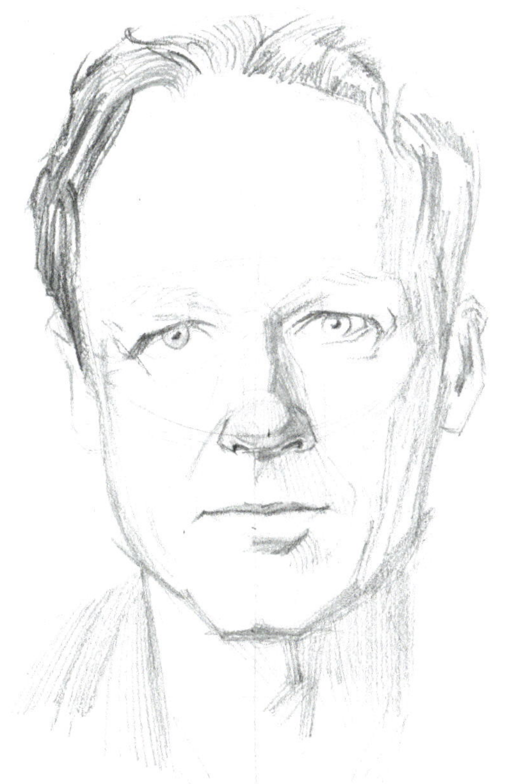

STEP 4

Determine the volume of the hair and sketch in tone. Use the white of the paper in the light areas to create the highlights.

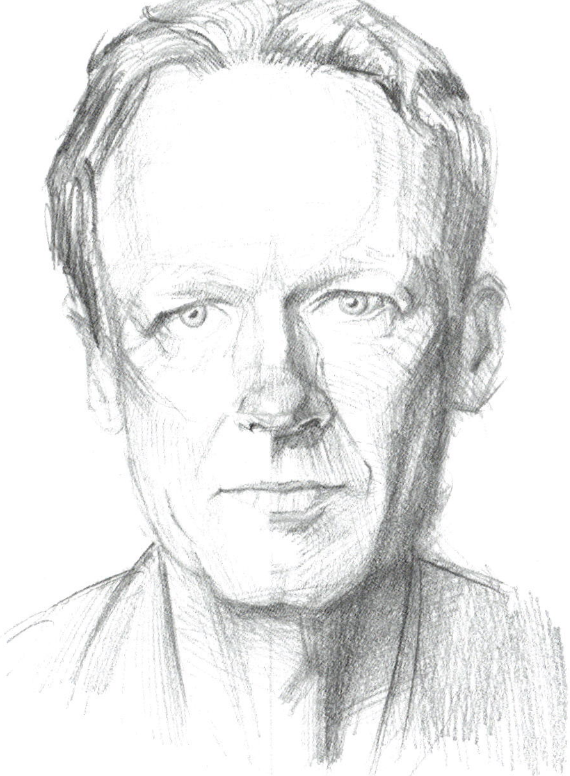

STEP 5

Cheekbones are more prominent in older people. To show this, use diagonal lines to shade these areas, and add details such as eye wrinkles.

Continue shading the portrait to create a range of tonal values that suggest the three-dimensional shapes of the face.

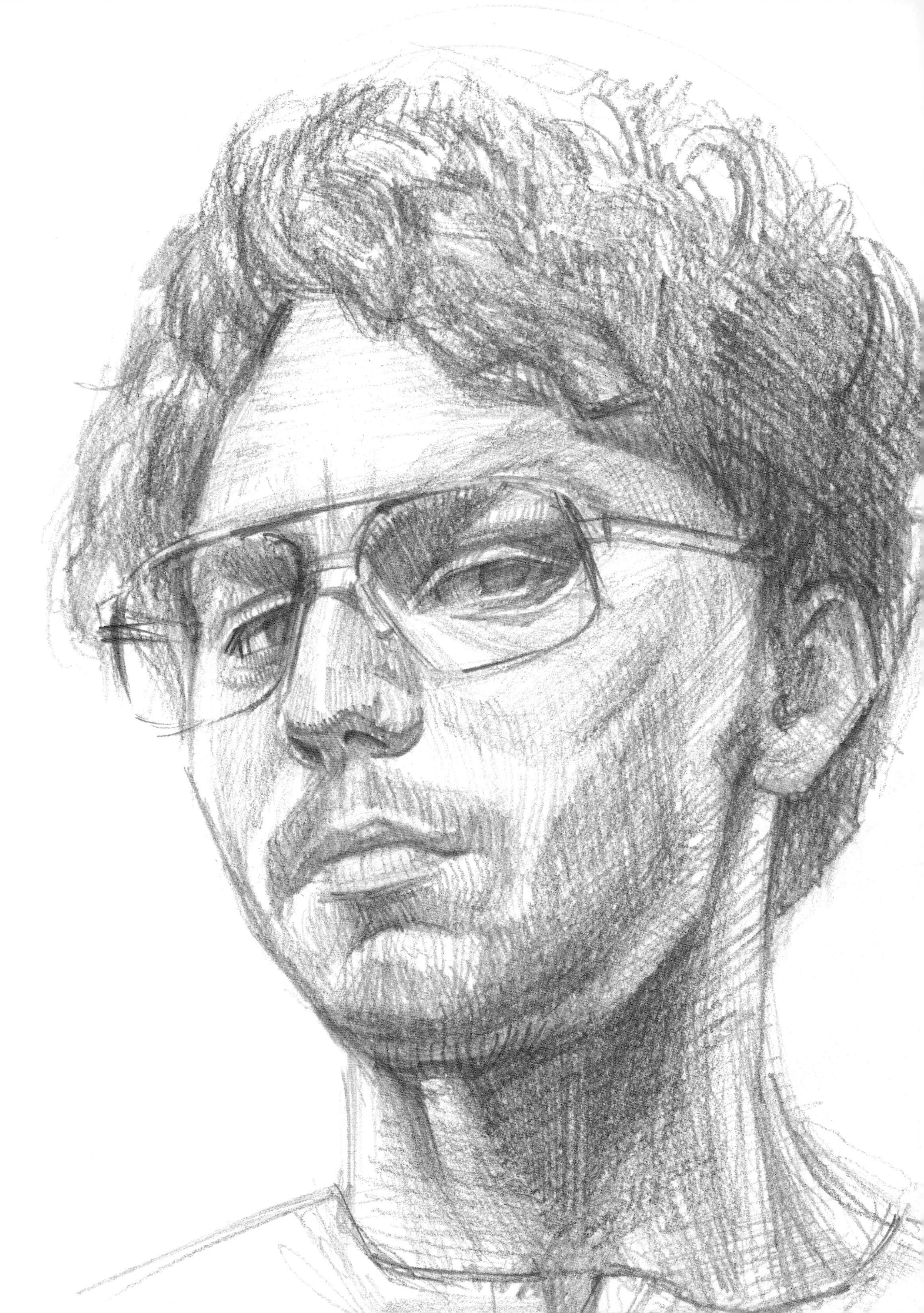

PROJECT 18

ANGLED
THREE-QUARTER VIEW

When drawing a diagonal, or angled, portrait, determining the correct position and composition of the face and features is an important first step. You'll use more slanted lines as you sketch in the overall structure of the face, and the facial features fall differently on the face. Pay close attention to your reference, and use additional guidelines as needed to help place the features and draw them in the right perspective.

Perspective is especially important in a portrait from this dynamic angle. To express perspective correctly, it's important to understand how objects change in relation to distance. Objects farther away will appear smaller, and those closer will appear larger.

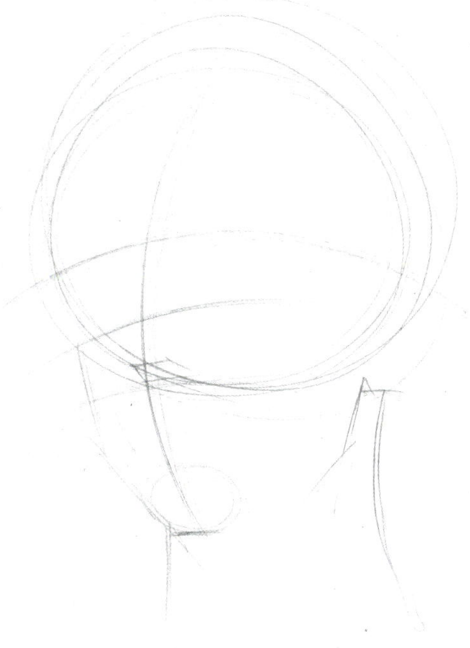

STEP 1

Start with a circle for the face. After dividing the circle in half with a horizontal line, add a vertical line in the direction it is facing. These lines should be slightly slanted to account for the angle of the face. Now you have three equal parts: The bottom segment of the circle is the nose, the middle is the eyebrows and eyes, and the upper third is the forehead and hair.

STEP 2

Determine the overall proportions of the portrait, including the basic points where the eyes, nose, and mouth will go. Lightly mark these basic proportions and think about how they will be placed in a diagonal position. Outline the eye sockets. Designate the nose toward the bottom of the circle. Explore the mouth and jaw structure. Continue exploring with light lines. Observe the ear and neck connections.

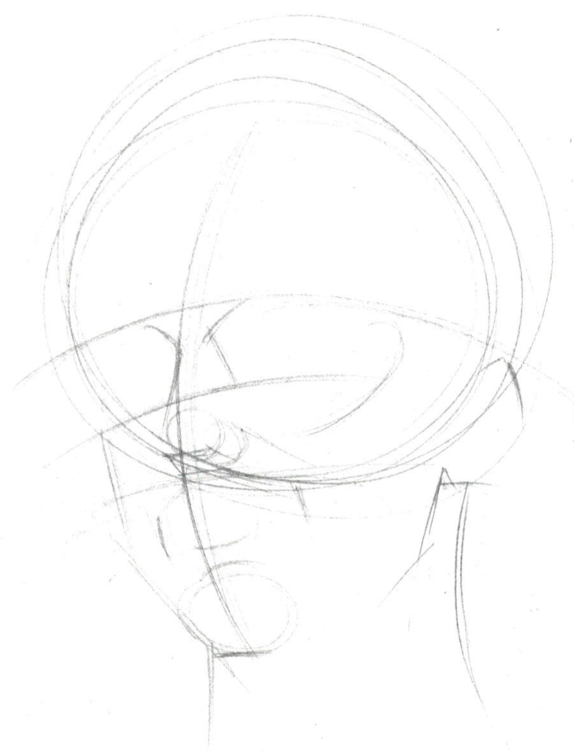

STEP 3

Lightly clarify and outline the general contours of the face. Mark the position of the eyes, nose, mouth, and chin. When drawing a diagonal portrait, perspective is important, so drawing facial features should be done with this in mind. Investigate the position of the glasses and draw the boundaries of where the hair extends.

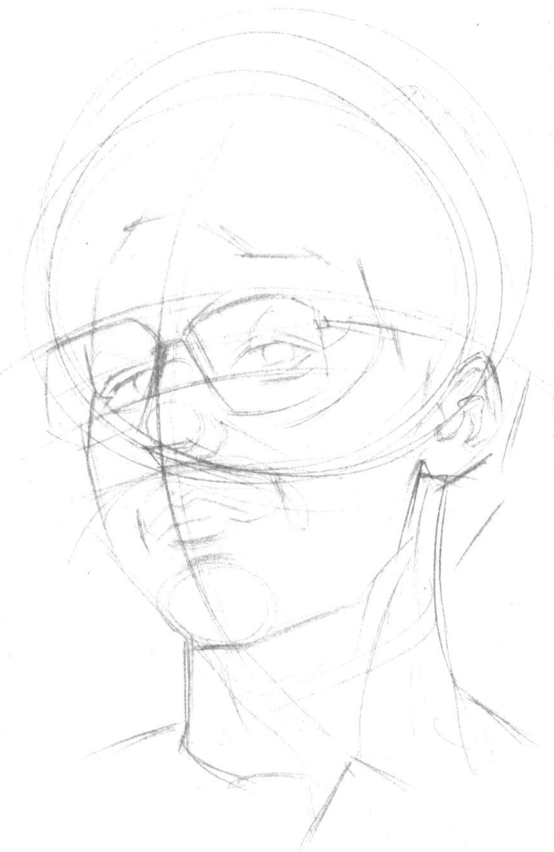

STEP 4

Shading is an important way to add depth and a sense of volume. Identify the light source and begin to apply the darkest shadows in that direction. Lightly shade the space between the eyebrows and eyes, and the shadows under the nose, lips, and chin, and behind the ear.

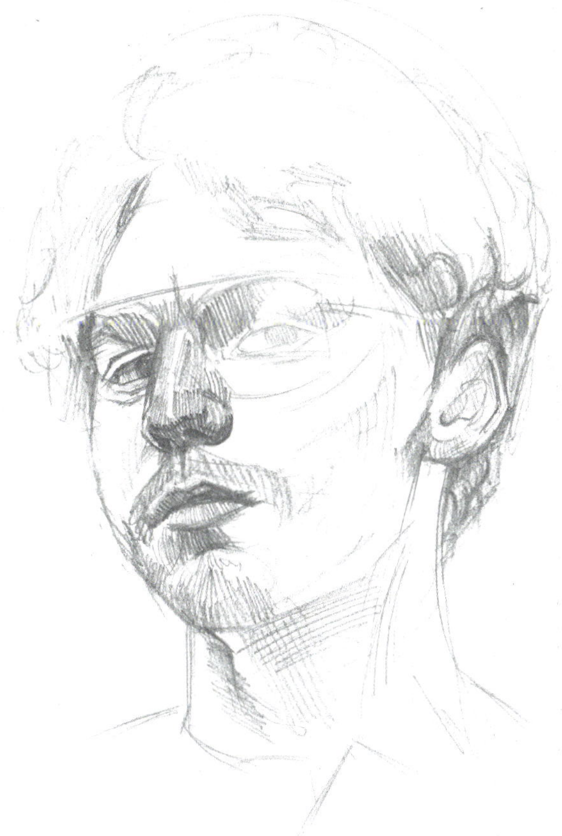

STEP 5

Developing these shadows to reveal your portrait can help you notice mistakes made in earlier steps. As you continue to develop the shadows and shading, frequently look at your portrait from a distance. Seeing the whole drawing from a distance allows you to notice and cor-rect mistakes early on in the process.

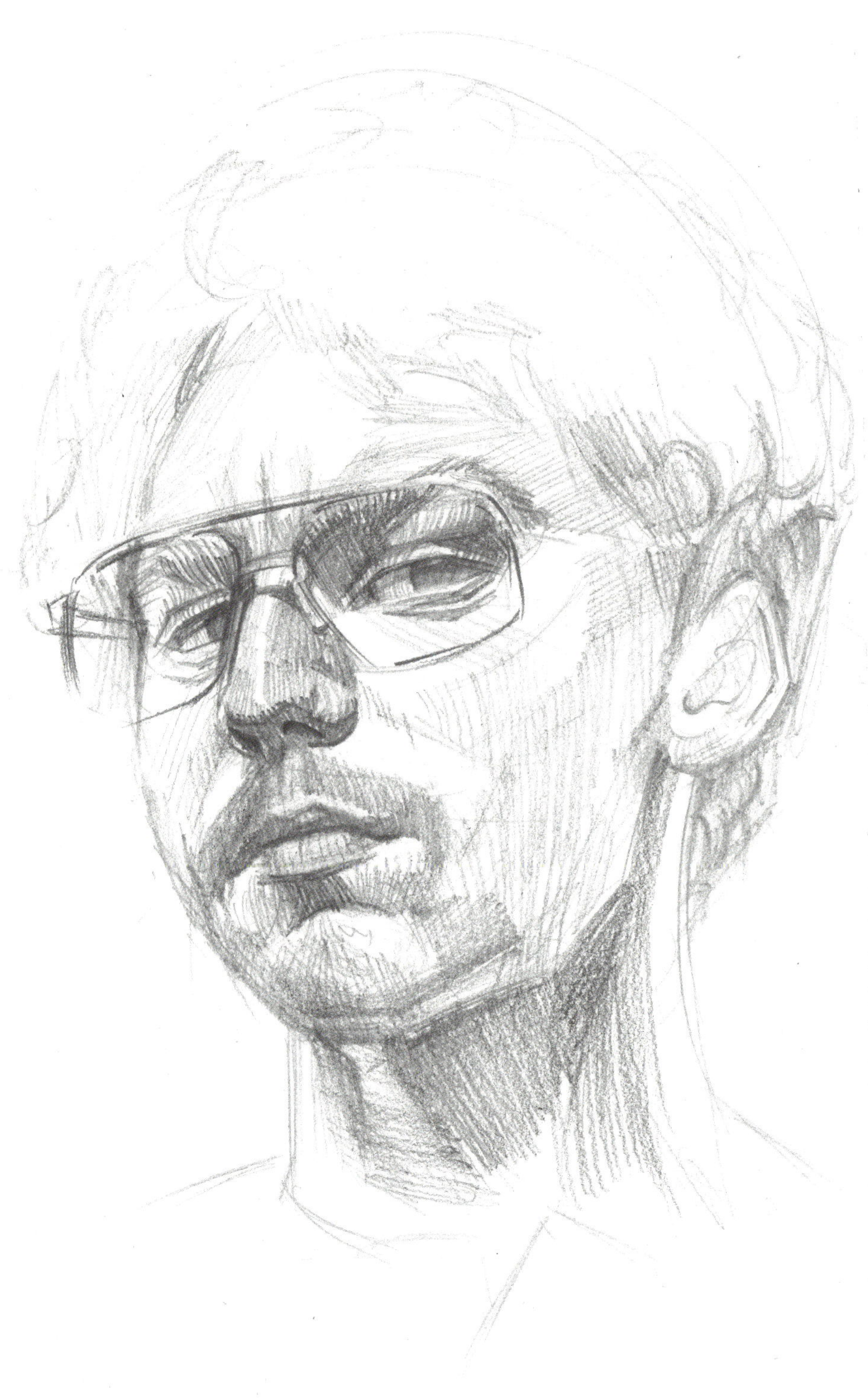

STEP 6

Continue working from dark to light as you develop
the darkest shadows with hatching and crosshatching, erasing any remaining guidelines as you go.

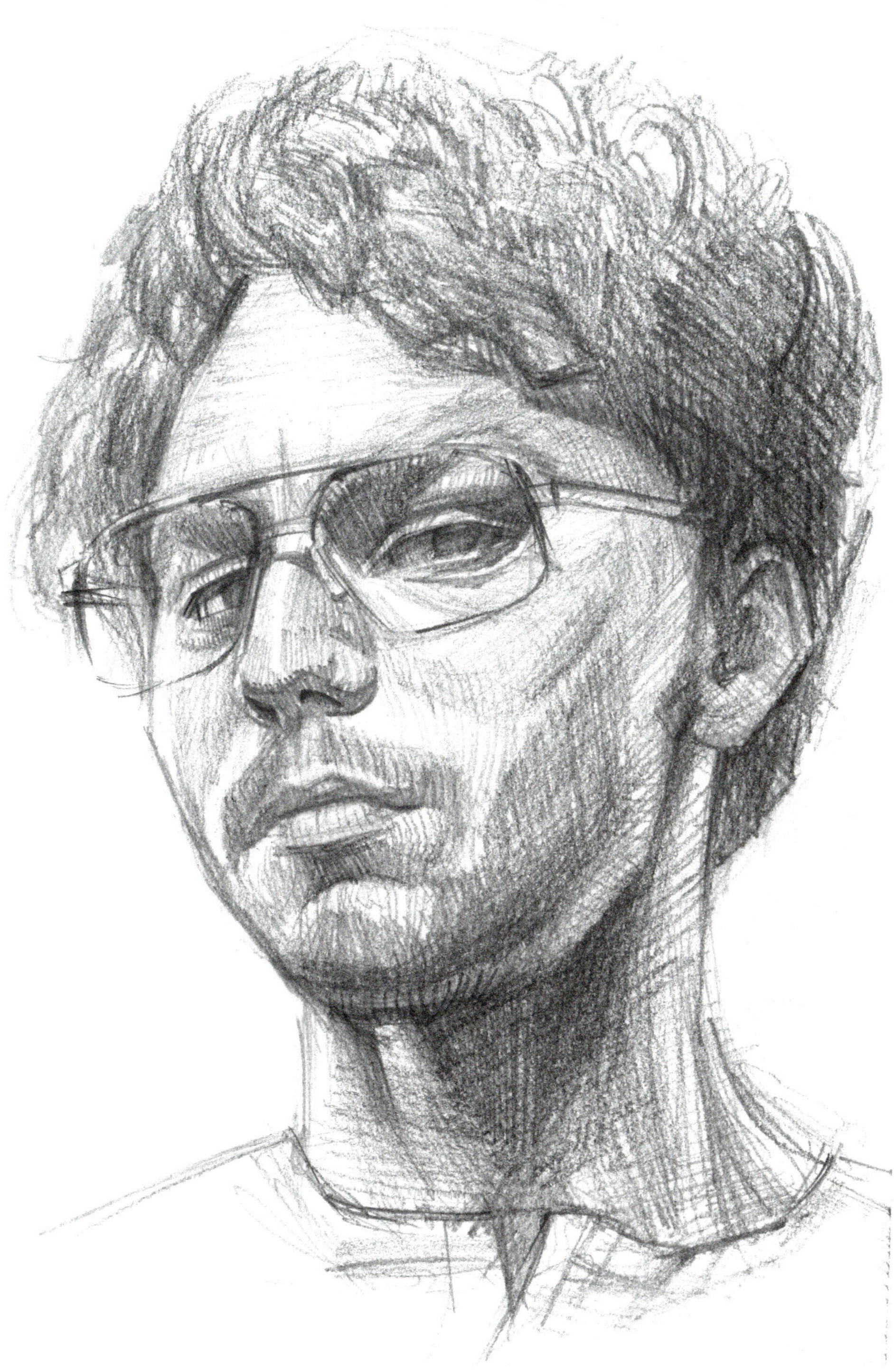

STEP 7

Detail your portrait and complete it with finishing touches. Emphasize the details of the eyes, eyebrows, nostrils, and mouth. Emphasize the tone of the hair with dense lines. Tighten the darkness under the chin with close pencil strokes. Use an eraser to pull out the highlights.

Review the tonal value of the portrait and intensify your lines where necessary. If the dark tones are not what you want, use a softer pencil, such as a 4B or 5B.

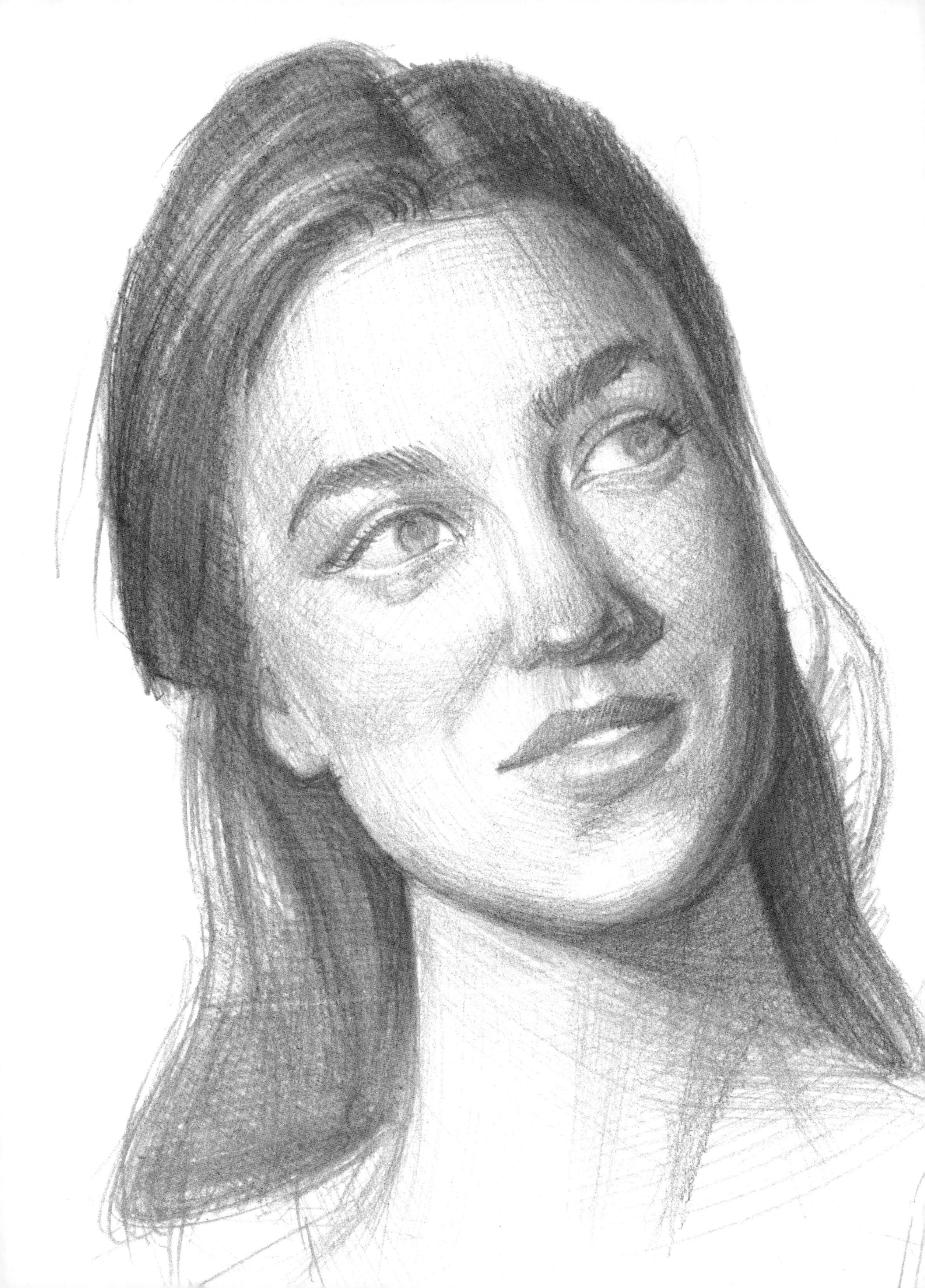

TILTED FEMALE HEAD

The model in this portrait is tilting her head, looking up and away from the viewer. When drawing a portrait with this kind of angle, the starting point is usually the eye level of the portrait, the center of the face. This is a point where the eyes fall horizontally in the center of the drawing paper. Determining the eye level will help you set the height and proportions of the portrait correctly.

Once you have established the starting point, it is important to place the other facial features in the correct proportions. Work with specific proportions in mind, such as the distances from the top of the eyes to the beginning of the eyebrows, from the beginning of the eyebrows to the beginning of the nose, and from the beginning of the nose to the bottom of the chin.

TIPS

USING STRAIGHT ANGLE LINES: When adding other details of the portrait, be sure to accurately place facial features using straight angle lines. For example, you can use horizontal lines to locate the eyes and vertical lines to locate the nose.

ADDING OTHER FEATURES OF THE HEAD: Once you have determined the starting point and set the proportions correctly, add other facial features. Make details like eyebrows, nose, mouth, and chin more prominent. When adding these details, make sure they are positioned correctly with reference to the starting point.

STEP 1

First, identify the center of the face. This is often the top of the eyes or the beginning of the eyebrows. This spot will be the focal point of your drawing and will help you place other facial features around it.

Draw horizontal and vertical lines to correctly set the proportions of the face. Horizontal lines determine the placement of the eyes, nose, and mouth, while vertical lines determine the symmetry of the face. These lines will help you accurately adjust the proportions of the face.

Determine the position of the eyes. The eyes usually fall halfway down the face, so once you have determined the center point of the face, you can place the other features around the eyes. Mark the location of the nose as well.

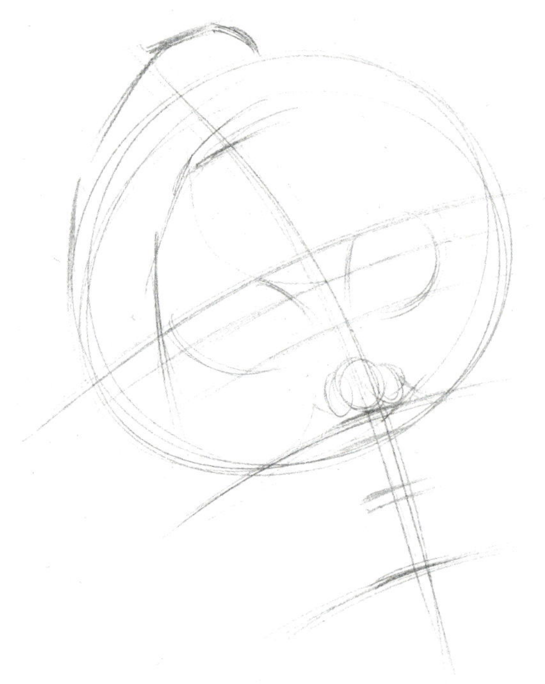

1

STEP 2

Under the nose, move on to drawing the mouth and chin. The mouth is located between the nose and chin and greatly affects facial expression. The chin forms the lower part of the face and is usually in harmony with the mouth.

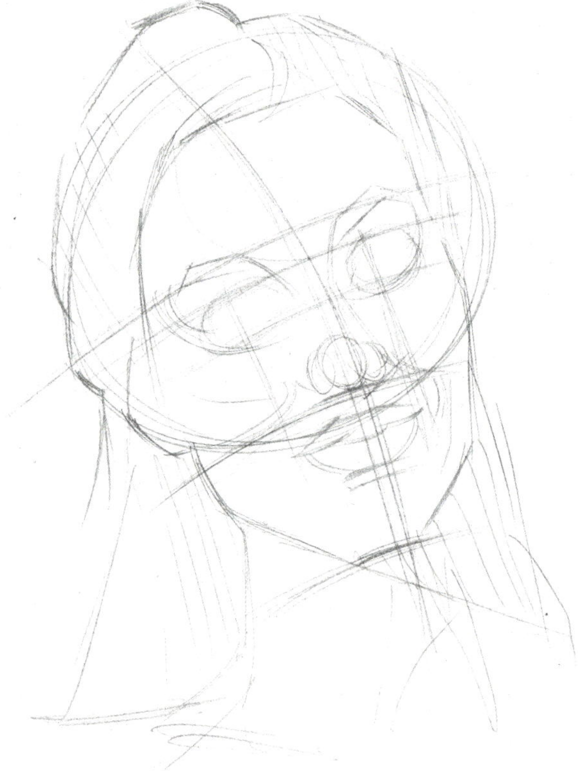

2

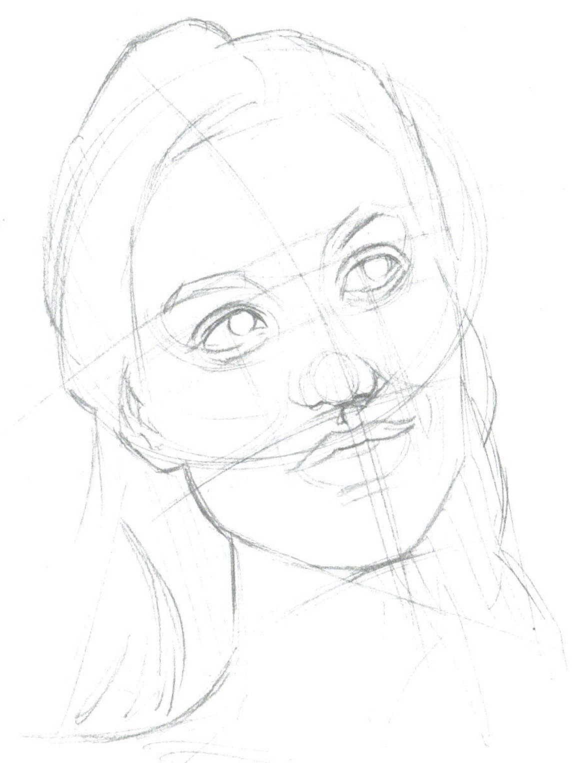

3

STEP 3

Draw the eyebrows above the eyes and then the eyes. Pay attention to the shape and placement of the eyebrows, as they can determine the expression in the drawing. Be careful when drawing the eyes and pay attention to their size and the direction in which the model is looking. Begin to detail the nose and lips and smooth out the outline of the face.

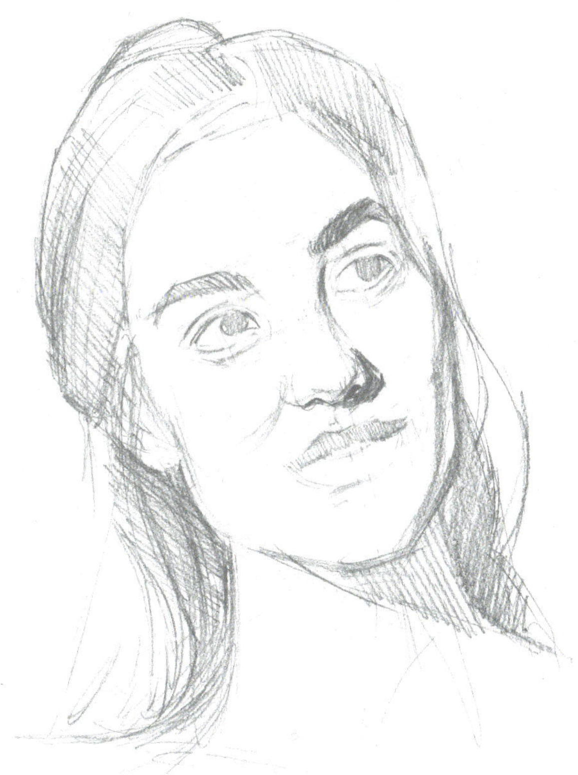

4

STEP 4

When drawing the nose, consider the height of the bridge of the nose and details about the tip of the nose. Darken the nostrils and add the dark shadow along the top of the bridge, which helps define its shape. Begin to fill in other areas of shadow, including along the neck and the darker tones in the hair and eyebrows.

STEP 5

The eyes are the focal point of the portrait, so add details of the eyes first. Carefully draw the folds of the eyelids, eyelashes, and pupils. Emphasize the shadows and subtle tonal shifts around the eyes to give a sense of depth.

Make the eyebrows look natural by defining the lines and hairs. Clarify the start and end points of the eyebrows and accurately express their arch.

Define the nostrils and shadows around the bridge of the nose. Accurately draw the shape of the mouth and the curves of the lips. Lip curves, fullness, and shadows are important in rendering natural-looking lips, so pay close attention to these details.

Make the facial features more distinct and accurately express the anatomical structure of the face. Make sure that the facial features are in the right proportions and reflect the serene facial expression.

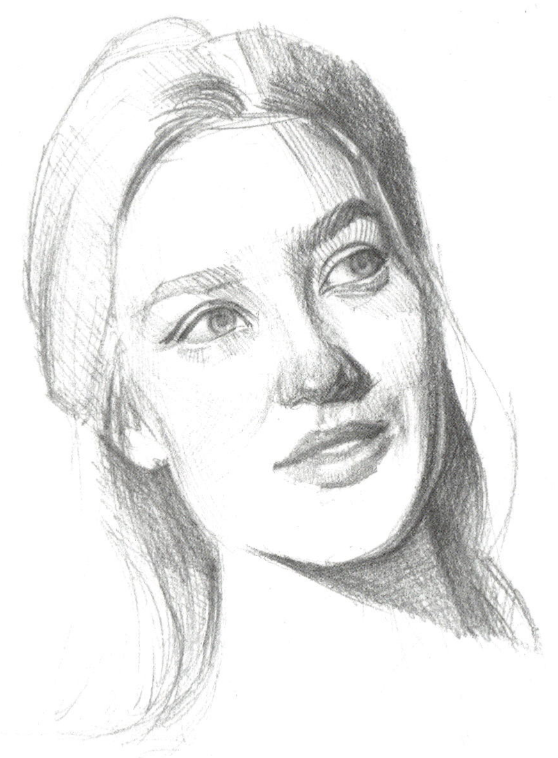

5

STEP 6

Identify the light source and add depth to your portrait by shading. Apply the shadows correctly, in harmony with the volume and shape of the face. Take into account the shadows on the protrusions and in the recesses of the face. Study the movement of the cheekbones and sweep with slanted lines to give a rounded feel.

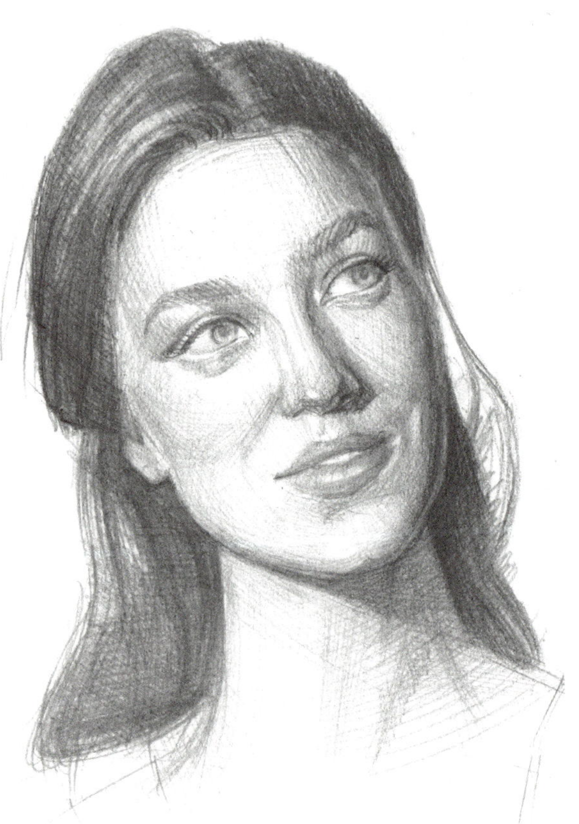

6

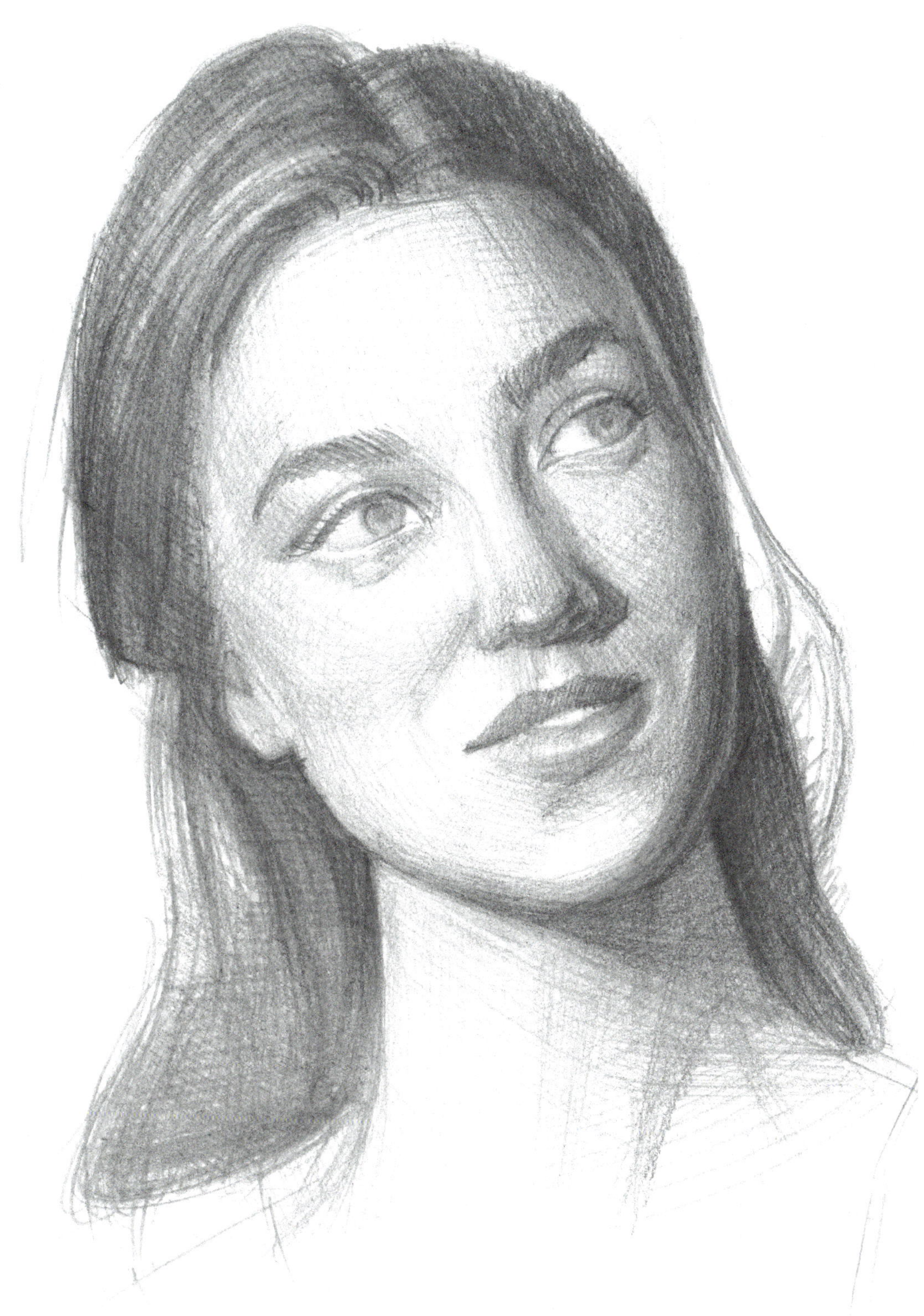

7

STEP 7

After adding details and shading, review your drawing and make final checks. Correct any areas that
look incomplete or unbalanced and fine-tune as
needed to complete your portrait. Add the finishing
touches to complete your drawing.

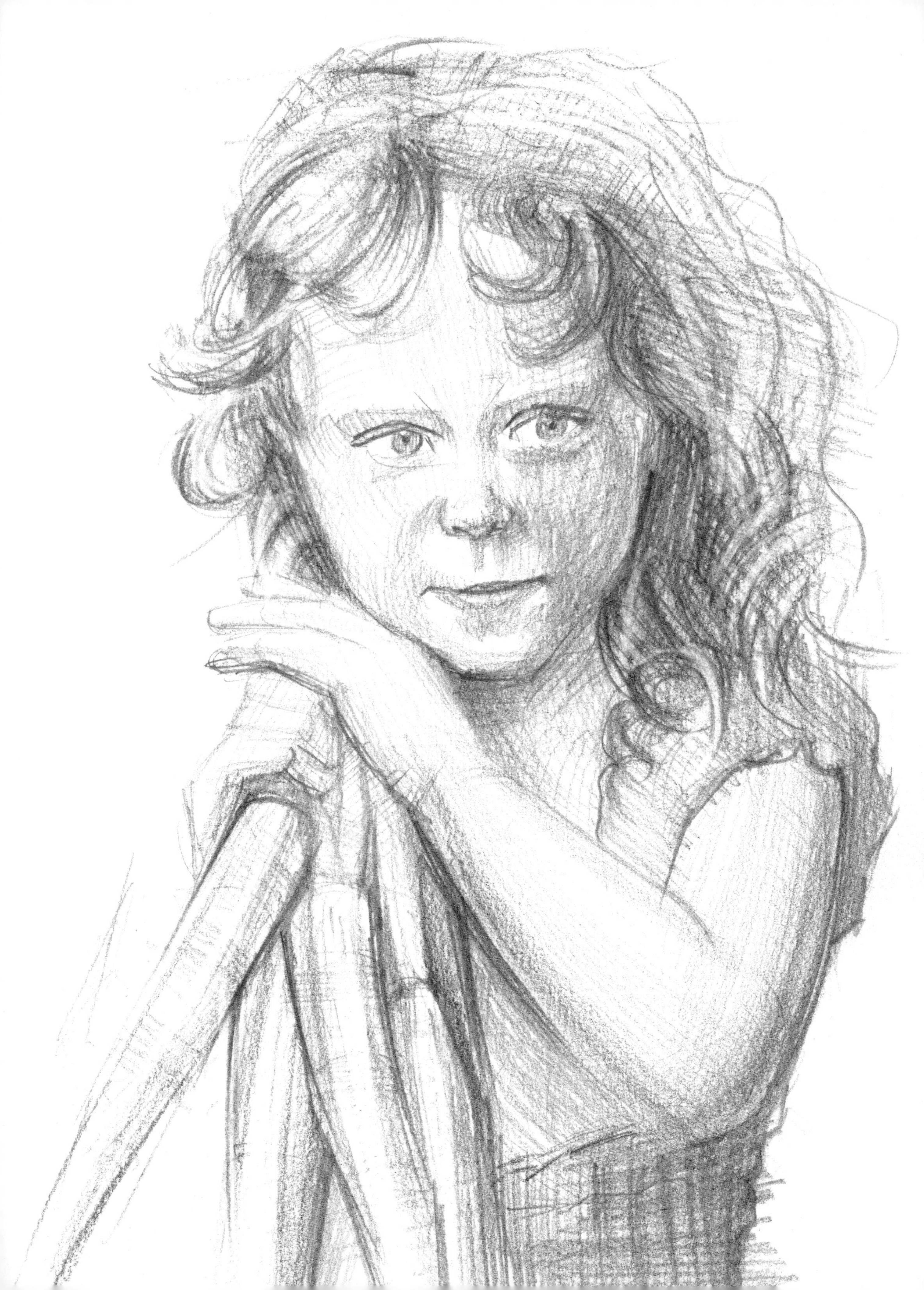

YOUNG GIRL

Drawing children's portraits includes some differences, compared to drawing adults. Children's facial features are usually softer and rounder, their noses and chins are smaller, and they usually have less pronounced lines.

Children often have different proportions than adults. The eyes may be larger, the nose smaller, and the face rounder. Consider these differences when setting proportions and make adjustments based on the age and gender of the child.

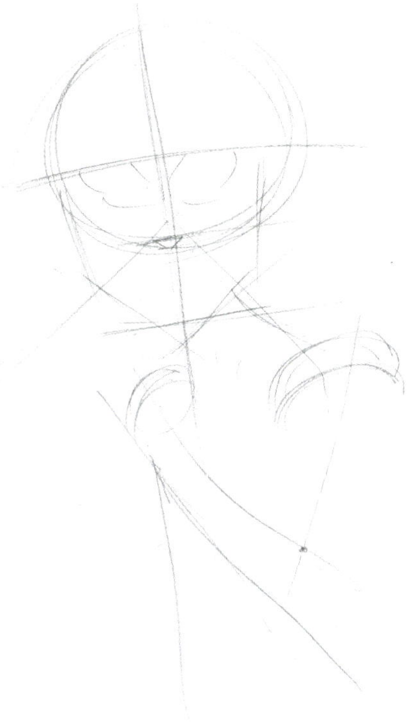

1

STEP 1

Draw a circle for the face, and use horizontal and vertical lines to accurately adjust the proportions. For example, draw a horizontal line through the center of the face to determine the eye level. This line will help you identify the key points where the eyes, nose, and mouth will be placed.

Once you have determined the eye level, mark this point with a marker or a light line. This will be the focal point of your drawing and will help you place other facial features around it.

After dividing the face into sections, determine where the eyes will be. The placement of the eyes can vary depending on the child's age and face shape, so make sure you get the proportions right.

Place the nose under the eyes and the mouth under the nose. Children's noses are usually smaller, so carefully adjust the size and position of the nose. The mouth is located below the point where the nose and chin meet.

STEP 2

Add the child's chin and other details of the face. Remember that children usually have a softer, rounder chin. Highlight the jawline and carefully adjust the facial features to reflect the child's expression. Sketch in the child's arm and toros to begin developing these forms as well.

TIP: Start with soft and light lines to create the overall structure of the child's portrait. Because children's facial features are usually softer and rounder, use more vague lines at the beginning to establish the overall facial form.

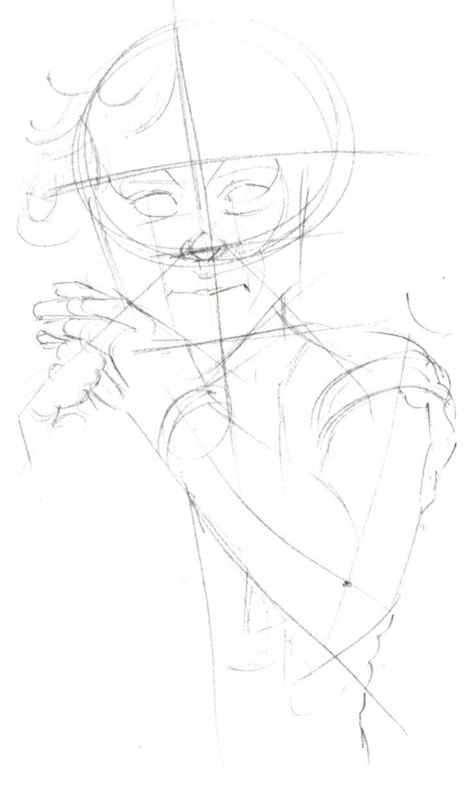

2

STEP 3

Detail your drawing by making the eyes, eyebrows, nose, and mouth more prominent. Add eyelids, eyelashes, and the curve of eyebrows and nostrils. Take care to accurately express the child's characteristic features. Sketch in the overall shape of the hair.

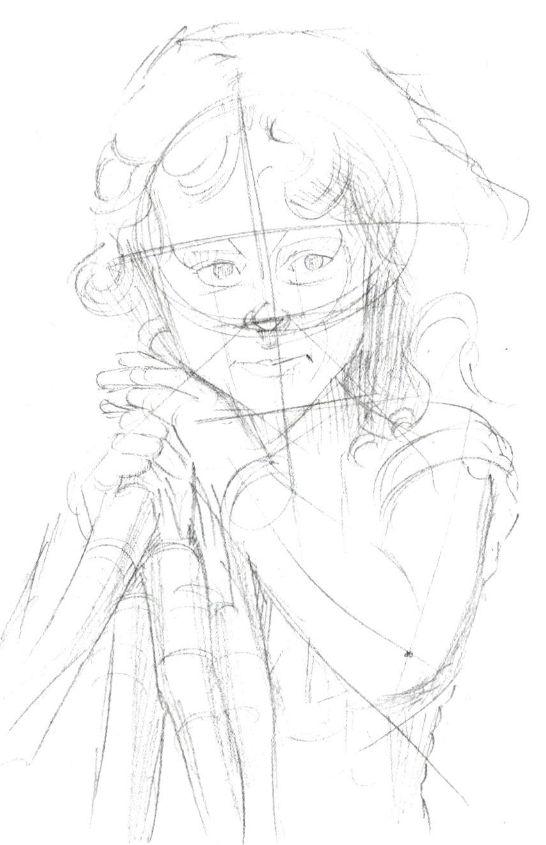

3

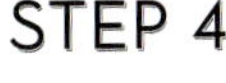

STEP 4

As you refine the facial features, erase your guidelines when you're confident in the placement and proportions.

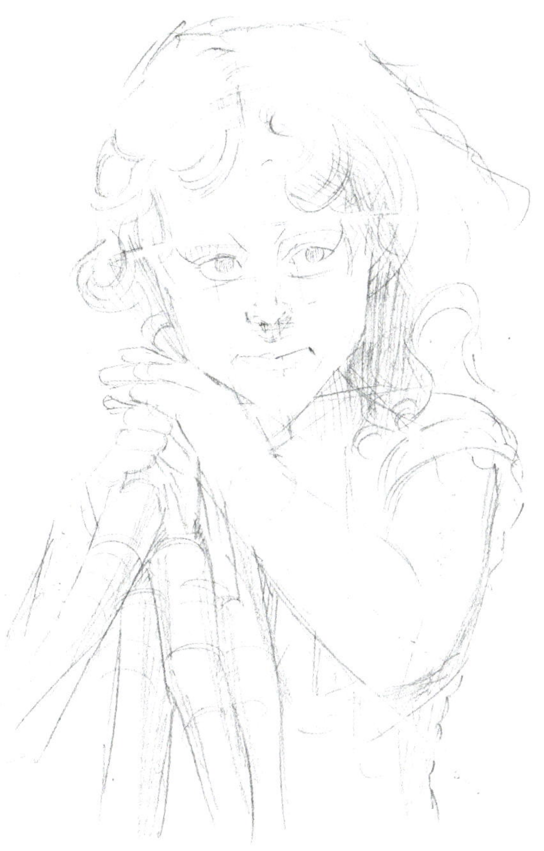

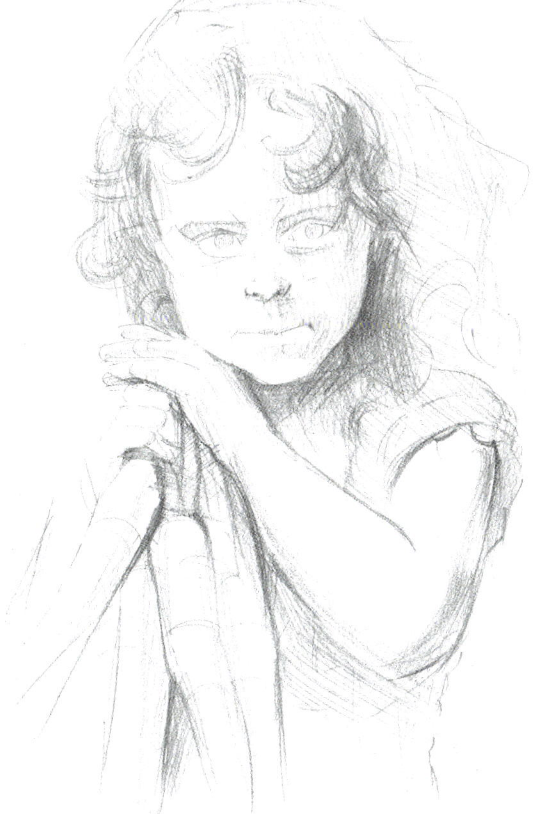

STEP 5

Begin to add shading, starting with the darkest shadows and tones in the hair and under the chin. When creating shadows, focus on soft transitions. This makes the shadows look more natural and realistic. You can blend the shadows softly using a soft brush, blending stump, or tissue.

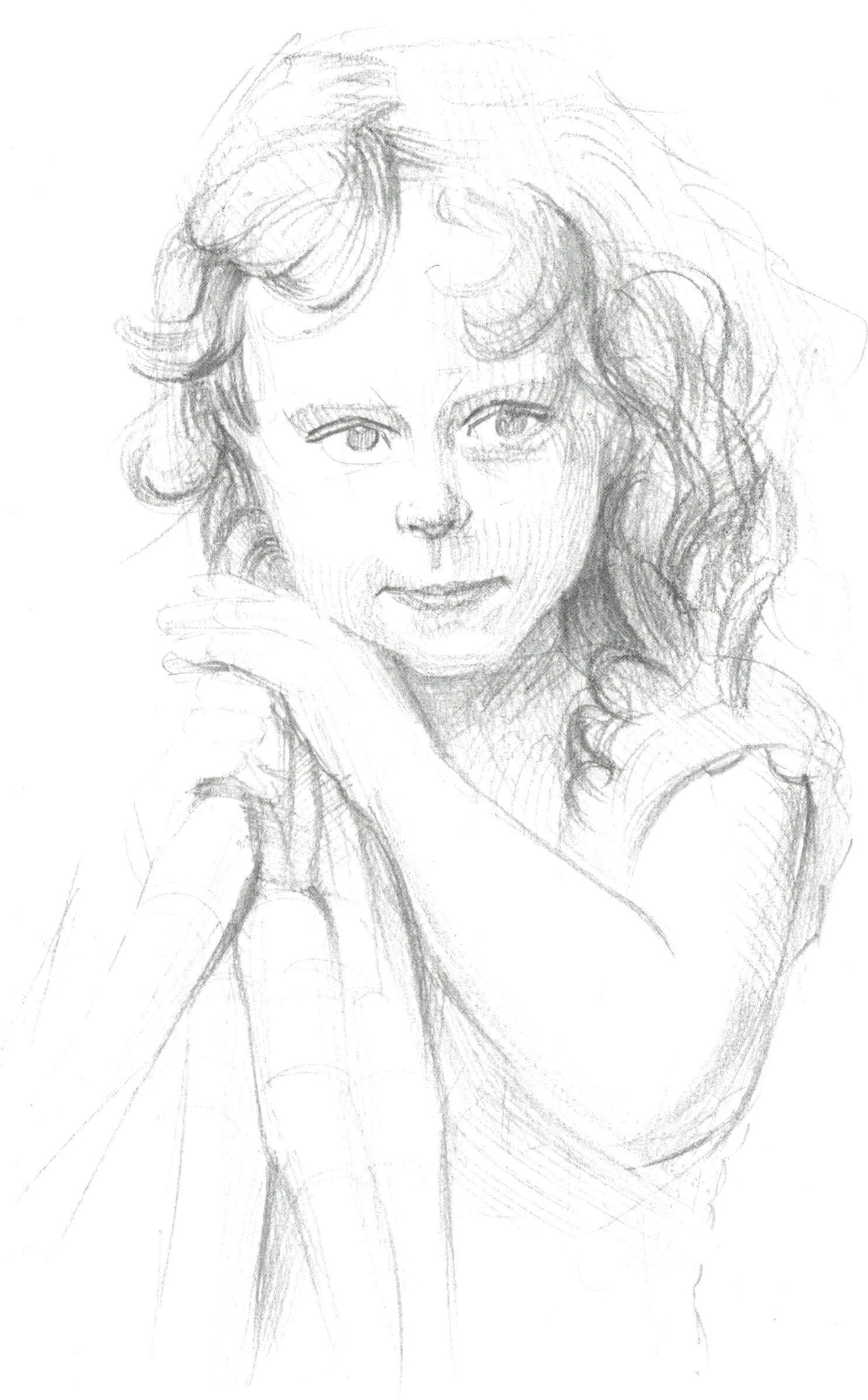

STEP 6

The intensity of the shadows varies depending on the angle at which the light falls and the strength of the light source. When drawing a child portrait, you can achieve a more natural look by keeping the shadows lighter and more subtle. Use light strokes to continue to develop the tones in the hair and on the face leaving the white of the paper for highlighted areas.

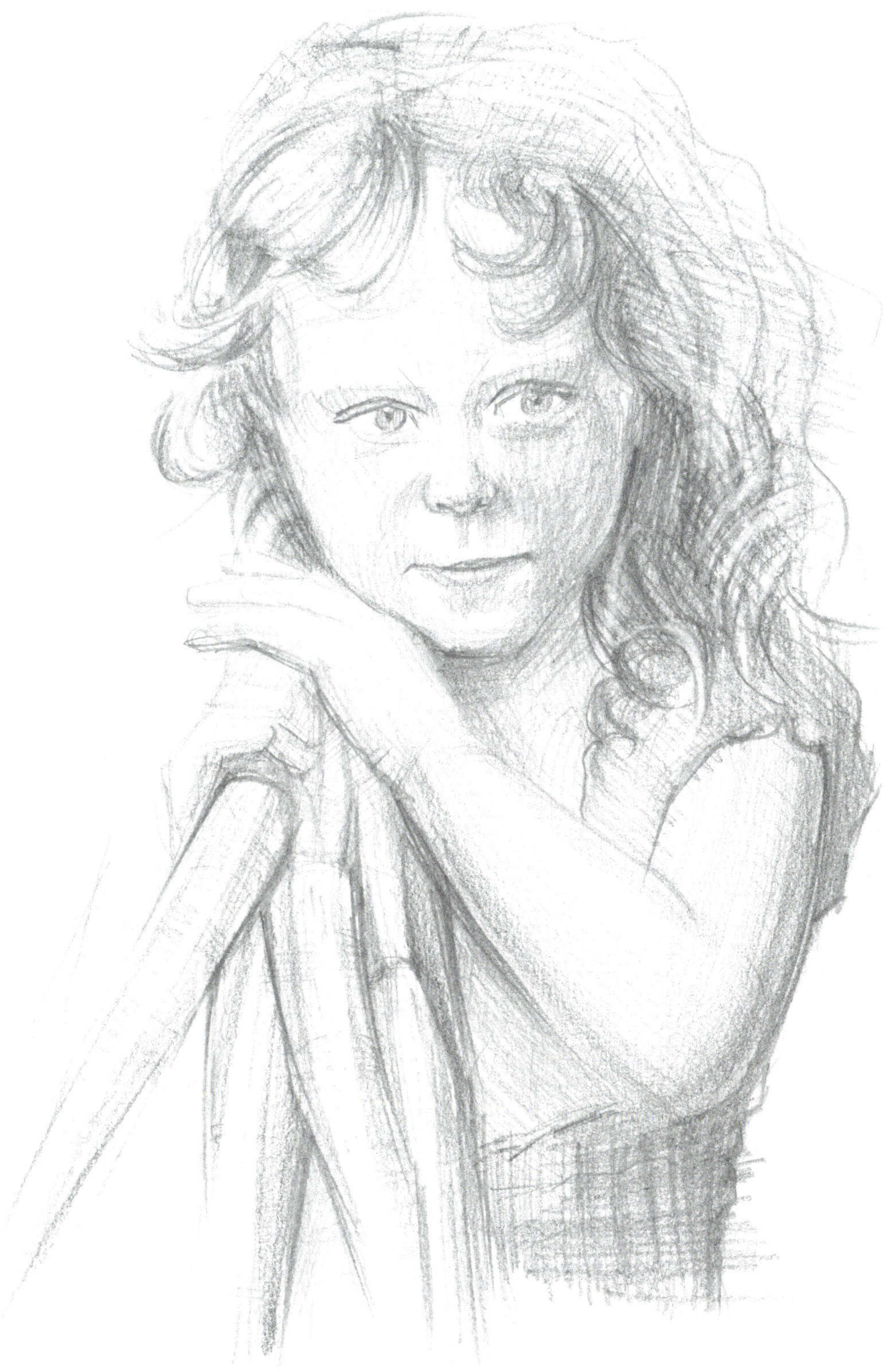

STEP 7

As you finalize your shading and details, note that children's lips and the area under the eye often have light shadows. Add light shadows to emphasize these areas, but don't overdo it, and do not overdefine the facial features. Keeping it simple and light will reinforce the youthful character of the child.

ABOUT THE ARTIST

Samet Türkan is a young artist living in Istanbul, Turkey. He is @clsamet online, and his passion for art and approachable drawing style have allowed him to build his large, engaged following quickly. Now a full-time artist, Samet seeks to help others learn to draw as well.

INDEX